Worked Over

Worked Over

The Corporate Sabotage
of an American Community

Dimitra Doukas

Cornell University Press

Ithaca and London

First published 2003 by Cornell University Press
First printing, Cornell Paperbacks, 2003

Printed in the United States of America

Library of Congress Cataloging-in-Publication Data
Doukas, Dimitra, 1948–
   Worked over : the corporate sabotage of an American community /
Dimitra Doukas.
      p. cm.
Includes bibliographical references (p.) and index.
   ISBN 0-8014-4092-0 (cloth) — ISBN 0-8014-8861-3 (pbk.)
   1. Big business—Social aspects—New York (State)—Mohawk River
Valley.   2. Social values—New York (State)—Mohawk River Valley.
3. E. Remington & Sons—History.   4. Local government—New York
(State)—Mohawk River Valley.   5. Distributive justice—New York
(State)—Mohawk River Valley.   I. Title.
   HD2356.U52 M643 2003
   306.3'09747'6—dc21   2002014618

Cornell University Press strives to use environmentally responsible
suppliers and materials to the fullest extent possible in the publishing
of its books. Such materials include vegetable-based, low-VOC inks
and acid-free papers that are recycled, totally chlorine-free, or partly
composed of nonwood fibers. For further information, visit our
website at www.cornellpress.cornell.edu.

Cloth printing   10 9 8 7 6 5 4 3 2 1

Paperback printing   10 9 8 7 6 5 4 3 2 1

To the memory of Marion Bradley Doukas

and George Agesilaos Doukas,

my first and best teachers

Contents

Preface

Many stories of "the Valley" could be told. Many are. Some would be more upbeat than mine. Some would not. You can't please everyone.

It is often the fate of anthropological and sociological stories to be hated by the people of whom they are told. Words and deeds have been lifted out of the contexts in which they were said or done and twisted to fit the arcane purposes of a nosy stranger. The people feel *used*.

I wish to make it perfectly clear that I did *use* the words and deeds of the people I studied. I put them together into a story that no one in "the Valley" would tell. But it is, I wish to say, a story that needs telling, that could matter to our future as a free people. With apologies to anyone whose words or deeds I have misinterpreted, this story is offered to "the Valley" and the nation to which it belongs in the spirit of honest inquiry into what has gone wrong in "the land of the free and the home of the brave."

Acknowledgments

I have many people to thank for making this book possible. The support of Faye D. Ginsburg, Claudio Lomnitz-Adler, and Constance R. Sutton was invaluable throughout the long research process. My many debts to their insights and intellectual commitments are visible to the discerning eye on every page. I am also very grateful to Thomas O. Beidelman and Karen I. Blu for their careful readings and challenging comments. I thank Jennie Tichenor and Karen Hewitt at the New York University Department of Anthropology for countless acts of kindness, and the New York University Graduate School of Arts and Science for the Dean's Dissertation Fellowship that greatly assisted this work. For fertile discussions and disagreements about "middle Americans" I thank Thomas O. Beidelman, Marilyn Thomas-Houston, Fred R. Myers, Owen Lynch, Antonio Lauria-Pericelli, Nick Salvatore, Daniel Rogers, Adam Arkadi, Rob Riggs, Bonnie Blanding-May, Christine Walley, Brian Larkin, Nina Browne, and Thomas Burgess. I am grateful to Thomas Burgess, too, for generous bibliographical assistance.

Without the kind and timely recommendation of Jane Fajans, this project might never have met the sympathetic ear of Cornell University Press's extraordinary Editor-in-Chief, Frances Benson. The thoughtful and provocative comments of two anonymous reviewers did much to sharpen this book's focus and head off some of its less tenable conclusions, and the Press's careful copyeditors saved the readers of this book much confusion (and its author some embarrassment). Thanks also to participants in the Cornell seminar I taught for two semesters, "Equality and Dominance: Historical Ethnography of the U.S. before 1900," and to the participants of the Cornell University Social Sciences Seminar, for thoughtful comments on sections of this work.

My debts of gratitude in Central New York are extensive. I thank the Village and County officials and former officials who graciously consented to be interviewed. Jane Spellman and the staff and volunteers of the Herkimer County Historical Society were unfailingly helpful and hospitable to me—Town of Columbia historian, Doris Huxtable, and Town of Fairfield historian, Jane Dieffenbacher, were especially kind. I thank, too, Janice Estey and Kevin Cornell at the Remington Arms Archive, and Sue and Ken Greene for opening the opportunity for me to work in that archive. I would also like to thank Jerrold Swinney of the Remington Society for a key discussion about Remington scrip and for his careful work on the Remington era. Louis C. Parker III was kind enough to lend me his fascinating manuscript on the Parker Gun Works, and I must thank Arthur Kerr and Dr. Roger Weeden for that connection and for illuminating discussions of early industrialization at the Remington shops.

To former Director of the Ilion Free Public Library, Christine Lozoski, and my coworkers there, I am extremely grateful for innumerable professional courtesies, personal kindnesses, stimulating discussions, and my daily bread. I would also like to express my gratitude to the late Pearl Wheeler, my predecessor at the Historical Room for her irascible wit and historical vision, and to Bruce George, the Library's current Director, whose interest in the region's history will preserve the ILHR collection for future generations.

I could not possibly thank the Concerned Citizens for Ilion's Environment enough for my eye-opening education in grassroots politics, for letting me participate in their work, and for sharing their knowledge of the past and the present with me. I am profoundly obliged to the proprietors of Clapsaddle Farm for their continuing friendship, gracious hospitality, and astute analysis of our world.

This study benefited immeasurably from the considerable intelligence, wit, and research skills of the late Barry J. Wilson, whose generosity I can now never repay. Without the loving assistance of the late Mr. Paul Kinney, who introduced me to Ilion, shared with me the insights of a long and thoughtful life, and cared for me as a daughter, this research could not have been conducted.

The emotional support of my sisters, Leslie and Andrea Doukas, and my dear friends, Bill and Brenda Fleming, helped me stay the course. Finally, the intelligence, "moral imagination," and practical help of my late mother, Marion Bradley Doukas, sustained research and researcher against the tide of fashionable indifference to the predicament of the majority.

Part I
Encounters

At the beginning of this marvelous era it was natural to expect, and it was expected, that laborsaving inventions would lighten the toil and improve the condition of the laborer; that the enormous increase in the power of producing wealth would make real poverty a thing of the past.

HENRY GEORGE, *Progress and Poverty*

1

Introduction: The Other American Culture

It is a curious kind of democracy we live in where the largest political party in the United States is the nonvoters.[1] But is nonvoting so irrational in a society where decisions of any consequence are made "above our heads" by great wealth, allied with the photogenic politicians we may choose among in election day ritual? This book looks at how a great democratic project went wrong when the resources of a nation, material and cultural, were gathered up into the hands of a few giant corporations.

This is not a book of large-scale statistical arguments and the doings of famous people.[2] It studies the corporate ascendancy from the perspective of "ordinary" people in a Central New York State manufacturing region: how they used to live, how the corporations changed their lives, what people thought, what the corporate boosters tried to get them to think, and where they are today. It is a study of great transformations at close range, through the lives of working people, the people most exposed to risk at the front lines of social change.[3]

The working people of Central New York State, like working people all over the United States, don't trust (as many of the people I studied put it) "people who think they're better than us." That means politicians, bureaucrats, pundits, most of the bosses who employ them, and the "do-gooders" who cannot solve their problems. Why they do not trust such people is an important story for understanding the United States and its possible futures, but it is a largely untold story because not only does it have deep roots in the much-forgotten past of precorporate America but also because the mistrust is mutual.

The problem of mutual mistrust haunted me since I first encountered it, setting out in 1993 on eighteen months of ethnographic fieldwork in Central New York. I brought to my research exactly the kind of question that "people who think they're better than us" *would* ask. For years scholars and commentators have been concerned about a "turn to the right" on the part of the U.S. working class, an apparent rejection of the New Deal coalition that had, among other things, instituted a social safety net and legitimated the political voice of labor unions, policies that have greatly benefited working people. I wished to investigate the working people's alleged change of heart through the close-up methods of ethnography, but mistrust was embedded in my question—it assumed that these people do not know what's good for them.

My question sat uncomfortably in the company of the greatest works of my discipline, cultural anthropology. (Appendix 1 discusses in detail this book's theoretical and methodological orientations.) Such a question could not even have been framed if I were going off to do research in the New Guinea highlands, say, or the South Pacific, instead of the U.S. hinterlands, because resisting derogatory descriptions of the people we study has long been an anthropological point of honor. The strange customs of "the natives," anthropologists insist, make perfectly good sense in terms of their own culture and circumstances. Our task is to understand the world as *they* understand it. When we succeed in this task, we find that "the natives" do "know what's good for them," and they act as wisely (and as foolishly) on their knowledge as anyone else does.

Why should it be different in Central New York? That I *could* pose a research question that embedded the assumption of "native" ignorance is an artifact of the mutual mistrust I was discovering. But fortunately, it took only a few weeks "in the field" for me to realize that the working people of Central New York are keen analysts of and careful actors in their world. My task, like that of any cultural anthropologist, was the challenge of understanding their world as they understand it.

And it was challenging. Much about them was perplexing. The more I lived and worked among them, the clearer it became that they did not fit either of the molds that the social sciences had prepared for them, neither the dominant one of working-class "turn to the right" nor the leftist one of class-conscious radicalism. Early on, a local political activist gave me a provocative clue. Local people, he said, cling to "old values" that they grew up with and still "appreciate," even though these values have been "tested" by ridicule. What these "old values" are, exactly, he did not spell out—he was challenging me to find out for myself. And he was, I suspect in hindsight, trying to determine if I were one of those "people who think they're better than us."

Again and again the people I studied tried to lead me to the recognition that the "people who think they're better" had got them wrong, seriously, consequentially wrong. And they were right. At the heart of the matter is a central finding of this book, that the working people I studied, and many others across the United States who share their predicament,[4] do not wholly subscribe to the mainstream American culture that is grounded in individualism, optimism, and upward mobility (Spindler and Spindler 1983, 1990; Moffatt 1992). They are not unfamiliar with it—indeed, they "speak" that culture quite fluently—but they also transmit and act on ideals that are diametrically opposed to the ones that are supposed to be at the core of American culture. Among these ideals (as we will see in Chapters 2 and 3) are strong sanctions against conspicuous consumption, respect for hard work well done, a commitment to the integrity of community—thus, a cautious appraisal of individual upward mobility—and a reasonable pessimism about the larger world in which they live. Mutual mistrust, in other words, is undergirded by cultural opposition.

A central puzzle of this book is the nature and source of the oppositional, even counterhegemonic, culture I encountered in Central New York. Historically, I argue, U.S. culture was bisected by the consolidation of corporate capitalism at the turn of the twentieth century. In the brief span of a generation, a handful of businessmen and their political allies rocked the foundations of American life by concentrating the control of hundreds of thriving, independent local economies into their own few hands. This book is the story of one of those independent local economies. The puzzle of the "old values" in which my Central New Yorker friends put such stock leads back in time to the social world of their ancestors, before the corporate giants held sway, and forward from there, through the massive transformations to which their world has been subjected under corporate rule.

The consolidation of corporate capitalism could not have taken place without an immense cultural campaign, intended to overcome the nearly unanimous anticorporate sentiments of the populace. (Chapters 8 and 9 describe and analyze the local version of this campaign). The rise of the corporate giants, this book proposes, upended a culture of "traditional American values" that had jelled around the virtue of hard work and suspicion of great wealth, in pursuit of a sustainable "equality." The local culture of the people I studied in Central New York, with its respect for hard work and distrust of would-be "social betters," looks intriguingly like the "old values" of a historical American people that, still touchy about their hard-won dignity, viewed concentrated wealth as the greatest threat to their freedom.[5]

Observers in the years that bracketed the turn of the twentieth century registered the presence of a new cultural force through the many lenses of the old. The trades unions looked through the lens of their long struggle for the fruits of their labor, and saw arrogant capitalists dictating lifelong "wage slavery"—forcing a man "to beg his fellow-man's leave to earn a living." If the capitalists succeed in their quest for power, unionists asserted, "then the sign of a free country might as well be taken down."[6]

Journalists of the era, looking through the lens of middle-class anxiety, were alarmed by "the strange new conditions of business life in America"—"seizing special privileges, . . . criminal underselling, . . . manipulating the stock market"—and, worse, by what the concentration of corporate wealth would do to the moral and political "life of the nation."[7] "Free and just play" of constitutional principles, an indignant journalist asserted, would see to it "that the profits from the cooperation of all the people went *to* the people," but "the great drainage companies fastened upon America's prosperity" saw to it that "the proceeds of the labor of the many [went] into the pockets of the few."[8]

Big capital, looking defensively through the lens of its unstable new magnificence, across a landscape of unanimous disapproval, formulated its ideological offensive. As Andrew Carnegie put it in his infamous "gospel of wealth": "We accept and welcome, therefore, as conditions to which we must accommodate ourselves, great inequality of environment, the concentration of business, industrial and commercial, in the hands of a few, and the law of competition between these, as being not only beneficial, but essential for the future progress of the race" (1889:655). Big capital "welcomed" the very conditions that appalled the vast majority of the society. Indeed, it bid to lead that society, guiding it to the forefront of social evolution.

Hardly! retorted one of this country's most original and probing social thinkers. Thorstein Veblen ([1899] 1979) registered the conspicuous consumption of the new "leisure class," and the "pecuniary emulation" of the wanna-be nimbus that floated obligingly about it, through the lens of evolutionary theory too—but as "late barbarism," not as progress. The "captains of industry," he argued, are moved by a feudal code of prowess that heaps honor on seizure by force, and finds labor "irksome." To the contrary, in Veblen's view, the evolution of the human race rests on the "industrial classes" and their "instinct of workmanship." The unequal distribution of wealth, on which the leisure of the leisure class rests, Veblen argued, directly *inhibits* the future progress of the race ([1899] 1979:204–205).

The consolidation of corporate capitalism produced a decades-long cultural war of titanic proportions, played out on local battlefields across the United States. Victory was not swift, judging from the vicissitudes of the Central New York case (Chapters 8 and 9), nor has it been complete. If the "industrial classes" have stood their ground on the "instinct of workmanship," it is in part, at least, because the "great drainage companies" made sure that their wages were not equal to "pecuniary emulation." But is there more than economics to the story?

This is the puzzle. Could that "old" culture have persisted, transformed but continuous, against the tide of competitive consumerism that corporate mass-production promoted (Fox and Lears 1983; Horowitz 1992)? This book proposes that it could, and did—that the American culture of individualism, upward mobility, and competitive consumption is a distinctive cultural adaptation of those social groups who benefited from the new corporate order. Those who did not continued to develop "traditional American values," centered on work and its just reward. And the widening gap between them filled up with mutual mistrust.

It is time to bridge the gap. The corporate order has pulled up the ladder of success, not only for the many millions, like the people I studied, whom corporate leadership rewarded for years, even generations, of service by replacing good jobs with a "service sector" of poorly paid, insecure work, but also for the small-business owners whose customers used to be a prosperous working people and for the middle managers who could once confidently predict secure futures for themselves and their children. The United States now has the greatest inequality of any industrialized country.[9] And this country looks fat and happy compared to the "developing" countries who have been admitted into the corporate order as suppliers of cheap labor and raw materials.[10]

Thoughtful people of every nation and ethnicity are dismayed at what looks like the wholesale purchase of planet earth by corporate giants bent on "processing" every inch of it for their own profit. Since the 1990s a multinational "anti-globalization" movement has mounted protests against corporate abuses on the campuses of prestigious universities and on the streets of major cities, filmed by the cameras of the international media. But way underneath the media's radar, working people mount their own protests in neighborhoods and small towns (see Chapters 3 and 11), reclaiming their right to take part in the decisions that affect their lives.

The two sides do not know each other. If they could meet, it is possible to imagine that the perpetrators of corporate abuses would face an irresistible democratic challenge in the land of their headquarters, the United States of America. This book aspires to bridge a century-old cultural gap because democratization cannot succeed without genuine democracy, which must entail commitment and cooperation across the unrecognized divide of American culture.

The View from Anthropology

Cultural anthropologists study cultural diversity. It was our discovery, a century or so ago, that different peoples do not just *act* differently, they see the world differently. The discipline arose in the historical context of European colonization, when Europeans took on the task of figuring out "the natives" in whose land, labor, and resources the colonizers were interested. In most cases these were not *states*. That is, they were peoples who managed to keep their lives in order without many of the social institutions that we take for granted, like powerful leaders, police, prisons, armies, land titles, even money. They were immensely fascinating, and immensely disturbing. How could they live together without these institutions? What kept them from theft and murder and rape? Intimate contact with these cultures had a way of shaking up what the anthropologists had long assumed to be natural in human social life.

There was only one way to get good answers to our big questions.

That was to move in, share their lives, and work our way through the thick fog of mutual incomprehension. Ethnographic research is unique in this. It does not take polls, administer questionnaires, or test people in laboratories. Ethnography is the *live-in* study of human social life. And we succeed—if we succeed—by weathering no end of awkward moments on the path of learning what it is to be human among the people we study.

The view from anthropology, then, has been shaped by close encounters with societies in which the researcher's own cultural knowledge was useless. After a few rounds of these encounters, there was no alternative but to rethink, from the ground up, what human society and culture is all about. This is the source of our strength—we can take nothing for granted.

Most anthropologists still go abroad to conduct their research, but many of us have turned back to our own societies, concerned that the standard methods of polls and surveys are not painting an adequate picture of the cultural diversity among us.[11] Pollsters pose a question and give their respondents a set of choices, such as "strongly agree," "agree," or "disagree." But what if the only honest response is that the pollster's question is irrelevant, or worse, to the respondent? There is no choice for that. To a cultural anthropologist, such methods assume the very thing that needs to be investigated—cultural homogeneity. Survey methods can only produce useful data to the extent that the questions and the range of choices reflect the shared concerns of both pollsters and respondents; that is, to the extent that they share the same culture. The extent to which they do *not* will remain invisible—or worse.

It is an intriguing consistency of cross-cultural mistrust that the peoples involved think that they *do* understand each other—the other guys are simply primitive, have bad manners, eat disgusting food, and probably do immoral things with their kin. There is no end to this kind of "knowledge" in the annals of cross-cultural encounters. And we can see just this sort of "knowledge" in much (not all) literature on U.S. working people. At best they show up as people with economic and intellectual "disadvantages" whose "culture" is a poor reflection of the genuine article. At worst they are contemptible. Their "authoritarianism," "moral absolutism," "anti-intellectualism," "parochialism," "apathy," and "intolerance" were diagnosed in the early years of the Cold War by an influential group of social scientists whose work[12] has cast a long shadow over research on the United States. (Chapter 3 returns to this problem.)

Mistrust across cultural borders is nothing new, nor is the use of ethnographic research to bridge it. What is new is the recognition of a cultural border across the broad middle of an American culture widely acclaimed for its individualism and optimistic pursuit of upward mobility. From the perspective of this American culture, the people I studied must look like "failures." They are not, as they see it. They do not measure themselves against the standards of "pecuniary emulation." The culture that animates the working people I studied poses a serious challenge to conventional views of the United States.[13]

"The Valley"

The people I studied live in the Mohawk River Valley of Central New York, a place of stunning natural beauty where steep, densely wooded hills slope dramatically to "the flats," the rich bottom lands on which most of the region's population clusters. Since time immemorial the flats have produced abundant harvests of corn, for most of those years under the skilled hands of Mohawk women, members of the easternmost of the Six Nations, the mighty Iroquois whose diplomatic prowess tipped the balance of power between the warring New World empires of England and France.

Where I lived, the valley bottom is called "German Flatts" because the first European settlers there spoke German. They were Protestant religious refugees from wars in Europe that brought their ancestral homeland, the Palatinate (between France and Germany), under French rule, a domination that targeted them for forced conversion to Catholicism, or genocide. With the aid of the British colonial government—happy to have a buffer between their own settlements and an increasingly restless Iroquois Confederacy—the Palatines purchased land from the Mohawk Nation in the 1720s.[14] The oldest families in the region today proudly claim Palatine descent.

Whatever wary coexistence the Mohawk and the Palatines worked out was shattered by the American Revolution. The Mohawk Nation sided with the British.[15] Most Palatines took the rebel side.[16] When the tide of war finally turned to the Patriot side, the Mohawk, firm in their allegiance to the English, fled with them to Canada, and this fertile land attracted the attention of a new wave of settlers. New England Yankees by the thousands fled their rocky soil for "the West": the "new" lands of the Mohawk Valley.

The Palatines and their new Yankee neighbors eyed each other with mutual suspicion, guarding the separation of their linguistic, religious, and commercial worlds into the 1820s, but in the end, their differences were less prepossessing than their shared view of what life ought to be. They were both farmers of their own land, who spun yarn and wove cloth for their clothes, made cheese, forged tools, cobbled shoes, and built furniture in their workshops, ground grain, pressed oil, and sawed wood in their mills, and traded their surpluses along the Mohawk River.

Early in the nineteenth century the Mohawk Valley was reshaped by the most monumental engineering feat of its day, the Erie Canal, completed in 1825. For a century the Canal cut a long, straight path of glowing prospects across New York State—363 miles long, from Albany west to Buffalo—linking the state's fertile hinterlands with the emerging trade routes of the Great Lakes and the teeming port of New York City, down the Hudson River. By the time the Canal was dug, Palatines and Yankees were poised to build up their mills and workshops into "manufactories" (as they called them), ushering in a century of prosperity. (Chapters 4–6 give more detail on these developments.) The cities of Utica, Syracuse, Rochester, and Buffalo grew large on the commerce of the Canal. But more interesting than the large cities, for the "old values" that the people I worked with "cling to," were the scores of small towns that line the Canal like beads on a string.

In the middle of the state, along the Canal's oldest section (opened in 1817), four towns cluster on the flats and spread up the wooded hills just south of the Adirondack Mountains. Like most Canal towns, these four—Herkimer, Mohawk, Ilion, and Frankfort—grew up on the mix of agriculture and manufacturing that was characteristic of the nineteenth-century Northeast. I follow local usage in referring to these four towns and the farms that still surround them as "the Valley."

Who lives there? They are, most of them, members of a group that a recent study argues is "America's best kept secret," the 62 percent of the United States' population who work nonsupervisory jobs at the bottom of the country's power structure, with little autonomy or security (Zweig 2000:28–34). They are overwhelmingly white (as I will discuss further in Chapter 2), and they are a people of a particular place whose understanding of the world has been shaped by a singular past, the often surprising twists and turns of which will unfold in the chapters that follow. But the outline of their past is not theirs alone—it is shared by communities across the Northeast and Midwest "rust belt," the longtime heartland of U.S. heavy industry.

In the nineteenth century, they enjoyed a measure of prosperity. They worked hard for it, building homes, farms, workshops, factories, churches, and town halls, as settlers did all over the United States. But near the end of that century the fruits of all their labors seemed to slip from their hands. The manufacturing enterprises they built were taken over by the "trusts," the disreputable ancestors of many of today's most powerful corporations. (See Part II for discussion of the trusts). Step by disturbing step, the trusts-turned-corporations took control of the most important decisions in their lives. When the corporations were willing, or pressured into it, people could enjoy a modest comfort and security. But it was the corporations' call—they held the reins of local prosperity.

Beginning in the late 1960s the corporations left in pursuit of "cheap labor" elsewhere, and the people of the Valley, like millions of others across the rust belt, found their own work cheapened. By the 1980s they shared the standard predicament of the working majority today, negotiating the shifting sands of unpredictable, "temp," low-wage jobs.

Not surprisingly for a people who have seen radical social change, little of it for the better, the people I studied spend a lot of time thinking and talking about the past. They have been, for several generations now, avid conservers of artifacts and lore from the local past which, taken together, compose the rich treasure-trove of local history that this book gratefully plunders (described and discussed in Appendices 1 and 2). So the people I studied are not only the living people whose daily lives I shared but also the people of their past about whom they tell stories and whose things they have saved in their homes and in local historical collections.[17] No name looms larger in the memorabilia of the Valley than Remington, the family who, for three generations, blazed the trail of regional manufacturing.

For three-quarters of a century, from the 1810s to 1886, the varied enterprises of E. Remington & Sons were the backbone of a thriving local economy. The Remington manufactories, like others of their day, arose on the skills of local "mechanics" (or artisans), and made common cause with surrounding farms to the mutual advantage of each. Contrary to the standard picture of a farming nation collapsing before the hard imperative of industrialization, in the Valley and elsewhere farm and factory created markets for each others' products and work for each others' people—the slack seasons of the agricultural year became the busy seasons of the manufacturing year.[18] Skilled "mechanics" were the pillars of a local society that had every reason to believe in the rewards of hard work under democratic self-rule. They lived well, working at their own pace and pursuing their musical, dramatic, religious, historical, literary, and sporting interests in scores of formal and informal associations. Time and again, the Remingtons acted to sustain the prosperity of the community through hard times, even when that commitment meant their taking on a heavy burden of debt. (Part II tells the Remington story.)

Then came the big change. In the decades around the turn of the twentieth century, the trusts, numerically tiny but connected to big capital on Wall Street and abroad, managed a coup that subordinated places like the Valley, across the industrialized United States, to a moneyed foe that looked suspiciously like the Old World aristocracy their democratic ideals had long condemned.

The trusts sent charismatic speakers to persuade the conquered multitudes that their new distant rulers were the harbingers of a more efficient way to produce the goods they desired. But working people desired more than goods. They desired a good life in which their views mattered. This the neo-aristocracy could not provide. Its view of efficiency meant that it alone made the decisions (Chapters 8–10).

Fought out in public arenas across the country, the ensuing crisis engaged the most significant debate in the history of the United States: What kind of a country was this to be? What could democracy mean when distant capitalists—with no place in the Constitution of this nation—could override the will of a loyal and industrious people? How could the founding vision of popular sovereignty survive such an imposition? The corporate capitalists could not answer these questions then, and they still stand unanswered.

The Valley's story is a regional variant of a larger story, the corporate sabotage of American democracy. Today we hardly have the words to remember it. And we do not because the corporate coup was not only a matter of controlling production, land, jobs, natural resources, and money. It quickly became a matter of thought-control, of *cultural* production. In the 1890s, with unprecedented resources at their disposal, the trusts-turned-corporations' "cultural revolution" sought to substitute the traditional ideal of democratic prosperity with their own ideal: "survival of the fittest," a philosophy that would relieve them of responsibility for the people whose work made their wealth (see Chapter 9).

Few of us are willing to embrace the necessary implication of "survival of the fittest"—that poverty and desperation among us are natural and unavoidable—but we are inundated with corporate propaganda, so inundated that we hardly see it. And if we do not see it, we cannot see through it. "Watching" the corporate cultural campaign in the Valley as it tries to legitimate a new cultural order (Chapters 9 and 10), first clumsily, then gaining in sophistication, offers an opportunity to see the corporate manipulation of American culture afresh. Through this story the antidemocratic coup that shaped our times is forced out of its historical hiding place.

The American culture that the corporate cultural revolution produced did not fully take root among the Valley's working people because it had nothing to say to their predicament, except that it was the fault of their own inferior "fitness." They know better, and we can too. This book tells their story through the voice of an anthropologist who was ill-prepared to recognize the deep roots of their discontent. Theirs is the story of stubborn clinging to *genuine* "traditional American values" that see the nations' wealth as the creation of everyone who works, every one of whom ought to receive a fair share of the wealth they create. Their story pulls democracy back to earth, back from the self-serving propaganda of a regime that has won its legitimacy by effectively disenfranchising the working majority.

The corporate neo-aristocracy owns and controls not only the food, housing, and work that are the basic ingredients of decent human life but also the media through which images of ourselves as people and as a polity flow. The rootedness of U.S. democracy in the work and prosperity of the whole nation is not a story that the corporate order has wished to tell. Our cultural forgetting is their cultural production. Our remembering is a step toward rebuilding democracy.

2

The Valley

You can enter the Valley from the east, exiting the New York State Thruway onto the busy streets of Herkimer, but the western approach from Utica offers a spectacular panorama. A couple of miles east of the Utica train station you round the crest of a hill—and suddenly the Valley spreads out before you like a vast homemade quilt. Ancient hedgerows define field and pasture, outlining "patches" that each season recolors, deep hazy greens, red and gold, speckled white. The practiced eye can trace one plumb-straight line to which all others orient, the ghost of the old Erie Canal and, snaking alongside it, the silver thread of the Mohawk River. It's a fertile, well-cared-for land.

Only toward the end of your long, steep descent do the towns come into focus. You first touch bottom at Frankfort, westernmost of the four towns, technically "villages" (the smallest incorporated units of New York State government), that make up the Valley in local geographic reckoning. Once the site of a major canal dry dock (and red-light district), a match factory (infamous for a tragic explosion), a railroad yard, and a sparkling "modern" milk-processing factory, Frankfort today hosts a few acres of boarded-up factory buildings, the outpost of a tool-manufacturing firm, and the county fairgrounds.

Continuing east on Main Street, exactly parallel to the old Canal, is a sparsely settled stretch that local people call "the reservation"— once a colony of Southern Italians whom early twentieth-century entrepreneurs imported to do the dirty work of the Valley's industry. Some of their descendants still live in the bungalows of "little Italy," just outside the next village, Ilion, my base for eighteen months of ethnographic fieldwork.

Ilion has been home since 1828 to the varied manufacturing enterprises that bore the name of their founding family, the Remingtons. By 1960 these enterprises had swelled to four huge "plants," employing upward of twenty-five thousand. Here, generations of workers have turned out vast quantities of just about anything made of metal—agricultural implements of all kinds, automobile parts, bicycles, cotton gins, firearms, iron bridges, sewing machines, trolley cars, the first commercial typewriters in the world, and UNIVAC computers (see Part II for a discussion of these varied products). Now a single factory complex seems considerably too large for its thousand or so full-time employees. Ilion was, and even in its shrunken state remains, the industrial center of the Valley.

Continuing east along the Canal's path, the third inhabitant of the Valley's shared Main Street, the village of Mohawk, comes into view. It feels more "country" than its neighbors—no factory buildings, but gift shops and an old-fashioned ice-cream parlor line Main Street, along with a cluster of unmistakably governmental buildings. Mohawk is the administrative center for the Town of German Flatts, which encompasses Mohawk, Ilion, and their surrounding countryside. (It surprises some of my Western friends that we are so comprehensively governed in the Northeast as to have township government intermediating between municipality and county.)

You have to cross the Mohawk River to get to the fourth and easternmost village of the Valley, Herkimer, the administrative center of Herkimer County. Here the courts and jail, the county legislature,[1] social services, and innumerable other administrative offices are the village's major employers.

In the 1850s a group of Herkimer men bid to challenge Ilion's industrial might with a textile manufacturing complex. It was a costly failure. The problem was, in part, the magnet of better-paying work in Ilion's factories to the west, but probably more significant was the established textile center at the city of Little Falls, just east of Herkimer. Despite its geographic proximity, Little Falls tends to fall outside local reckoning of the Valley proper. The cultural logic of Little Fall's exclusion offers an important insight into how the people of the Valley understand themselves.

The Message of a Borderline

Why this exclusion from "the Valley"? For one thing, Little Falls let itself become a city. In the Valley proper, a cadre of wealthy citizens promoted city-dom with a series of early twentieth-century initiatives, but every one of them was firmly voted down by the populace (see Chapter 8). What *city* meant to them was not how they wanted to be. Most Herkimer County residents today are proudly, even defiantly, *not* urban.

For much of the twentieth century the city of Little Falls has been smaller in population than the villages of Ilion and Herkimer, but, interestingly, it has a palpable citylike feel. What gives Little Falls its urbanity eluded me until the implications of a fascinating conversation I had at the Herkimer County Historical Society began to infiltrate my ethnographic awareness.

A couple of well-informed local historians had been trying to describe for me the particular character of the Valley. "We don't have social class here," one volunteered with evident pride. But Little Falls *does*, another added. Little Falls, they told me, has "real wealth"—people who drive luxury cars, they said, and regularly vacation in Europe.

Was "real wealth" what made Little Falls different? Real wealth and its necessary opposite, yes. In this small city grand homes perch high above street level a few blocks away from dingy rows of "worker housing." By contrast, the Valley appears strikingly homogeneous. Everybody dresses with casual tidiness and drives modest, U.S.-made cars. The typical house has two stories, with basement below, attic above, and porches fore and aft, and with the well-mown summer lawns and well-shoveled winter sidewalks that signify "house-proud" inhabitants. The occasional run-down house only serves to point out the general well-keptness of the place. In time I discovered that wealth differences were a major topic of gossipy speculation, but no self-respecting Valley resident indulges in visible conspicuous consumption—indeed, the putatively wealthier residents are likely to underplay their status with older cars and well-worn clothes.

Appearances can be deceiving, certainly, but to an ethnographer's eye they are never arbitrary—they are symptomatic of people's ideals and expectations. "We don't have social class" may not stand the test of sociological scrutiny, but it certainly suggests that somewhere in the consciousness of all those Valley people who take care to present themselves as *like* their neighbors in dress, house, and car, there dwells some ideal of equality.

Not having social class has been a dream of tremendous significance for the United States of America. And what follows from that dream can cast a long shadow over the legitimacy, the appropriateness, even the patriotism, of this country's increasing division into a handful of "the rich," a growing multitude of "the poor," and a shrinking "middle." If we listen to the voices that speak through the media—including the textbooks with which we educate our young—the explanation of our decreasing equality is simple: It's the economy. The economy changes, and we have to adapt as well as we can. When the economy "limps along" (as it is while I write these words) businesses must let employees go. When it picks up, so will employment.

This may sound reasonable unless, perhaps, we were among the millions who lost a good job over the past couple of decades and, even in the 1990s when the economy was supposedly "booming," could find nothing but insecure, temporary, part-time, poorly paid work. That, in fact, has been the hard fate of many Valley residents. When a supposedly "booming economy" produces nothing but hard times across the visible social landscape, economic explanations do not explain the problem.

Valley people are likely to explain their own and their community's predicament in terms of *greed*—corporate greed, a predictable component of their working lives, and political greed, which strongly arouses their indignation. This country is supposed to be a democracy, they often observe, but the politicians whom they put in office to serve the people "serve themselves." They do not, as one put it, "care one bit about us working people." Democracy, in their view, has fallen prey to greed.

But greed, surely, is nothing new. Why should it suddenly strike and leave communities of hard-working people in trouble? From the Valley's perspective, there is no debate over the fact that their lives used to be better. Some of them know this personally because they have lived long enough to see major, long-term change in this society. Others can know it through the treasury of stories about the past that circulate whenever Valley people get together (Chapters 3 and 4). Where was the greed then? To this anthropologist, what needs explaining is what changed between then and now to "liberate" greed, to remove whatever barriers must have once held it at bay long enough for the Valley to have lived well and dreamed of not "having social class." What changed, I argue, is American culture.

The border that Valley residents implicitly maintain between themselves and Little Falls can stand as a symbol of the cultural transformation that is a central subject of this book. Little Falls feels like a city because of its visible class divisions. For most of a century, its textile mills sustained a working class of renters and an elite of "real wealth." Ilion's manufactories, in contrast, sustained home-owning working people and an elite who did not invest in conspicuous consumption to distinguish themselves from the people who worked for them.

This is the lesson of the invisible border that separates Little Falls from the Valley. Little Falls, if I may speak for the Valley's perspective, has come to symbolize the kind of America in which a few can live extravagantly while the majority live in insecurity. So it stands outside the Valley that, for all its present difficulties, has come to symbolize an America in which everyone can live in modest prosperity.

Natives and Newcomers: Class, Race, and Social Capital

As well it could. Street upon street of spacious, well-kept homes testify to the comfortable living that the Valley's local economy once provided. But here looks *are* deceiving. For most Valley residents, holding onto those homes requires negotiating a job market of temporary, part-time, low-paying work. It takes at least two of these jobs, often supplemented by a home-based business ("on the books" or not)—like child care, motorcycle repair, or the varieties of commerce that pass under the name of "garage sales"—to pay mortgage, insurance, taxes, upkeep, and stay decently well-fed and clothed. It's all you can do to keep the roof over your head, people complain—it's impossible to "get ahead."

Who are these people? Three characteristics of the Valley's population stand out. First, they are people sociologists would label working class, but, like most of the United States, they identify as middle class. Second, they are white people. Third, most of them have lived in the area for more than three generations.

Sociologically speaking, the Valley is, and historically has been, working class. Until the 1970s, a comfortable and secure living could be earned, without postsecondary education, in local factories and in the many small businesses that thrived in a population of well-paid factory workers. (In the mid-1990s, only 14 percent of Ilion's adults had postsecondary school education [Dembowski 1994:25].) Most residents of the Valley, however, identify their status as firmly middle class. These contrasting judgments on the matter of social class point to a very interesting problem.

In the United States we are culturally shy on the question of social class. We do not, at least in public, like to talk about this society as divided into a few who have much and, in most cases, always will, and many who don't and, in most cases, never will. As scores of sociological studies note, "everybody" in the United States claims middle-class status. The school janitor might hedge his bets by describing himself as *lower* middle class, and the college student living on a million-dollar trust fund might admit to being *upper* middle class, but we rarely describe ourselves as "working class" or "upper class."

This nearly universal claim to middle-class status distresses many social scientists. They see in it an irrational cultural denial of social facts that are clearly evident in every industrialized society. Our propensity for identifying with the middle class, these scholars argue, is merely ideological. It is ideological, yes, but the ideology at stake is a very significant one. Despite (and perhaps because of) the differences we can see in education, wealth, and style among the people of this country, we prefer to insist, at least in public, that our common ground as persons and citizens matters more, that we are, in truth, "created equal."

Social class, as a social scientific principle, however, can help us understand why the dream of a classless society has been so hard to realize. Social class is, at one level, a pattern of minority control over the sources of wealth we call capital—money, land, machines, wells, mines, shipping, airlines, the media, and so forth—and the influence over political and legal regulation that wealth generally enjoys. In business as in government these resources are managed by hierarchies through which a few people make rules and decisions that affect millions of others, and those at "the top," owners and managers of capital, see to it that their own work is richly rewarded.

Needless to say, perhaps, people who have little or no capital—the great majority of us—are less likely to view this reward system with enthusiasm. As we'll see throughout this book, the view "from above" that makes capital the weight and measure of all value has long been countered by a view "from below" that makes *work* the ultimate determiner of value. The long history of competition between these two class-cultural perspectives in the Valley (see Chapter 8) will demonstrate a depth of cross-class cultural difference that our view of American culture typically ignores.

Across this country, still today, we set aside our ideology of class-lessness in the heat of political conflict. As it happened, I bumbled into just such a conflict in the Valley, the meaning of which will occupy much of this book. What was plain to see, in that charged atmosphere, was an unraveling of the "classlessness" on which the Valley so prides itself. As local officials announced the next year's budget figures or the next increase in utility rates, angry citizens laid claim to something that looked very much like a separate class identity. They were "the *working* people," they said, as opposed to politicians, government em-ployees, and corporate managers. They were "average Americans" or "the little guy" or, simply, "the people" as opposed to the "higher-ups," the "big guys," or the "people who think they're better than us." Chapter 3 will return to these conflicts and the conflicting class iden-tities they forced into the open, and succeeding chapters will trace their roots down the winding road of the local past. These contradic-tory views of social class, in the Valley and in the larger U.S. society of which it is a part, are the central conundrum of this book.

Second, the people of the Valley are overwhelmingly white people. With 97.8 percent of Herkimer County's population classified "white" (according to the 2000 U.S. Census), the area is actually more non-white than it has ever been. (The county was 99.2 percent white in the 1990 census.) This absence of racial diversity is not untypical of nonurban areas, but it presents special problems for social research.

No problem has vexed social research on the United States more than race. With the idea that the Valley's racial homogeneity might have some useful clues to this problem, I proposed a research question on "the social construction of whiteness." This concept (see Franken-berg 1993 and Roediger 1991) recognizes that racial friction is not nat-ural but, rather, is taught and learned, thus, "constructed" in social interaction. I suspected that I would be able to study some of the processes through which white people socially construct the superi-ority of whiteness. The social construction of whiteness contends that race inflects the views and positions of every social identity in the United States.

But I was unable to garner any insight into the "whiteness" prob-lem.[2] During my eighteen-month research period, I heard (and duti-fully recorded in my fieldnotes) a total of three remarks that could be construed as racist, all to the point that specific African Americans, historical and present-day, were "not willing to work." The same was said of many whites, especially those at the top of the local social hierarchy.

Does this mean that the Valley is not racist? The people I worked with, if I broached the subject directly, insisted that they were not, but in this racially homogeneous region there were few occasions that put that claim to the test. In short, my findings do not support the contention that race inflects the views and positions of every social identity in the United States. Indeed, in retrospect, I would suggest that, at the close range of regional study, we should not expect it to—and for precisely the reason that today's scholars must emphasize race in historical and ethnographic research: Race has been sadly neglected. Why? Because for nearly two centuries the prevailing view, scholarly and popular, was that the United States *is* a white, European culture and society.

In a universe where "American" is assumed to be white, and the people among whom one lives are white, being white does not have to provoke self-consciousness of whiteness. It is the assumed, the unmarked category.[3] In the Valley, historically, race or skin color did not distinguish people. I do not wish to represent the people I studied as exceptionally virtuous. Historically, they distinguished the social differences that impinged on their lives: "people" (British and Palatine) and "Indians" or "savages," for example; "people" (Yankees) and "Krauts" (Palatines); or "people" (Protestants) and "dagoes" or "wops" (Italian Catholics). If African Americans settle in the Valley in considerable numbers, "people" (whites) and "blacks" may come to bear a set of complex meanings, but, for now, race is a rather abstract concept in local social life, not a daily social tension, and the people I worked with have chosen what they see as the morally correct position of nonracism.

Third, and crucial to understanding the people of the Valley, is that a large proportion of local families have been in the area for many generations, a fact that has important consequences for their lives, material and cultural. There are two kinds of people in the Valley, as I began to discover when I asked a local historian how long her family had been in the area. She replied, with a certain embarrassment, "oh we're relative newcomers—only thirty-five years." As an architect who had "only" lived in the area twenty-five years explained it: "You gotta be three generations here to call yourself a 'native.'"

In an economically depressed area like the Valley, where there is no job market to attract immigration, "newcomers" are rare. The area has been, predictably, losing population over the last few decades. Newcomers are likely to be professionals, come to the Valley for administrative jobs, or commuters to such jobs elsewhere who have discovered its depressed real estate market—rust belt towns are great places to find beautiful old houses at bargain-basement prices.

"Natives," though, the majority of the local population, present a more complicated question for analysis. Why do they stay in a depressed region? While population loss has been steady since the 1970s, that loss (about 2 percent countywide in the 1990s) is minuscule compared to the hemorrhaging of good jobs. Thanks to a demographic study commissioned by the Ilion school district (Dembowski 1994), we have some statistics that can take us part way toward puzzling through the "natives'" seemingly irrational commitment to their economically depressed hometowns.

Considering their general identification with the middle class, Ilionites' median annual household income, $22,115 (Dembowski 1994:14), is decidedly low. Forty-six percent of Ilion's households take in less than $20,000 a year. Three fourths make less than $35,000 a year, and only 12 percent take in $55,000 or more. About a third, "30 to 35 percent of our population," a local official informed me, claim public assistance of some kind.

And yet 65.5 percent of Ilion's houses are owner-occupied, well above the national average. Many people of the region pride themselves on the "old value" of thriftiness, but with those income figures, thrift alone cannot account for such high rates of home ownership. What can? The answer is directly connected to "natives'" residence in the area across generations. We could call it transgenerational "sweat equity"—today's residents are heirs to the work of past generations.

Many of Ilion's home owner–occupants are living in houses that were built by their kin and inherited (or purchased for less than market value) from the parents, grandparents, or other kin who built them—three-fourths of the village's housing stock was constructed before 1930 (Dembowski 1994). "Sweat equity" capital, unlike money capital, is not readily transferable to someplace else. Entering the housing market of another region, at a level that could duplicate their Valley standard of living, would take forbidding amounts of money. Leaving the Valley, then, would likely mean acute "downward mobility."[4]

But even less transferable than "sweat equity" capital is "social capital" (Bourdieu 1977, 1990); that is, people's knowledge of each other, their reputations, the esteem in which they are held by others in the community. As French anthropologist/sociologist Pierre Bourdieu defines it, *social capital* is the ability to maintain a network of social support (1990:35). In the Valley many people call it "neighborliness," the relations of reciprocal sharing, helping, and watching out for each other that can make the difference between a satisfying life and a desperate life, especially when money capital is in short supply.

Though they would not put it in such a calculating way, we could say that Valley natives strategize with deliberation and ingenuity to stay in a depressed region because their nontransferable capital in homes and land, kin and friendship add up to a quality of life that they could not reproduce anywhere else. How would they put it? Many people told me that they lived in "the most beautiful place in the world" and that they would never want to live in a city where everybody is a stranger. They have invested their lives in this place for generations, and they feel it as deeply wrong that they or their children should not be able to continue their lives there.

So they fight, many of them, to preserve their community, against corporate and political foes who seem bent on selling them for scrap. The Valley owes much of its image of middle-class well-being to prior generations—today's residents are living in the "hand-me-downs" of a prosperity that, under present conditions, they cannot reproduce. And they are keenly aware of this. "What will be left for our children and grandchildren?" is a comment I heard daily in conversations about wages, health care, the environment, taxes, and politics. Reproducing their community is the driving force of the Valley's grassroots politics.

The Ethnographer in the Valley

The goal of ethnographic research is to produce careful, valid accounts of the cultures we investigate. In this sense, our ends are scientific. But ethnographers are not microscopes, we are living people, and the ethnographic encounter is necessarily one with unique personal dimensions. The product of this kind of research is an account of a people by a trained observer—in this case, myself—but of course they were observing me too. Who was I to them?

For one thing, I was someone who could appear to be one of them.

I had a curious experience over my first weeks in the Valley. People stared at me—politely, out of the corner of their eyes, but persistently and, for me, unnervingly. Did I have New York City written all over me? Was I going to get categorized as one of those people who "think they're better than us" and never be able to connect with them? My sister came for a short visit and saw it too, but, to my great relief, she interpreted their stares differently. "It's not that they're suspicious of you," she said, "they're trying to figure out whose daughter or sister or niece you are—they think they *ought to* know who you are." They were trying to place me. They do not expect total strangers in their world. I could have been one of them, and of course they did not want to be un-"neighborly."

In time I made friends who introduced me to their friends and it quickly became clear that "anthropology" was not necessarily a meaningful description of what I was doing there. One evening, on the steps of the Ilion Free Public Library, I tried another self-description. I was, I said (drawing on a once-prominent ethnographic genre), doing a "community study." The response was striking. *Of course*, their community was worthy of study. Important things had gone on there in the past, some people noted. But more often the response was to the effect that it was "high time" their community got some attention: They had worked hard for generations, and fought every one of the nation's wars with tremendous personal sacrifice—but today, nobody wants to hear about their problems. I did.

In another sense, I really could have been one of them. I have a genealogical connection to Ilion and the Valley. My mother, granddaughter of an Ilion toolmaker, daughter of an Ilion clerk and factory worker, returned to the village to attend high school. Although she moved away for good after graduation, my connection to the region through my mother opened doors for me—some of the people I worked with saw it as entitling me to a share in local knowledge that a total stranger could not claim.

But it was probably more important in the long run that I was, as a county legislator put it, "a good listener"—at a time of great local uncertainty. Remington Arms, the last large factory in the Valley, was up for sale. Corporate and political officials denied this, but no one, justifiably, believed them. It was sold in December of 1993 to a New York City investment firm, and, some people say, it is on the auction block yet again. In such a tense environment, people are inclined to explain themselves to a "good listener" as they try to understand the shifting sands of their world and think about their alternatives for the future.

The Valley and the Nation

The people of the Valley cannot be said to represent the people of the United States, nor to be a "microcosm" of the country as a whole. Central New York has its own regional traditions, and the Valley is certainly less racially diverse than any big cities of the United States. But the people I studied are not, on the other hand, unique. Many hundreds of smaller communities, especially in the Northeastern rust belt have been shaped by the same large-scale historical processes that shaped the Valley.

Here manufacturing developed in the early 1800s, in partnership with local agriculture (see Chapter 5). Canals, and later railroads, increased the numbers of manufacturing workers and their potential customers. In the decades that bracketed the year 1900, however, across the industrialized United States, thriving, locally owned enterprises were likely to be taken over by an ancestor of today's corporate giants, to eventually be integrated as a subsidiary division in a corporate empire. From this point forward, local decisions of any consequence could be preempted by the plans of corporate headquarters, which held the sword of impoverishment over local prosperity. In the later decades of the twentieth century, corporate headquarters dropped that sword, moving manufacturing processes to points south or abroad in search of cheap labor.

On this historical skeleton, hundreds of communities could flesh out the particulars of their past. The Valley is a place that offers a fresh, though not unique, vantage point from which to tell this important story about the United States.

3

Local Knowledge

It was stuffy in the Village auditorium on a warm night in the late summer of 1993, and it rapidly got hotter. The scene was the monthly public meeting of the Board of Trustees of the Village of Ilion. The mayor, a youthful forty-something man in shirtsleeves, stood red-faced at the podium, shaking his finger at a group of citizens who were seated together on one side of the auditorium. One of this group, agitated and defensive, was trying to make himself heard over loud heckling from another group of citizens, seated together on the opposite side of the auditorium.

"Oh *sure*! LIAR! Don't trust him!" they called out. Neither the mayor nor the board members, seated on the auditorium's stage, tried to quiet them.

"You don't have a permit," the mayor charged. "You're not a non-profit organization," a trustee interjected, "so you need a permit."

"Yes we *are*," insisted a vigorous white-haired spokesman. "We're the Concerned Citizens for Ilion's Environment," he said, rising to his feet, raising his voice, and looking around the room for acknowledgment. *"You know who we are!*—we have regular meetings, every Tuesday night at the library. The public is welcome."

"You sure knew who we were when we *sued you*," shouted a long-haired man who rose to stand beside the spokesman.

"You are not a *legitimate* group!" the Mayor charged angrily. Lowering his voice and staring hard at the spokesman, he asked pointedly, "What is your *real* purpose?"

"To fight injustice," the spokesman replied forcefully. The other side of the room burst out in contemptuous guffaws.

It was my first Village meeting. I expected reports from the water, sanitation, recreation, police, and fire departments, delivered in the measured tones of bureaucratic efficiency to a handful of salutary citizens. I had read nothing about this "concerned citizens" group in the newspapers. And nothing in the mountains of studies I had poured through prepared me to find white Americans organizing themselves to "fight injustice."

Social scientists have been nearly unanimous in their dim view of "average," home-owning white people.[1] They are supposed to have, as one sociologist put it, an "enclave consciousness" (Plotkin 1990), ignorant of and uninterested in "larger issues." Their only political commitment, many commentators believe, is to their property values. They live "microsocial lives," a respected sociologist writes (Gans 1991:ix,xi). They're NIMBYs ("Not In My Back Yard"), according to this scholarly consensus, who block the construction of good projects like halfway houses and homeless shelters in their neighborhoods. And they're probably racists too. People of the white majority "admire the rich" and "despise the very poor," writes a professor of journalism with undisguised contempt (Willis 1998:18–19). Average, white, home-owning Americans are not supposed to be concerned about injustice.

Maybe they really aren't. Maybe the Concerned Citizens' idealistic statement was just rhetoric, intended to cover up a "hidden agenda." As I soon found out, that is precisely what their political opponents— Village officials and their allies in business and county government— thought.

Ethnography thrives on conflict. Such is our human bias in favor of social peace that only in controversy do the fault lines of a social scene fracture and become visible to an outside observer. Had I struck ethnographic gold? I quickly decided, of course, to go to the Concerned Citizens' "regular public meeting at the library." Mr. Paul Kinney, octogenarian elder brother of my mother's closest high school friend, a retired factory worker and respected elder, enthusiastically agreed to go with me.

The white-haired spokesman of the Concerned Citizens, Mr. Kinney told me, was Jim, the owner of a venerable local institution, the old South Ilion cider mill. It had been in his family for generations. Last year, Mr. Kinney said, Jim had led a group of some four hundred citizens in protest against the construction of a "cogeneration plant" (a privately owned electricity plant) on the hill behind Remington Arms, a neighborhood of old Victorian homes. Hmmm. Maybe they *were* just NIMBYs defending their property values.

Mr. Kinney and I were two of twelve men and women that night who took places around the large conference table at the Remington Room of the Ilion Free Public Library for the Concerned Citizens' weekly meeting. "Let's introduce ourselves," Jim suggested. (A nice way to find out who we were, I thought, since they surely knew each other.)

Around the table were factory workers, retired factory workers, farmers, small-business owners, a school teacher, a rock musician. At my turn I said that I was an anthropologist from New York University, here to do a community study, and that I was very interested in what the group was trying to do.[2] "Everyone's welcome," Jim said— "We're totally democratic here."

The meeting began with talk about the Village Board meeting. "That was *mild*," a large, gregarious man remarked—"last year they called us *drug dealers* and *welfare cheats!*" "They'd say anything to discredit us," a middle-age woman added.

On that evening's agenda was a new videotape from a statewide activist organization, the All-County Taxpayers Association (ACTA), with which the Concerned Citizens had recently affiliated. Jim interjected (for our benefit?) that the leader of ACTA, is "a Jeffersonian, not a radical." (What did it mean, I wondered, to be "a Jeffersonian" today?)

The subject of the videotape was "backdoor borrowing," a set of private arrangements by which the state government dispenses publicly funded financial benefits to large corporations. Such corporate players as CBS, Bear Stearns, Prudential, Morgan Stanley, the *New York Times*, General Motors, and the New York Mercantile Exchange had all received loan guarantees, tax abatements, and outright grants, ACTA alleged, representing a massive transfer of public funds to private pockets.

The use of state funds for private business, "any private corporation, or association, or private undertaking," is explicitly forbidden in Articles 7 and 8 of the New York State Constitution, ACTA's leader declared, quoting chapter and verse. "ACTA people," he said, have brought suit against this practice. "Join the lawsuit as a plaintiff!" "Show up in court to support us!," he pleaded—"stay well, stay vigilant."

This was shocking information to Mr. Kinney and me, but none of it was news to the Concerned Citizens. Some members had already signed onto the ACTA lawsuit.

"Act globally, think locally," Jim declared, as the meeting turned to a discussion of local "backdoor borrowing." The Concerned Citizens had, as they said, "a thick folder" on the county's Industrial Development Authority (IDA), the leading local channel, they all agreed, through which public moneys flowed to private pockets. Like the 170 or so other IDAs in the state, the Concerned Citizens noted, the local crew borrowed money, bought property, and arranged loans, supposedly to create jobs.

Millions of dollars had changed hands, various Concerned Citizens observed, readily citing the figures, but the jobs never materialized. In fact, they argued (to us? surely the contents of the "thick folder" represented a situation of which they were well aware), IDA projects were further squeezing an already hard-pressed people. By arranging exemptions and abatements on property and sales taxes, the IDA was removing their "developments" from the regular local tax base, at the same time that these projects were major consumers of public services, like police, garbage, and sewers. Our taxes go up, they argued, so banks and real estate dealers can make a profit.

"Is this fair when our people are barely able to hold onto their homes as it is?" "The ____s—that have the farm east of us?—they just sold their life insurance to pay off their property taxes." "So did the ____s!" "What will be left for our children and grandchildren?"

It *was* hard times in the Valley. Many people, including many Concerned Citizens, were scrambling for work, any kind of work, day and night, to keep roofs over their heads. Many were charged more in taxes than they owed on their mortgages.

I asked village, county, and corporate officials about this, and they were unanimous on one thing: It was not their fault. They were working hard to improve conditions in the Valley, but the majority of the people, they said, simply did not understand how complicated the situation is. Yes, taxes are high at a time when a lot of people are underemployed, but this, they said, is because the State mandates expensive social welfare programs and leaves the problem of funding them to local government. Local government has no choice but to raise taxes. And, in the middle of all these *real* problems, the officials lamented, irresponsible troublemakers start stirring up people's anger. They meant, among others, the Concerned Citizens, who were, officials wished to believe, a tiny group of chronic malcontents.

People used to respect their public servants, many local officials told me, but now they are completely "cynical" about government. A well-known local politician made the point this way: "No one believes *anybody* who's involved in government, no matter how well-intentioned or how effective they are, by virtue of the fact that you *are* involved in that process there must be something wrong with you."

Was it possible that the Concerned Citizens (and other critics throughout the county) were merely reacting out of cynicism? Local government does have a hard job. At the bottom of the political chain of command, local government faces hard-pressed residents with a very circumscribed range of power. Still, it did not seem warranted to dismiss the citizens' concerns so easily. "Cynicism" may be a helpful explanation for local officials, but if people are unhappy with their political leaders, the ethnographer needs to find out why they are unhappy, from *their* point of view.

At another hot Village Board meeting I got a crucial clue. At the top of the agenda that night was the touchy subject of the village budget. After a series of well-reasoned arguments for budget increases by various department heads, a Concerned Citizen stood up, exasperated, and made a simple observation: "There are jobs in the paper for *experienced people* for $5.50 an hour. You know, I'm paying your health insurance when I can't afford my own!" He touched a nerve. The auditorium resounded with calls of, "RIGHT," "Right on," "That's right," "YEA."

The Remington Room was packed for the Concerned Citizens meeting that took place after this outburst. The Citizens were angry, but the village budget had taken second place to another concern. The county legislature, against a full tide of citizen disapproval, had just announced substantial pay raises for its administrators.

Discussion was animated. "I got no sympathy for someone who can't live on $32 thousand," a factory worker remarked. "Any of you make that this year?," he asked, already knowing the answer. "No!" "nope," "no way," came the replies.

Clearly, in their view, the County was giving raises to people who were already better off than the vast majority of Valley people. County officials argued that they had to pay these people large sums in order to attract qualified applicants to government jobs, but this argument carried little weight with the Concerned Citizens for reasons that the next line of discussion soon clarified.

A newcomer to the Concerned Citizens heatedly observed that a particular administrator was driving a Lincoln Continental because "he's been at the *public trough* all these years!" "It's a *moral* question," the man continued, and, addressing the absent official, he asked: "How can you keep *feeding off us?*"

"That's exactly what we say," Jim excitedly agreed, "it's a *moral wrong.*" "Their title is civil *servant,* not *master,*" another member added, to the hearty agreement of the group.

A moral question? At the level of fact, the majority of the Valley's taxpayers were struggling with layoffs and insecure part-time jobs in the private sector. Their "public servants," meanwhile, were living in relative comfort, backed by the secure pay and generous benefits of state employment—funded, of course, by the taxes levied on the majority. Was that the moral question? That was part of it, I discovered, but there was one thing more.

At the next Concerned Citizens meeting, discussion turned to term limits, a popular grassroots issue at the time, even in New York City. Valley activists generally agreed that if politicians' terms of office were strictly limited, they would not be able to set up "old boy networks" and "serve themselves," rather than "serving the people." (Politicians, with few exceptions, were adamantly opposed to term limits, arguing that long experience in office allowed them to serve their constituents more effectively.)

"None of them [the politicians] wants term limits," a Concerned Citizen quipped—"*They'll have to go out and get a job!*" Everyone had a good laugh, but it was no joking matter. Stories circulated widely in the Valley about government employees "reading the paper" all day, watching videos to pass the time on long, lazy afternoons, "double dipping" the pension system, and reporting two and three times the number of hours they actually worked.

Here was the key, though it would be years before I understood enough to use it. The moral issue was not that some people were paid more than others but that they did not *work* for it. These people, I was shocked to realize, still believe in something like the old "Protestant work ethic." They are, after all, "working people." Of course they believe in the value of work.

As working people they maintain this belief against the grain of a mainstream American culture that often mocks the "Protestant work ethic" as a thing of the past. And maybe it is, but the past in question is one that the mainstream culture has forgotten. The old Protestant idea that work is virtuous and ennobling (Weber 1976 [1904], chap. 3; Hill 1964) did not arise in a vacuum. It arose at the moral center of a revolution in human social relations of which the vast majority of us have been beneficiaries: The dignity of work was the winning argument in the "common people's" long-prosecuted case against aristocratic rule. Aristocrats, so the argument went, placed themselves "above" work and so lived immorally off the work of others (Faler 1981, Lazerow 1995).

This was exactly the gist of the Concerned Citizens' argument. The politicians and their friends reaped unjust rewards because they did not, in the working people's view, work for those rewards—they "fed off" the work of a hard-pressed public.

The Concerned Citizens did not content themselves with reproducing this ancient complaint—they acted. In campaign after campaign they brought this moral reasoning to bear on public decisions in which they should, as they understood democracy, have had a voice. But their reasoning went unheard by public officials who took for granted the inequalities that aroused the Concerned Citizens' indignation—as well they might, since most officials did not have to live out the consequences of those inequalities.

The officials were clearly wrong about this group's being a tiny band of malcontents. "They're famous," a Herkimer politician observed, "for targeting one person as a troublemaker when they know that thousands agree with him." While there were never more than sixteen members at weekly meetings, and often as few as eight, the Concerned Citizens had a wide network of support across the Valley, including "spies" in administrative offices, a large number of "correspondents" who brought problems to the group's attention, and strong collaborative relationships with other organizations throughout the county. It was, of course, a matter of self-interest that officials diminished and discredited these critics, but no neutral observer could fail to note the cheers that resounded in every public forum when the Concerned Citizens and their allies spoke out.[3]

The Valley's public officials could afford allegiance to mainstream American culture and roll their eyes knowingly if the "Protestant work ethic" ever came up in conversation, as could many of us. The

intriguing question, at this point in time, is how the Valley's working
people have been able to hold on to the old-fashioned idea of the dignity of work.

Old Values

There's a great number of people [in the Valley] who have old
values that are in their heads. They don't know why. They're
there from their grandparents or parents, certain ways of doing
things, a certain persistence or stubbornness, a certain appreciation of their values that they grew up with—and they have
seen those values eroded and destroyed and, in fact, put to the
test of being ridiculed.

JIM 1993

I had asked if I could interview Jim and his wife, Hilda, core members
of the Concerned Citizens. They agreed without hesitation. I was welcome. Would I like to visit them at their farm?

I jumped at the opportunity. We settled into their comfortable living room with glasses of freshly pressed cider. I put the tape recorder
on the table between us and turned it on. Jim spoke first. He had, it
seemed to me, thought out beforehand what he most wanted me to
understand. He wanted me to understand the Valley's "old values." He
did not define them, nor speculate about why some people grew up
with them and "stubbornly" kept them, while others ridiculed them.

We went on to talk for nearly two hours about how they had gotten
involved in grassroots activism. Hilda started it. She had read Rachel
Carson's *Silent Spring* in the 1960s and it set her on fire: She "had to
do something." With the support of other mothers from her sons' Boy
Scout troop, she initiated a recycling system that became the model
for a successful recycling program throughout the Valley.

Hilda was characteristically modest about her achievement. For her
and Jim both, this modest revolution in their hometown followed naturally from their values. Thrift and frugality would surely be on the
"old values" list, as would being a responsible member of one's community. Still, it seemed paradoxical that "old values" would dispose
people to the progressive cause of environmentalism. What were these
values and where did they come from—and what was the "test" of
"ridicule" to which they had been subjected? For the deep questions,
the questions to which the people we study do not have direct answers

to give us, ethnographers can only stay engaged and try to understand the connections.

The Landscape of Social Memory

The [Village] clock was removed in the 1930s. Old timers are still seen glancing in its direction "to see what time it is."

Observer-Dispatch 1961

Curiously, from my first day in the Valley, most everyone I met wanted to tell me about what "used to be" here. At every turn, a house, store, road, barn, shop, machine, or feature of the geography prompted them to tell stories about what "used to be."

The building I moved into, divided into three apartments and a law office for decades, "used to be" the home of a state senator, so the men who moved me into it told me. That side used to be a separate house— he built it for his daughter.

Where was I living? asked a man I met at the Ilion Free Public Library. I told him. Well, he told me, the man who built that house invented Lydia Pinkham's Pills in the nineteenth century and made a fortune off them.

"Oh you live *there*," said a woman I met at a funeral. Well, one of the ways her father worked his way through high school was by going into that house every morning before dawn—used to, nobody locked their doors—to light the downstairs fires before the family got up. "They were real good to him," she remembered.

What "used to be" here was important enough to the people I studied that even landmarks that had not existed for decades, even for a century, called forth stories. "This used to be" where the Erie Canal ran through—right up there were the old dry docks and the "house" where the canal men met their ladies of the night.

"This is where" the old Remington "mansion" used to be—tore it down years ago—"it's a pity but, you know, the Remingtons were modest people, never wanted to live like that anyway." Two decades after Urban Renewal flattened the red-brick downtown that some "natives" call "old Ilion," dozens of people I met could name off each building that used to be along the old Main Street.

Every spot in the landscape seemed to have a dual existence, how it is now and how it "used to be." What did this mean to them?

A long chain of social research suggests that place anchors social memory; that is, places seem to "hold" the past. People and the stories of what happened to them, so the theory goes, can stay alive in memory because they have their place in the shared landscape. And, contrariwise, these researchers find, transience thins social memory, depletes the shared past.[4]

And indeed, in the Valley, it was "natives" who had all the stories. "Newcomers" might speak in historical vein—about which local notables of the past owned this or that fine house, for example—but "natives" had a seemingly boundless treasury of stories about things and people that "used to be." In this sense "natives" and "newcomers" do not quite live in the same Valley. Newcomers only know the place as they see it. Natives know it as it is, but also as it used to be, when things were different and, for them, a good deal better.

Of the past that lives in the Valley's landscape, the most often told is not necessarily what we think of as history. It is not about the great deeds of famous people but about the remembered past, the everyday deeds of people who acquire symbolic currency for what their words and deeds come to mean. Stories of this past are the conversational stock of everyday life—in the car, at work, on the street, at get-togethers, on the phone—whenever the place and the company prompt them. (I scribbled them down as soon as I could, in as close as I could to the conversational styles of the storytellers.)

These stories seemed so much a part of the fabric of everyday life in the Valley that I did not at first register their significance. Coming forth as they often did in reference to a particular place, and in the context of local people's telling an interested newcomer about their community, it was easy to take them as simply objective information. But one evening at a birthday party, I saw the people I was studying engaged in telling stories of the remembered past *to each other*. It was a cross-generational group of nine or ten people, the youngest in her twenties, the eldest in his eighties.

The elders led, catching each others' eyes as they proceeded to the next turn of the story. The younger guests commented and questioned, often turning the story down another avenue of connections. A woman in her mid-fifties started one stream of stories when she mentioned to a younger woman that her mother worked because her father had died when she was a girl.[5]

"So I was a 'latchkey child,'" she said, "Well, not exactly—we never locked our doors. Nobody did in those days, but I could always go over to the Miller's after school. They'd share their supper with me when Mother had to work late."

"You knew old Mrs. Miller, didn't you?" she asks the eldest man. "Oh yes," he responds, Bill and I used to work evenings "over to the greenhouse." The greenhouse, now a ruin, was owned by a relation of "old Mrs. Miller"—the speaker assumed that the listeners knew this. "They treated me like one of their own," the woman concludes, smiling, looking around at the others' faces. They smile at her, at each other, approvingly.

"That old greenhouse on Prospect?" asks one of the younger men— "what happened over there?" "*Well*," say two elder men, almost in unison, catching each others' eyes often as they tell the story together, latching onto each others' remarks.

"When old Mr. Wilkins passed away," one of them notes, "Dan inherited the business." The man who asked about the greenhouse looks puzzled. "You know Ted," says a younger man, filling in the genealogy, "Sue's brother? lived over to the old Johnson place? That's his uncle." "Oh *him*," says the man who asked. "*Well*," the older gents continue: "He didn't care one bit about the business. He just wanted to spend money. He was a regular ladies man. Liked expensive cars. Went way over his head in debt. Let the place go to ruin. What a waste. Best tomatoes in the Valley." People watch each others' reactions. "Too bad," "what a shame," some say. Others shake their heads sympathetically in unspoken agreement.

They went on to another story in the same chatty way. This one pivoted on the plot of land that two of the group, a couple, had recently purchased. They'd heard some strange things about the former owner. "Oh yes," said one of the elder men, warming to the subject. It was owned for years by an eccentric farmer who supposedly made a lot of money in land speculation. "And his widow," someone adds, she had "pillows stuffed with money" but she lived "like an animal," never cleaning the place, wearing four or five tattered dresses at once, one on top of the other.

Through another chain of associations the story-scape moved to South Ilion, where the boundaries of village and township converge. "You remember that terrible fire years ago?," an older man asks. Several tellers contribute, recalling whose house it was, just where it was, what time of night it was, how many were hurt, before the man who had brought it up continues. Three children burned to death before the fire companies got there, not because nobody called for help but because the town and village dispatchers, crackling on their radios, argued about which was responsible for the call.

As each detail entered the picture, with whatever clarifications the listeners and alternate tellers needed to make, there was that taking stock of each others' reactions. And when they reached the end of a story, there was that thoughtful pause, that demonstration of agreement.

That's when I saw it. Spoken or unspoken, there was a *moral* to these stories of the past. The moral of Lydia Pinkham's Pills, like that of the greenhouse story, was about the waste and vanity of pretentiousness, of trying to look "better" than one's neighbors. The rich farmer's wife was about the folly of hoarding wealth—what good might have been done with it? The latchkey child was about a neighborly kindness that, as I would hear again and again, is all too rare these days—little children burn to death for its absence.

Stories of the remembered past, I began to see, are about the living processes of building moral agreement, or values, together, every day, with the bricks and mortar of local places and people. They are about producing a "We" that stands for something, that is larger than the sum of its individual parts.

The more I became aware of this process the more I could hear and observe. Take the following example, prompted by the recollection of a particular house.

> Money was her *God*. When you went over there, she couldn't even offer you a cup of coffee. She got [her aging husband] to put everything he had into real estate. Joe was sent to jail the *day* Sandy came back from the hospital with the baby. They had no place to live. He [the husband] told her they could stay in the Carson house but then *she* stepped in and said, I have a cash buyer standing right here—you'll have to be out in thirty days! Imagine!

The outline of the story is perhaps clear: A young couple had been renting a house, owned by a kind elderly man. The husband of the young couple was arrested just before the wife gave birth, but this did not keep the elderly man's greedy wife from evicting the desperate young mother in favor of a "cash buyer." The moral of the story: Money is not God. By implication, being kind to those in need *is*, a moral direction to which this woman, who "couldn't even offer you a cup of coffee," had no commitment.

Take another example, prompted by a drive around Ilion and reflection on the old downtown that "used to be here" before the disaster of Urban Renewal.

> He doesn't have a shred of decency, and she's just as bad. Years ago, they caught him with his hand in the [government agency] money but they didn't press charges, probably because they were *all* lining their pockets. I guess he didn't get *enough* because then he borrowed ten thousand from [his brother and sister-in-law]—so *she* could ride around in a new Buick and say, "Look how successful my husband is." To this day he hasn't paid back one red cent!

The central character in this story had been a high local official who sought to increase his family's status through his position, with the energetic complicity of his wife. The moral of the story is, again, the vanity of pretending to be "better," but here it is combined with another significant element, the special temptations of public officials.

One further example places the moral values of "natives" in confrontation with those of certain "newcomers."

> Old Mr. Thomas who just passed away? Had a farm up on McVicar Road? He was *renowned* for his knowledge of antique cars. People came from all over to ask his opinion. Well, what really happened is that some new people bought lots out there and built these hundred-thousand-dollar homes. They didn't like the *look* of all those old cars in his yard, and they got a court order to make him "clean up." They had him thrown into jail! On Christmas Eve! He had a heart attack in jail and never got his health back.

"Natives" are likely to understand old cars in the yard. They have skills. A handy old car means handy spare parts when the one you depend on breaks down. And for old Mr. Thomas and the many antique-car fans who consulted him, they meant even more. For the "new people," though, old cars were simply an eyesore, perhaps a symbol of rural poverty. Trying to appear "better" than their neighbors, in this story, claimed the life of a respected elder.

The moral of this story describes "old values" under siege, suffering ridicule, as Jim suggested (above), and it provides a major clue to understanding the others: All these stories are told and listened to against the backdrop of "new" values that glorify the appearance of "being better," the pursuit of wealth for the competitive consumption of status symbols.

I was struck early on by how Valley people cultivated the appearance of "being the same" in their presentation of themselves, an appearance that seemed to support the local claim of not having social class (Chapter 2). Through stories of the past, I was finding out that their appearance of homogeneity was underpinned by a lot of cultural work, a steady effort to build and maintain a moral consensus in which the flaunting of wealth differences was a major moral fault. Why does this matter so much to them?

Neighborliness

Look again at these stories. Who helped, who refused to help, who was stingy when neighbors were in need, who "thought they were too good" for their neighbors—these are recurrent themes. "People used to trust each other, look out for each other." "Nobody locked their doors—most people didn't even *have* locks on their doors." Trust and open doors are key symbols of the "neighborly" way it "used to be." By contrast, they say, people don't even *know* their neighbors in the city, much less trust them.

The people I worked with put a great deal of effort into living their neighborly values, as I discovered first-hand. When a friend of a friend at the library fixed my bicycle, when Mr. Kinney quietly left bags of fresh vegetables at my door after his weekly visits to local farm stands, when half a dozen people helped me diagnose a problem on my phone line, I thanked them effusively, only to be told "it was nothing"—they were just "being neighborly."

I was not sure how to respond until an idea from anthropology came to mind—one of our best ideas, summed up in the word *reciprocity*. Anthropologists historically studied peoples who did not have markets and economic systems as we know them, and the question arose: How are goods distributed among them? The answer was reciprocity, give and take. You give to me today, I'll give to you tomorrow. We give what we can, not wishing to calculate whether our gifts are of equivalent value.[6] A classic study called these "gift economies" (Mauss 1967 [1925]). Was I seeing something like that in the Valley?

There was just one way to find out: Reciprocate. When I stopped looking at "neighborly" kindnesses as exceptional favors and started reciprocating in kind, I found myself in a network of neighborly exchange. I do not wish to romanticize. Sometimes, frankly, being neighborly is a lot of trouble. Sometimes responding to a neighbor's request is a bother and a distraction. Sometimes a favor is unwanted, but one still has to take the time to come up with a reciprocal favor. Still, when people learned that they could count on me, I could count on them, and this was deeply gratifying. It was a revelation.

Neighborly reciprocity is the moral imperative of countless stories through which people of the Valley teach each other—and tried to teach me—that neighborliness is worth the trouble. Neighborliness is the reward, the "profit," of the social capital they can "save" and "invest" by holding onto their homes in the Valley, against the tide of economic logic that would send them south or west in search of better jobs. The trust and open doors of one's neighbors make all the difference to people who know and expect hard times. (Chapter 10 will consider what developments over the long past could produce the expectation of hard times.) Neighborliness—helping, borrowing, lending, "watching out for each other"—makes hard times livable. Imagine a whole community knit together by networks of neighborly give-and-take and you are close, I believe, to Valley "natives'" ideal of classless social good.

As many of these stories suggest, the single greatest threat to neighborly reciprocity is disparity of wealth. Neighborly give-and-take can only operate within narrow tolerances of inequality. Too great neediness next door to too great opulence can only make for mutual suspicion—wealth feels oppressed by the unrelenting demand of need; need feels oppressed by dependency on wealth.

Early in my fieldwork an elder woman suggested just this connection when she told me about a recent visit to New York City. She was "appalled," she said, by all the homeless people she saw on the street. I expected her to continue with a comment like, they should get a job or be moved into shelters, but I had seriously misjudged her perceptions. "I was so upset," she said, "that it was weeks before I could enjoy what I have." The desperation of the city's homeless cast a moral pall over her homely comforts (she was not, by any means, a wealthy woman). She could only enjoy what she had in a social universe where everyone else had comforts like hers.

This is, I believe, close to the bedrock of Valley natives' moral reasoning. Neighborliness requires a certain equality so that both giver and receiver are dignified by the mutual recognition that they will, in the fullness of time, change places—giver will receive and receiver give. Hard-core poverty, no less than entrenched wealth, destroys the equation, stealing dignity from both sides. Relative equality is the precondition of neighborliness.

In the Valley today, neighborliness is pushed up against a competing ethic that, from the neighborly perspective, idealizes appearances over substance, "hustling" over hard work, fun over duty, luxury over saving for the future, conspicuous consumption over helping a neighbor in need. All of the past that "natives" recall and share and teach each other pushes back against the "new values" in which one's own and one's family's dignity rest on "being better" than one's neighbors.

And what does "being better" rest on? I believe its secret is what the old idea of the dignity of work stood against: living off the work of others. Living by one's own productive contribution to the community, not "feeding off" the work of others, would certainly tend toward equalizing wealth. And it is just that kind of productive ideal that Valley "natives" preserve in their local history, the history of the past before memory.

4

Local History

> I have seen my father's face darken when he told of Cherry Val-
> ley, and the dread that was in the homes around Fort Herkimer
> in 1776. And so there are some things that occurred before I
> had a memory that are vivid to my mind.
>
> WALTER C. GREEN, "Early History in Ilion," 1916

Mr. Walter C. Green, storyteller son of a long line of storytellers, came
to the bustling little settlement on the Canal—it would later be the
village of Ilion—from his family's farm on the Flatts (Town of German
Flatts) in 1849, at the age of sixteen, to earn some money in construction. The hamlet was abuilding. E. Remington's forge was finding a healthy market for the guns and agricultural implements that
were its major products. The skilled men who filled the boarding-
houses a few years back were now marrying and building homes of
their own.

Mr. Green in time bought into a sawmill, secured his own family's
modest comforts, and pursued his avocation, collecting stories from
the old-timers. Later, as an old-timer himself, when the Valley was
just taking its place in the industrial heartland of a vast national economy, he became a valued source of local history.

Mr. Green did not write history books. He witnessed history, tromp-
ing through the woods with his old friends to find the cellars that
marked long-lost cabins or the stand of hemlocks where a local hero
outwitted the ruthless Tories and their Indian allies. Things that occurred before his memory stayed "vivid" in his mind because they had
their place in the landscape.[1]

Still today the Valley's local history stays vivid in places and things
that bear—in contrast to the everyday, remembered past (Chapter 3)—
the special mark of history proper, history before memory. There are

Walter Green, local historian, probably 1916, cleaning what may have
been the second rifle produced by
Eliphalet Remington. Courtesy, Historical Room, Ilion Free Public Library.

now a few books about local history, built out of the memories of people like Mr. Green, but local history remains most vivid, and most ac-
cessible, in the landscape of special places. The Valley's history before
memory is, most notably, history before industrialization, history of
the days when people lived on what they produced themselves and exchanged among each other.

Places of the Past

Jim and Hilda's farm is one of those special historical places. Still
named for its original Palatine owners, Clapsaddle Farm has always
been "in the family," as Jim sees it—he proudly claims Palatine descent on both sides. The farm occupies the southern half of one of the
original patents (land parcels) that the Mohawks sold to the Palatines
in the 1720s. On the northern half sits Remington Arms. "*We* sold the

land to Eliphalet Remington," Jim told me the first time we met, at the Millers Mills Ice Cream Social, a special place of local history that I will describe shortly.

The elegant old barns of Clapsaddle Farm no longer hold the farm's prize-winning Hereford cattle nor Hilda's flocks of hens—too expensive to maintain these days. But two of its venerable sites remain productive, the old cider mill and the fragrant evaporator shed. Every fall the cider mill pours forth gallons of fresh apple brew. Every spring the evaporator yields gallons of the Valley's dark maple syrup. And each, during their annual heydays, attracts storytellers.

A neighborly request by Mr. Kinney brought about my first visit to the cider mill. He could drive a team of horses as well as any man, he liked to say, but he never took to cars, and he was too blind to start now. He needed cider, though, two gallons for now and two for the freezer, he said, and I really ought to try it. I could hardly refuse— that's neighborly reciprocity.

In one left-hand turn we left the town behind. Rumbling across a shaky bridge and down a rutted dirt road, we parked in front of a huge, old, red barn, next to a battered pickup truck. Hand lettered on its side was the curious motto:

Clapsaddle Farm
"200 Years Behind the Times"

Jim greeted us warmly. Did we want a tour, he asked? Yes, indeed. He'd had to add this and that shiny stainless steel accessory to the cider press in order stay up to state code, he noted, but the central mechanism, lovingly maintained for a century, was "brand new" in 1890 when his great-grandfather installed it. Works like a charm, he said. They don't build them the way they used to.

As he shows it to us, he's reminded of the farmers who used to line up in the fall with horse-drawn wagons full of apples, come to press them into cider. They took it home, sealed it up, and let nature take its course—"Couldn't get farm hands in those days without hard cider," Jim says with a wink. There was no order of boss and subordinates. Everybody pitched in unloading the apples, hoisting them onto the chute that tumbled them down to the cider press, filling up the jugs, and loading the jugs back onto the wagons. The farmers paid for the pressing with a share of the cider from their apples, which Jim's grandfather and great-grandfather fermented in the Vinegar Works upstairs. Everybody worked and got what they needed.

I went to the cider mill often after that, in part for the cider, which is sublime, but in part because the place was a magnet for natives and their stories. So too, in the blustery northern spring, was the cozy evaporator shed.

You can see the steam from the evaporators rising into the air before you even get off the bridge. The first thing you notice when you enter the shed—or, rather, the second thing after the sweet fragrance of simmering maple sap—is that the walls are hung with chairs, ready to be pulled down next to the evaporators for a cozy bout of storytelling. The shed's steamy warmth is welcome refuge that time of year, and what better entertainment than recollecting the time before memory.

Clapsaddle Farm is not only for old-timers. It is, among other things, a popular destination for the field trips of local schoolchildren, where sweet tastes, stories, and rowdy hayrides across orchard and field induct them into farm life "200 years behind the times."

But probably the most popular place in the county for soaking up time before memory is just south of the Valley in the Town of Columbia. The people of the Valley sometimes boast (and sometimes rue) that the county does not have a single shopping mall. People in the Town of Columbia boast that they do not even have a single incorporated village. The Town of Columbia is defiantly rural, and its exemplary center is the hamlet of Millers Mills.

I had only been in the Valley a little over a month when I heard the buzz about the Millers Mills Ice Cream Social. Everybody was going. On the happy day, our carful of merry-makers headed through the Ilion Gorge—the deep valley behind the Valley where, people say with a certain awe: some of those dense forests are primeval, never cut, never cultivated. South from the gorge we climbed into the bright sunlight on a rolling plain where ancient hedgerows border some of the county's oldest (and few remaining) dairy farms.

At the end of a long dirt road a young man in jeans waved us into a fresh-mown field, one of three that were, for the day, parking lots. We had come for the 118th annual Millers Mills Ice Cream Social. We parked and walked with the crowds through a green yard where thousands of flowers bloomed all over and around a rusty collection of

1920s-vintage farm machinery. We admired a brightly polished Model T Ford, ceremoniously parked in front of a Victorian "gingerbread" house. Next to it was a hand-lettered sign,

Down Town
Millers Mills
Population 29+

Country humor. As we neared a large pond, the multitudes slowed down, fanning out to the left and right of a new wooden bridge, festooned with red, white, and blue streamers. We had arrived in time for its dedication. A preacher blessed the moment and passed the megaphone down the line of dignitaries. Last to speak was the Town Historian, a descendant of the hamlet's founder. "We are about to have a christening," she announced, directing all the children in the crowd toward a young woman in nineteenth-century dress who stood beside a huge, old-fashioned milk jug. She dipped out a full ladle of fresh milk and poured it on the bridge, then one by one the children followed her lead, dipping in and pouring out, some kidding around, some with solemn concentration. Cameras snapped, video cameras whirred, until the milk jug was empty and the happy throngs crossed the bridge.

On the other side was a gently sloping hill dotted with crafts booths and old-fashioned games. Nearby were take-off points for hayrides and pony rides, and down by the pond rowboats awaited. At the crest of the hill was the Millers Mills Grange Hall where all could partake in bowl after bowl of the hamlet's famous ice cream, still made to the exacting specifications of a secret 1870s recipe.

Of course those exacting specifications did not include an electric ice cream freezer. But as anyone in the July crowds could have told you, Millers Mills' famous ice cream did not need electric freezers—they did it by hand. The summer festivities are supported by winter festivities that draw crowds of equal size to the Millers Mills Ice Harvest.

Some weekend, usually in February—the Grange members, as one put it, "let the Lord decide the date"—the community holds a winter festival around the project of turning a large section of the hamlet's pond into blocks of ice. Visitors are encouraged to take a hand in the work with an assortment of fantastically shaped old iron saws, hooks, and tongs. Then there is the work of loading the blocks of ice onto horse-drawn sleds and hauling them to the storage shed. There, insulated with sawdust and burlap, they will miraculously stay frozen for half a year.

We pitched in. The frozen pond was thick with ice-cutters, most of us in desperate need of the experts who circulated among us with helpful advice. But not everyone worked. A hundred feet away from us young people ice-skated, showing off their grace and prowess as they had for more than a century. Others preferred to thunder across the scene on snowmobiles, and nobody seemed to mind the antinostalgic visitation.

It was winter in the north country. There was work and fun, as there had always been.

The Valley touches historical ground at Millers Mills. If the people of Millers Mills had not been able to reproduce their festivals of local history year after year, perhaps it would have been a bit easier for the Valley to get accustomed to its postindustrial predicament. But winter and summer, the rhythms of Millers Mills alternate with a regularity that puts the Valley's busy, worrisome days into a certain perspective: Life was not always so anxious and hard. There was hard work, yes, but people worked together for what they needed with no bosses over them. Thus the past presses in on the present, so that when those who are inclined to a critical view of the present propose that it doesn't *have to be* so anxious and hard, others will have grounds to agree.

The Other Local History

But there is another local history that does not press in on the present. It is not a popular history. Patronized by the Valley's elite, native and newcomer, it is a history made of books, lectures, journals, and museums.

"It was here that America was truly born," a historical novelist told a meeting of politicians, educators, and businesspeople, gathered for the purpose of stimulating the Mohawk Valley's flagging economy with historical tourism (Herkimer County Community College, 10/18/93). The novelist echoed a venerable commitment of the Valley's local historians, establishing the region's place in the creation story of the United States.

Here, local historians write, Mohawks and Palatine settlers joined British colonists to repel the French in the 1750s, and, here, in 1777 the Stars and Stripes were unfurled under fire for the first time at the Battle of Oriskany. As local historians understand it, Oriskany foiled the British three-pronged strategy to divide the Colonies, and Patriot losses in that battle, the "bloodiest of the Revolution," convinced the government of France to aid the Patriots' independence struggle.[2]

"Clubs and organizations that preserve local history," the longtime Executive Director of Herkimer County Historical Society (HCHS) told me, "are always elite." The HCHS (founded in 1892) has indeed worked hard to preserve local history, but this is not all it does. Its gala fund-raisers and annual tour of the county's "historical homes" have served as important meeting places for the Valley's "important" people, and those who wish to be so.

The (now retired) Executive Director is critical of the academic historians whom she meets at various conferences: "They do statistics," she says, "we do people." Indeed, a large part the Society's history is genealogy, especially the histories of local notables (conscientiously including notable women). These include the namesakes of local landmarks and institutions as well as the ancestral stories of still prominent Valley families, often researched and written by a descendant. As happy byproduct, this work provides a veritable who's-who for socially ambitious newcomers to the region.

This local history establishes the ancestors' claims to social status, and by extension, the claims of their descendants. But what is most interesting about these claims is that they are grounded in the ideals of equality, modesty, and hard work, as the following examples from *Legacy*, the quarterly journal of the Herkimer County Historical Society,[3] illustrate.

He loved "tinkering" from boyhood. He developed his talents at E. Remington and Sons, walking to work five miles a day for five years. Starting with products he himself invented and patented, his business thrived. "With all his successes in life, he remained humble and unpretentious. . . . He was proud of his heritage in a quiet way . . . and never lost sight of his origins." [1988 3(2):14–23]

"A test of character in a small town is mirrored in what people think of each other, and no one had a critical word for [her]." Of Palatine descent, she grew up in the "essentially rural" Town of Columbia. Such was her talent and hard work that this "quiet, unassuming country girl from Herkimer County" was able to "travel and work in highly sophisticated environments." [1988 3(3):9–13]

And nobody, as we'll soon see, outdid the Remington family for claims to hard work and modesty. But for today's descendants of the great ancestors, egalitarian ideals are largely "history." No guest or on-looker at the gala events of today's local elites could describe them as "unpretentious" or "unassuming"—quite the opposite. At gatherings of local high society today, the ideal is elegance in food, wine, music, dress, and conversation.

The past of elite local history does not press on the present. It draws, rather, a firm dividing line between the past and the present. This line is clear in the most frequent references to history in the local press, around the "historical" performances on which local elites rest their hopes for regional tourism. This is a history sealed off from the present so securely that it can become an escape from the present.

> [T]he annual Horse-Drawn Sleigh Rally at the [Cooperstown] Farmers' Museum on Sunday will truly create a sense of stepping back in time. . . . Amid the sounds of muffled hooves, crunching snow and jingling bells, visitors are invited to join in the fun . . . [ET 2/19/94:12]

> Members of the New York State Muzzle-Loaders Association will be taking a trip back in time—some 200 years back—when they gather for the group's annual Primitive Rendezvous in northern Herkimer County. Members "will be living, dressing, eating, and sleeping in the manner of their forefathers" for a full week. [ET 10/1/93:5]

Unlike a visit to Clapsaddle Farm or Millers Mills (they're free), admission to these events will be costly. Participants pay handsomely for "stepping back in time" to escape from a complex, modern world.

But nowhere did the segregation of the past from the present impress me more than in an interview with an important local official, himself an accomplished local historian. This man grew up in the South and spent his childhood summers at his grandfather's farm, just east of the Valley. He remembers these summers fondly:

"I can remember as a kid growing up, riding the milk truck with my Grandpa. On we'd go to Canajoharie and there were milk trucks from Fort Plain and St. Johnsville. Every community had its own creamery—its own local economy."

Our talk turned to local history. After a fascinating discussion about Ilion's prosperous beginnings under the leadership of the Remington family, he drew in his breath for a concluding comment. "It's kind of a sad commentary," he said, "because some of those things *that we lost* . . . ethics, values, morals . . . we're never gonna get those back. They're not gonna return."

The Concerned Citizens would no doubt find it believable that this politician saw ethics, values, and morals as a thing of the past. He has been consistently antagonistic toward the group. Indeed, when I pressed him on the question of the Concerned Citizens' political activities, he became visibly annoyed.

One comment succinctly illustrates the political advantages of a history that is, by definition, removed from the present. Nothing annoyed this official more than the Concerned Citizens' years-long opposition to the cogeneration plant (Chapter 3), which he supported. "Let go of it!" he said, as if addressing them—"Let go of it! [The plant] is built, it's up, it's running, it's functioning. It's past news. It's past history."

What is he arguing here? He is arguing from the position that history is *over*, that what happened in the past—in this case only a couple of years earlier—regardless of its effects in the present, is not a legitimate topic of political controversy. Having ruled out "the past," he is free to discredit the Concerned Citizens as ignorant, disruptive "trouble-makers." And he does.

For the "native" majority, through stories of the remembered past and the history of work and satisfaction "before memory" that lives in their special places, they remind each other that life has not always been the way it is. This understanding of what has gone before them fuels their sense of duty in the present and responsibility to the generations that will follow them.

For the more comfortable minority, though, the past is *over*. It has a certain value for explaining the existing order of social distinction, and on its back ride great expectations for tourist dollars. But otherwise, the past has no business in the present.

Grounding the Present

Months of ethnographic research had brought me some insight into the Valley's striking involvement with the past but nagging questions lingered. I could see that the "native" majority employed the past in support of neighborly reciprocity, a complex set of practices that could mean the difference between surviving hard times with dignity and falling into despair. I could see that their history before memory held up a social ideal in which the fruits of one's own labor should secure a respectable life, a vision that the Concerned Citizens, among others, brought implicitly to their political action and analysis.

I could see, too, that local elites used history differently, making a claim about their social position on the basis of their ancestors' hard work but, at the same time, drawing a thick line between the era of their ancestors and the world they live in today—a line that could immunize them against the criticism of local political dissidents.

But these are what anthropologists call "functionalist" explanations; that is, they explain behavior or belief by what it does, its functions. Functionalist analysis is part of the process of understanding, a part that can lead to important generalizations across cultures (e.g., we might look for a connection between reciprocity and stories of the remembered past in other cultures), but it does not address questions about why the people we study developed the *particular* cultural forms and practices we see, questions of where those forms and practices came from. For this we must have history; we must know what has happened across time to shape people's beliefs and practices in the present.

Two questions of this kind were foremost in my mind. For one, why did so many people in the Valley believe that their lives ought to be better? Not "could be" better but *ought*, as though the fact of their work entitled them to more than they were getting. Ideals of work and prosperity could be seen in the images they preserve of farming life, but why would these relationships apply to industrialized life?

The second question was the other side of the first: Why did local leadership *not* seem to share this belief that life ought to be better? Did they ever? If so, what events or conditions could have driven a wedge between the perspectives of the majority and those of the local elites?

I had to do my own study of local history, and it was clear from local historians' intriguing comments that I had to look particularly at the era of the Remington family. There were two things that local historians always said about the Remingtons.

One, the Remingtons were modest people. In the 1870s they turned their house next to the factory into offices and built a "mansion" on the hill behind it—but *not*, everyone insisted, because they wanted to live in luxury. They were, as one local historian put it, "quiet people with simple tastes." They built the mansion because it was expected of them, because they had to impress the important people who came to Ilion to negotiate contracts with them.

Two, the Remingtons were loyal to the Valley. Several times during the three generations that they presided over the Valley's manufacturing center, they faced serious business downturns. They could have cashed out and lived lives of luxury. But they did not. They plowed their money back into the shops, developing new product lines at their own expense. Again and again, they opted for the prosperity of the Valley over their own comfort.

What might these comments mean for understanding the long past that has shaped the Valley's local culture? I had splendid resources at hand for finding out. The Herkimer County Historical Society was one of the most active groups of local historians in the state. And at the Ilion Free Public Library were masses of documents that the Remington's neighbors had saved over five generations. So I dug into the materials at hand, and the more I found, the more amazed I became.

Part II
The Gospel of Work

There are those who believe that, if you will only legislate to make the well-to-do prosperous, their prosperity will leak through on those below. The Democratic idea, however, has been that if you legislate to make the masses prosperous, their prosperity will find its way up through every class which rests upon them.

WILLIAM JENNINGS BRYAN, "Cross of Gold" speech, 1896

5

The Remingtons of Ilion

After the American Revolution thousands of Yankees, crowded together for generations on the rocky New England soil ("crowded" by farmers' standards, that is), migrated west, to the newly surveyed woodlands of Central New York. Eliphalet Remington (that's E-*lye*-fa-let) and his young family headed west in 1799, along with some other families from Litchfield, Connecticut, to their new home in the hills southwest of the Valley (which they named Litchfield). The Remingtons built their house next to the new church, and set up a smithy next to that.[1]

Sometime around 1810 Eliphalet and his son Eliphalet (II) built an iron forge on Steele's Creek, just south of what would become the village of Ilion. There they did a brisk business making agricultural implements for their neighbors, paying local children to scavenge scrap iron for them, and taking on a couple of "hands" from time to time to help out.

Probably in 1812, Eliphalet (II), at eighteen or nineteen years old, began experimenting with forging gun barrels (Swinney 1987:14, 1994). It took exceptional skill to do this by hand. The craftsman has to heat and beat out the metal, over and over again, to an exacting standard of uniformity because the barrel will have to take the extreme stress of an internal explosion. Any weakness and the barrel can burst, causing serious injury or death.

His didn't. It was straight and sturdy. Eliphalet (II) soon earned one of the greatest compliments of his time—he was hailed as a "mechanical genius."

Historical "Spin"

This much can be ascertained through the layers of myth that encrust the Remington story. History is tricky. Each generation remodels the past for its own purposes, leaving layer after layer of "spin." To get at what actually happened, we have to figure out the "spin" well enough to separate it from historical fact, and even at our best this task will often come down to judgment calls based on experience, knowledge, training, and intuition. But for a cultural anthropologist this task can be complicated by a further consideration: The "spin" itself is data. It can show us the cultural preoccupations of the "spinners."

The Remington myth took off in earnest during the 1880s, the decade that saw corporate takeover of the enterprises that the family had led for three generations, as well as the death of Philo Remington, the last family head of these enterprises. The creation story of the Remington enterprises, hatched at this time, encodes the dreams and fears of a people who faced an uncertain future.

As an 1889 telling has it, "with rude tools" and "while but a boy" Eliphalet (II) "produced his first gun, and then his parents encouraged him, and from this small beginning has grown the immense works which have been the scene of life and activity for years" (Ilion *Citizen* 4/5/1889).

Dates and embellishments vary a good bit across different versions of this legend, but one theme is mysteriously consistent. Eliphalet Remington was *not seeking great wealth*—his success simply flows from his exceptional skill. Here it is in 1882: "Eliphalet Remington was a blacksmith by trade, and made a rifle for his own use. So superior was it to the guns in use at that time (1825) that those who saw the weapon insisted upon Mr. Remington making more of them" (*Utica Daily Press* (UDP) 12/9/1882).

And so it entered modern times. Here it is, still, in 1952, as local playwrights dramatized the Remington legend for the Ilion Centennial. Young Eliphalet enters a shooting contest with his homemade gun. It so awes the winner of the contest that he comes up to Eliphalet and says, "I want you to make me a rifle like yours!" Eliphalet protests, "Why, I'm really not a gunsmith . . . I'm a farmer actually." "Then it's time you changed your profession, young man!" the winner insists (Swarthout and Swarthout 1952:24–26, ellipses in original).

Soon after, a settler down the way, a pioneer heading west, and a visitor from Texas besiege Eliphalet with orders, as skilled craftsmen cluster around him, begging to join him in his work (*ibid.*). The rest is history—the company and the Valley grow rapidly into comfortable prosperity.

But this was not the way it happened. The best living historian of the Remingtons, Jerrold Swinney, has found good evidence that the family had every intention of becoming something like industrialists. Their shop was one of nine or ten small shops that were forging gun barrels in Central New York in the early 1800s. Evidently, the Eliphalets, father and son, had come up with important technical innovations that, they hoped, would give them the lead in producing low-cost, high-quality gun barrels (Swinney 1987).

In January 1828 they were confident enough to purchase one hundred acres of land—fronting on that wonder of the modern world, the Erie Canal—and start building a new and larger shop. Sadly, Eliphalet (I) died that autumn when an accident knocked him off the wagonload of timbers he was hauling down to their construction site. Eliphalet (II) carried on, borrowing substantially from friends (see Ingersoll Papers [IP]), digging a raceway (an artificial stream) from Steele's Creek to provide the new shop with water power, and building an inn across the road for the comfort of the customers whose business he confidently expected.

By 1832 some twenty men worked at the Remington shops. They still forged bar iron from scrap and made all the iron tools that their neighbors needed, but gun barrels had become their biggest product. By 1836 the Remington shops were generating $15,000 a year—a substantial sum at the time—representing, conservatively, a production of five thousand barrels per year, "far beyond the capacity of an ordinary shop" (Swinney 1987:17).

They had worked out a way to do it better, and the market was there. The region was filling up with settlers, and each one of them (so people believed in those days) needed a sturdy, affordable firearm.

In 1842, looking forward to his three sons entering the business, Remington purchased his first U.S. Army contract. To fulfill it, he invested heavily in machinery and enticed the brilliant William Jenks, inventor of the Jenks carbine, to Ilion—clearly he was committed to staying on top of the latest technology.[2]

During the 1850s, by then working closely with his eldest son Philo, Eliphalet (II) secured a series of army contracts and attracted a revolver expert from Eli Whitney's shop—he wanted to become a leading producer of this new technological marvel too.[3] In 1852 the Remingtons were prosperous enough to build a new factory for the Agricultural Works, across the Canal from the Armory.

The Civil War years were a period of intense activity at the Remington Armory. Hard-core abolitionists and staunch Lincoln supporters, the Remingtons made an all-out effort to support the Union side with massive quantities of low-cost, high-quality firearms. (One model, I am told, had a handy attachment for grinding coffee!) The shops of E. Remington & Sons ran round the clock, employing "every man and boy" in the Valley (Cent52:17). The intensity of the effort, they say, killed the aging Eliphalet (II). In 1861 ownership of the Armory and the Agricultural Works passed to his three sons, Philo, Samuel, and Eliphalet (III), who would run them successfully for two more decades.

The long Remington success story was, beyond a doubt, the result of exceptional skill, persistence, and business acumen. So why is it that the Remington myth presents us with Eliphalet Remington as a skilled but naive craftsmen who did not care about wealth? Here is where the "spin" gets revealing.

Two opposing cultural logics can explain this curious mythic twist. The second, in historical sequence, is the easier to describe because it is the ancestor of the American culture we know. It is the perspective of "the gun trust"—the cartel who ran the Remingtons out of business (see Chapter 7). The past as they wished it to be remembered *needed* the Remingtons to be naive about business. To put it simply, they did not want to be remembered as the bad guys. They wanted what was, in effect, a hostile takeover to look like, as one of their spokesman later put it, "the salvation of a great industry"—"saved" from the well-intentioned but bumbling Remingtons (see Chapters 8 and 9).

The other cultural logic leads us back to a different world, to the "traditional American values" that the American culture we know supplanted. In this culture the pursuit of great wealth for its own sake was simply not honorable—it was "worshiping Mammon."[4] Hard work was honorable. "Mechanical genius" was honorable. Put the two together and success *ought to be* the natural outcome. The Remington family operated in a world of small, relatively independent local economies, a world without the kind of labor markets that make working people dispensable. Dependent on the cooperation and goodwill of the Valley's working people, the family could not afford to be seen as "worshippers of Mammon."

The Gospel of Work

If you could have floated over the Valley in a hot-air balloon around the year 1880 you would have seen a place like most of the North-eastern and Midwestern United States at the time. It was mostly farm-land. Here and there branching country roads converged at small towns, towns where farm families—at least three-quarters of the 1880 population (see note 5, below)—brought to market what they did not consume at home.

At the center of the towns you would see shops, a hotel, maybe a factory building or two. You would see crates of local produce being loaded onto the canal barges and into the freight cars that rumbled to-ward other towns and, maybe, all the way to a city. Places that looked like cities (by today's standards, anyway) were few and far between.[5]

Surrounding the busy town centers you would have seen streets lined with tidy houses, church spires marking the street corners. In the long backyards of these houses, people would be busy with every-day chores, women bent over their vegetable gardens or wash tubs, small children playing at their feet, grandmother with her mending basket, older children tossing corn to clucking hens.

One or two houses, bigger than the rest, sat on broad lots next to the factory or mill. These had larger yards and gardens, a small orchard, and maybe a greenhouse. The chickens shared the big yard with a cow or two and a couple of horses. (Around the yard was the special hous-ing for each species, coop, shed, and stable.) These were the homes of local elites, the leading citizens of the towns. At the enterprises they owned, most men and women in the area came to work at some point in their lives. Work flowed with the seasons. During the winter months people looked for wage work, and if the business season was good, they found it. In plowing and harvesting seasons the factories and mills emptied out. Money was fine, the people might tell you, but you can't eat it.

An influential historian called these towns and the farms that surrounded them, "island communities" (Wiebe 1967). "Islands" be-cause, though they were tied together by water and rail, they were not dependent on each other for the necessities of life. Local farms pro-vided whatever the householders' backyards did not. Local workshops made the tools they used. Local grain was ground to flour at local mills—the miller took his wage in flour, which he could then sell to the baker and the grocer. Local grain was mixed with local hops and brewed into local beer. (Valley children, old-timers remembered, gathered hops for pennies a pound in the summer.) Local apples were pressed in local cider mills. Local wood was planed in local sawmills. Local clay was baked into bricks. The people of the "island communities" looked first to each other for what they needed.

I do not wish to paint an idyllic picture of this world. It was a human society with all of the usual squabbles, but it was different from the one we know in ways that will be important for understanding the Valley in the Remington era.

As the phrase "island communities" suggests, the United States was politically and economically *decentralized;* that is, what went on at the centers of government and finance had only slight or occasional effect on most people's lives. Communities had a degree of autonomy that is difficult to imagine today. Important decisions were made locally, and, while it would be unfair to represent this world as ideally democratic, it was certainly more difficult for local decision makers to hide from the public whom their decisions affected.

And, this decentralized political and economic world was lived in and understood through a culture much different than our own. Crucially, the people of this time understood the world in religious terms. Religion provided the single set of cultural resources that was shared across the country's boundaries of social class, ethnicity, and race. To be sure, the men of wealth who stood in the United States' most prominent offices often argued their positions in the elite language of the European Enlightenment, but, in the arenas of local decision making, these arguments were engaged in the religious language that everyone spoke.[6]

This American culture can be dated to 1800 when, after a decade of grassroots political organizing the like of which the world had never known, the people of these United States elected Thomas Jefferson to the Presidency, overthrowing the Federalist Party and the small circle of would-be aristocrats who had governed since Independence. It was this "Jeffersonian revolution" that made the American Revolution truly revolutionary (Appleby 1984). Never before had a state proposed to govern on the principle that the "common people" would act wisely in the public interest.

They could and they would, the Jeffersonians insisted, but if and only if they were truly free from the dead hand of aristocratic domination. With the greedy, luxury-loving heel of the New World's would-be aristocracy lifted off them, free to pursue happiness through employing their labor on their own land, free to enjoy the fruits of their own labor, the people would vigilantly guard their liberties. And the Jeffersonians acted on their convictions, pursuing policies that would open up land ownership to the working multitudes.[7]

Never before had "the common people" been offered such a deal. But, clearly, not all citizens subscribed, notably certain possessors of great wealth. Between the working people and the enjoyment of the fruits of their labor, again and again, stepped those who enjoyed the fruits of others' labor, whose interests in others' labor committed them to a political course that protected the privileges of wealth and opposed the aspirations of the majority.

But the "common people" were indeed vigilant in defending their liberties. When reason failed, they readily invoked the Word of a higher authority. The leader of a workers' movement that spread across the Northeast in the 1840s (the Mechanic's Mutual Protection Association) did just this in an editorial for the *Mechanics Mirror*, an Albany (New York) newsletter.

> Oppressors of mankind, ye who rob the poor of their bread—who reap the fruit of the working-man's toil, that you may flaunt in your gilded chariots and bask in the glories of earth-born splendors, beware, remember the scathing language of the great Law-giver, "Thou shalt not, therefore, oppress thy neighbor, but thou shalt fear the Lord thy God." [Robert McFarlane 1846][8]

Choosing the vanity of worldly splendor over the heavenly mandate to love thy neighbor, these "mechanics" argued, the "oppressors of mankind"—pointedly, greedy employers and their political and financial allies—robbed working people of the fruits of their own labor. In a culture that spoke religion, this was a potent argument, even an appeal to the luxury-lovers' self-interest: Robbing the poor of the fruits of their labor was not just unethical—it was a *sin* that would suffer divine punishment.

From Rochester to Baltimore, Philadelphia to Boston, arguments like McFarlane's could have been heard in local arenas across the nineteenth-century Northeast. Wherever people joined to attack low pay and long hours they evoked divine authority (Lazerow 1995). Had not God mandated, the logic went, that humankind should earn their daily bread by the sweat of their brow?[9] Then, did not those who lived off the work of others reject the Word of God?

We could call the complex of ideals that these arguments represent the "gospel of work" because the Protestant elevation of work to divine calling (Weber 1976 [1904]) was at the moral center of egalitarian thought among the working people of the nineteenth-century United States.[10] Historians, professionally shy about religion, refer to it as "producerism"—in contrast to the "consumerist" culture of our times—because it was as "producers of wealth" that working people laid claim to and shaped the democratic potential of the American Revolution. Producerism promoted the political interests of persons engaged in productive labor over the interests of those who lived (immorally) off the labor of others. Clearly by the 1830s it was a very robust current in national ideology—something like "gospel," as one historian observes, for all "political candidates and mass orators" (Kazin 1995:13).

Before then, historians give producerism varying pedigrees. The division of society into producers and nonproducers, Sean Wilentz suggests, comes from the work of British economist David Ricardo, entering U.S. politics with the immigration of English artisan radicals in the early nineteenth century (Wilentz 1984:158). Ricardo may well have found use for the producerist social dualism, and artisan radicals surely seized upon it, but its roots are, undoubtedly, among "the common people." Kazin finds "nascent versions" of the producerist social divide—"those that Labour for a Living" versus "those that git a Living without Bodily Labour"—in the rhetoric of Shay's Rebellion (1786–1787, Kazin 1995:13).

The "mechanic ideology" that Paul Faler finds, however, in 1790s Lynn, Massachusetts, is already full-blown producerism, undergirded by fervent Methodism (1981:45–48). In line with the anti-aristocratic politics of the Jeffersonians, Lynn's "mechanic ideology" envisioned turning the existing social order on its head, replacing the corrupt rule of nonproducers ("idlers, aristocrats, capitalists, lawyers, bureaucrats, and paupers") with a virtuous producers' democracy (Faler 1981:31).

Who were "mechanics"? Much reduced in our current vocabulary, the nineteenth-century version of this term extended across the spectrum of nonagricultural work. It represents, in fact, one of those great moments when an insurgent movement proudly seizes on what used to be a nasty epithet (like "Yankee," "black," or "queer"). In England

and in the Americas that England colonized, mechanics and farmers composed the "lower orders" of society, the vast "mob" whom their social "betters" considered unfit for political decision making (Blumin 1989:17; Williams 1983:201). But in the 1770s mechanics rose up in support of the American Revolution with enough valor and conviction to transform their social stature, and self-image, from lowly "mob" to the bearers of a new social vision (cf. Faler 1981:37; Ryerson 1976).

And the new United States, penniless and technologically inexperienced—the British empire had forbidden manufacture in the colonies in order to use them as markets for British manufactures—came to depend on the work and ingenuity of its mechanics. The bearers of a new, egalitarian social vision were also the bearers of the skills that would enable the new society to prosper. Across the country's manufacturing towns, the mechanics proclaimed a new ideal of respectability. Not luxury but a "competence," a modest but relatively independent living, would sustain the new Republic and allow everyone, as an almanac writer put it, "to live decently without acquiring wealth" (cited in Blumin 1989:36–37).

The "nonproducers"—predominantly "capitalists"[11]—did not give up their pursuit of great wealth, but for the first five or six decades of the nineteenth century they were held in check by the producers' successful claim to the moral high-ground of national ideology. It would be unimaginable today to hear words like the following spoken at the center of national power. While noting that capital indeed had certain rights, the speaker was clear about his and the nation's priorities.

> Labor is prior to, and independent of, capital. Capital is only the fruit of labor, and could never have existed if labor had not first existed. Labor is the superior of capital, and deserves much the higher consideration.

The speaker was President of the United States Abraham Lincoln, on the occasion of his first Annual Message to Congress in 1861. That's moral high-ground!

The Civil War was a pivotal moment for the "gospel of work." On the one hand egalitarian ideals had reached the pinnacle of national politics with explosive force, but, on the other hand, the demands of war—especially the government borrowing that provisioned the armies of the Union and the Confederacy with food, boots, and guns—

provided unprecedented opportunities for capitalists to gain conces-
sions from a government that was otherwise wary of capitalist privilege.[12]

By the late 1870s producerism was on the defensive. Politicians still
paid it lip-service but, under the surface of familiar political rhetoric
a new ideal of national "greatness" was gaining ground, a "greatness"
that would be measured in production statistics: more steel, more
coal, more oil—and more money. A new organization arose to defend
the interests of "the producing classes" with concerted political action, the Noble and Holy Order of the Knights of Labor. Any producer
could join, regardless of occupation, race, sex, or religion (ideally, anyway) but nonproducers, specifically, bankers, stockbrokers, lawyers,
liquor dealers, and gamblers, were unwelcome (Fink 1983; Licht
1995:176, 181). With "lodges" in virtually every U.S. state and county
by the mid-1880s, the Knights of Labor kept hope alive for a producer
majority under siege.

The Remington legend of unsought wealth has cultural roots in the
traditional American values of the "gospel of work." This family
whose success depended on thousands of mechanics and farmers, in
fact, was careful to identify themselves as producers, not—heaven for-
bid!—as nonproducer capitalists. Eliphalet (II), local sources tell us,
trained his sons at the forge. Philo, the eldest, "inherited, to a large degree, his father's mechanical genius" (*Citizen* 4/5/1889). Upon gradu-
ating common school (our eighth grade), he was already accomplished
enough to do the skilled job of barrel-straightening, and he "worked
his way up" from there (*ibid.*).

More is going on in these affirmations than meets the eye. Where
producerism was "gospel," Philo and his father emphasized their mechanical skills for good reason. There was a message there for the people of the Valley: The family's ownership of the Remington works was
earned by hard work, not simply inherited. Nothing was more suspiciously nonproducer than inherited wealth.

Whether or not they personally shared the producerist ideology, the
Remingtons lived in a face-to-face world, surrounded by and dependent on their fellow villagers. The kind of enterprises the Remingtons
operated—unlike the corporate kind of our day—were embedded in
their communities. The community's prosperity was an important
measure of business success, and of the family's prestige.[13]

Still, although it was clearly in their interest to keep up producerist appearances, the evidence is strong that the Remingtons were personally invested in the egalitarian ideals of their time.[14] The amazing extent of their commitment to the Valley's prosperity, detailed in Chapter 7, shows through in the Remington legend as humility, generosity, and high principles. Philo Remington "was ever one of the people," said one of the many eulogists at his funeral. He was "simple, modest, approachable by the humblest, a friend to all," said another (*Citizen* 4/12/1889). Fervent Methodists, the Remingtons "insisted upon occupying the poorest seat in the church" (*ibid*.). Abolitionists, they were rumored to keep a "station" on the Underground Railroad for people who had escaped enslavement in the South.

They were, wrote an editor of the local paper, the Ilion *Citizen*, "kind hearted, modest and unassuming."[15] "Accustomed to toil" himself, Philo was always "in sympathy with his workmen" and "had their confidence to a marked degree" (*Citizen* 4/5/1889). The evidence suggests that he did, as did his father and grandfather. There is no record of "labor trouble" over the three-quarters of a century that the Remingtons owned and operated the shops.

Indeed, it appears that no one ever had an unkind word for the Remingtons, and this may be the source for the last part of the Remington legend, the part about why they failed in business. Everyone I asked in the Valley said the same thing: The Remingtons were "too good" to succeed in business. They were "too good" to perceive the evil intentions of others in time to defend themselves. They were "too good" to be ruthless. The lesson is troubling, that goodness is weakness, that good people cannot succeed in business—that business cannot succeed without evil.

But the Remingtons did not fail in business because they were "too good." Their enterprises were targeted by a movement of big-city capitalists that was known at the time as "the trusts."

The Trusts

Valley people have had little choice in their efforts to understand what went wrong more than a century ago at that huge factory building in the middle of Ilion. What actually happened has been hidden in historical "spin."[16]

What happened to the Valley and to other "island communities"

was *the trusts*, secret—in fact, illegal—cartels of capitalists, organized
for the purpose of "cornering"—that is, monopolizing—particular
markets. And once they got respectable, they wanted to forget, and
wanted us to forget, where they came from. But by 1910 or so, changed
into the clean legal clothes of a modern corporation, they controlled
the productive property—factories, mines, wells, mills, refineries, railroads, telegraphs, telephones—of the United States. The trusts were
the disreputable ancestors of many of today's corporate giants.

Their goal, monopoly, and its means, incorporation, had long been
recognized as dangerous to freedom and prosperity. Adam Smith in
The Wealth of Nations (1776), like generations of European thinkers
before him (de Roover 1951), railed against incorporation of any kind.
Dating from Elizabethan times, the English anti-incorporation tradition was strong. Incorporation was a grant of monopoly. Any grant of
special privileges whereby any person is "restrained of any freedome
. . . , or hindered in their lawfull trade," wrote Sir Edward Coke in the
early 1600s, shall be illegal—because what "taketh away a mans trade,
taketh away his life" (Coke 1647:181). Incorporation, critics had
charged for centuries, gives special privileges to the few at the expense
of the many.

In the Old World, monopoly was a grant bestowed by the monarch
(for a share of the profits), which may have something to do with why
our Constitution makes no mention of it—no Crown, no monopolies.[17] (The French Revolutionary government, in contrast, made all
incorporations illegal in 1791 [Maier 1993:51]). But the early United
States had a special problem. With little capital in circulation, how
could it build the infrastructure—roads, bridges, canals, and, later,
railroads—that, as the leaders of the Republic all agreed, a prosperous
people required?

Tradition taught and experience would soon confirm the real dan-
gers of corporate privileges, when pet boondoggles of the Federalist
Party brought forth a range of criticism that drew on and extended
the English antimonopoly tradition. The privileges of incorporation
would create, Americans feared, a new aristocracy of wealth: Corporations would lock up resources against the prosperity of future generations, they would corrupt the political process, and they would be
less committed to public welfare than locally owned enterprises.[18]
These arguments would live on in the country's political discourse for
the next century and beyond.

Massachusetts Governor Levi Lincoln predicted in 1827 that "the grievous and intolerable pressure of corporate power over individual possession" would force a revolution to return property "to those, who by the laws of nature, had the original right to its enjoyment" (cited in Maier 1993:71). A New Jersey editorial of the 1830s saw incorporation as promoting "a class of privileged, if not titled, nobility" that "will ever be reaching forward to higher emoluments, at the hazard of . . . the rights of the public" (Trenton *Emporium and True American*, cited in Roy 1997:69). The merchants and mechanics of this country, a New York City editorial argued,

> are content to stand on the broad basis of equal rights. They trust with honorable confidence, to their own talents, exercised with industry, not to special immunities, for success. Why should the speculators, who throng the lobbies of our legislature, be more favoured than they? [William Leggett 1984 (1832)]

President Andrew Jackson, in vetoing the renewal of the national bank's corporate charter—an act that would be tantamount today to dissolving the Federal Reserve—put it bluntly[19]: the United States must

> take a stand against all new grants of monopolies and exclusive privileges, and against any prostitution of our Government to the advancement of the few at the expense of the many. [Veto Message, July 10, 1832][20]

These concerns were consequential but the problem remained: how to build those bridges and canals. Infrastructure projects take huge capital outlays, with no hope of revenue for many years. Individual entrepreneurs were in no position to risk their capital on such long-term projects, and the taxpayers were certainly in no position to shoulder the costs themselves (Roy 1997). The only answer was to charter corporations but regulate them vigilantly, and never grant a charter except in the clearest cases of public benefit. One by one, state legislatures anxiously chartered turnpike, canal, and railroad corporations, as well as the banks that would administer their capital, setting careful limits on the duration of the corporate charter, its maximum capitalization, and the exact nature of its business (Maier 1993). For clear cases of public benefit, the states were willing to protect investors against risk and to risk the danger of special privileges.[21]

Some capitalists, though, whose pursuit of wealth could in no way be construed as "public benefit," looked on with envy at the protections against risk that incorporation granted. They sought a way around the legal obstacles, and secrecy was the key.[22] A chamber of honest legislators would not give ten minutes to their petitions, but a cartel of powerful men might slip a few cronies into the legislature, provided they kept quiet about their friendship. (Corporate capitalism was "crony capitalism" from the outset.) After all, these men had much to offer a political "friend" with an easy conscience. Why, the politicians could say, their rich friends would surely benefit the public by increasing the commerce and "greatness" of the nation.

Charter secured, the cartel could then sell their stocks on Wall Street and embark in earnest on the serious business of securing a monopoly, where the real money was. It was for the purpose of securing monopolies that the trusts were organized. Invented in 1881 by an attorney for John D. Rockefeller, the trust as a legal device held the stock of constituent corporations "in trust," lest any of the gentlemen involved get weak-kneed and try to back out of the program.[23] The program was straightforward: "corner the market" by driving competitors out of business.

The trusts were capitalists, not producers. They monopolized a market by taking over enterprises that local producers, like the Remingtons, had built from scratch. Dodging the law at every step, it was surely a nerve-wracking way to make a fortune but, all things considered, it was a relatively easy route to fabulous wealth. You did not have to work day and night to invent something, or make something better, or find a better way to make something. Why build brick by brick when you can put together a group of powerful men and take it from the people who built it?

"Corner" a commodity or service and you can limit production. Limit production and you can keep prices high. Keep prices high and you can make yourself a king of Wall Street!

There are limits, presumably, to how high a price can be set before people refuse to buy. The trust-builders, wise to this problem, worked with commodities that people *had to* buy—the "necessaries," as people of the time called them. Among the first goods and services to be "trustified" were the fuels people used for heating, cooking, and lighting, coal and oil, and the urban transit systems that city-dwellers needed to get to work. Salt, a biological necessity, may have been *the* first proto-trust in the United States.[24] Sugar, flour, and the packaged meats on which city-dwellers depended followed shortly thereafter. Then came iron and steel, pharmaceuticals and canned goods, and our favorite addictions, whiskey and tobacco. In every case, monopoly brought wages down, prices up, and Wall Street booming.

Trust-building began in secret meetings, proceeded in stealth, and ended in court—because as soon as the people of an "island community" got wind of a trust in their area, they went to their legislators. The trusts were dogged by prohibitive laws and legislative investigations, in the states and in the U.S. Congress, that kept armies of trust attorneys up all night in search of ways to protect their clients' ill-gotten gains (and, by the way, left mountains of data for researchers).

The best way would have been to incorporate the trust, but no state permitted a corporation to own other corporations (Horwitz 1992)—that would amount to legalizing monopoly. The trusts' big break came in 1889 from a New Jersey crony legislature. Through its efforts, the state of New Jersey passed a law that not only made incorporation available "for any lawful business or purpose whatever" but it also granted corporations the right to own other corporations (Horwitz 1992:83). The modern corporation with its rank upon rank of subsidiaries was born.

The most successful trusts made their corporate "combinations" legal as fast as their lawyers could draw up the papers. Standard Oil, U.S. Steel, Anaconda Copper, General Mills, General Electric, Western Union, National Biscuit Company (Nabisco), International Harvester, American Telephone and Telegraph (AT&T)—to mention a few that have survived into our time under more or less the same names—all came into being in the decade or so after the New Jersey legislation.

The new behemoths fought among themselves over tariffs and trade, as they do today, but on one issue they seemed to be in complete agreement: The resources of the United States should be gathered up from many hands into a few—their own.

6

The Remington Success

The Remington enterprises failed in the 1880s, when mines, mills, and manufactories all over the country were being aggressively targeted by the trusts. The Valley was, of course, well aware of the trust movement. Like everyone in the United States at the time (except the trust-builders and their cronies), the Valley had nothing but contempt for the "unholy monopolists" and their "enormous soul consuming monopoly."[1]

"What if," an Ilion *Citizen* editor joked as the New York State Assembly was beginning its spring 1888 session, "the Albany lobbyists and 'bill workers' for trusts and corporations should all assemble under the Assembly roof. . . . Do you suppose Providence would let the roof fall?" (1/27/1888:4). Ilion stood with "the general public," the paper maintained, firmly "in favor of labor against heartless, bloated and niggardly corporations" (*Citizen* 1/13/1888:4).

By this time, local people spoke from bitter experience. But you have to dig in century-old newspapers and scrapbooks, as I did, to find out about that experience. The "gun trust" covered its heavy tracks very carefully.

The Remingtons do seem to have been "good," committed to the prosperity of the mechanics who depended on them and on whom they depended, but they did not fail, as local legend proposes, because they were "too good" to succeed in business (Chapter 5). They failed because vast wealth and well-placed political cronies wanted what they had, a thriving manufactory of a strategic "necessary" of life. How could a family who was "too good" to succeed in business have succeeded for more than seventy years? The Remingtons' long success provides a deeper look at the society and culture shaped by the traditional American values of the "gospel of work."

The Remington "Shops"

In 1872 *Scientific American* sent a reporter to Ilion to have a look around the famed Remington works. He was impressed.

> I saw some cotton gins being put together, and inquired what they were doing there. The reply was: "Oh, we make cotton gins of a superior kind here. We often make two hundred or three hundred gins a year." In the foundry, I saw men at work on heavy iron beams. "What are they for?" I asked. "Oh, we build bridges here about and in other parts of the State, railroad and other bridges." The fact is these Remingtons inherit a mechanical spirit and a restless activity. They cannot be otherwise than busy. If guns are not in demand, they make pistols; if pistols are not wanted, they make cartridges; should cartridges become a drug on the market, they burst out in sewing machines, horse cars, cotton gins, bridges, plows, mowers and reapers or anything else that strikes their fancy . . . They have created Ilion; they are bound to see that Ilion gets along. [*Scientific American* 4/13/1872]

The sheer variety of goods is amazing in itself. But surely the Remingtons *could be* "otherwise than busy," and may well have wished to be. More useful is the reporter's observation that they were "bound to see that Ilion gets along." The more product lines, the more employment for local mechanics. As we'll see, this was the commitment that motivated their "restless activity."

The operation that the Remingtons ran bears little resemblance to our standard image of a factory. For one thing, few people who worked there held a *job* as we know it. Most of the mechanics were hired as contractors by a contractor to the Remingtons. This contractor was typically a master mechanic who had successfully bid on a particular job—that is, "job" in the nineteenth-century sense, a task, a part of the manufacturing process.

The Remingtons had a steady crew of senior contractors, about thirty in number, from before the Civil War through the mid-1880s. Most were trusted friends, whose names are often linked with the Remingtons' in reports of church, political, and social events. Each senior contractor specialized in a particular aspect of manufacturing— for example, forging, polishing, woodworking, or engraving. They hired their own crews, some bought their own raw materials, most paid rent to the company for workspace and power (water power, plus,

E. Remington & Sons, advertisement c. 1875. The three Remington brothers, Philo, Samuel, and Eliphalet III, in cameo, surrounded by the remarkable variety of products that their mechanics produced, are depicted as exemplars of sober virtue. Courtesy, Historical Room, Ilion Free Public Library.

from the Civil War era, a huge Corliss Steam Engine). And when the particular task was finished, the contractors "sold" to the company the items their crews had completed. The thirty-odd senior contractors, skilled mechanics themselves, figured out how to accomplish the task and supervised the work. There were no professional engineers sending specifications down to the shop floor. The design of an object was part and parcel of making it.

The mechanics were not paid by the hour but by the "piece," the quantity of items he or she produced, at periodically negotiated rates. (Yes, there were women too, most of them employed in engraving stocks and grooving bullets.) Young people entered the shops after common school, learned from their elders and, by the time they reached young adulthood, could be productive enough to earn enough to think about setting up their own households. Mechanics could to some extent control their earnings, within the limits of their skills and their relationship with the contractor, by working more and producing more "pieces."[2]

The owners (in this case, the Remingtons) were paid through the rents they collected from the senior contractors, and the difference between the price they could get for the finished products and the price they had to pay the senior contractors. They also negotiated contracts, worked with inventors, arranged for marketing, and had the last word in piece-rate negotiations.

This was not an unusual system for nineteenth-century U.S. manufacturing.[3] And it was well-suited to producerist ideals. There was no management hierarchy with a chain of command that penetrated into every corner of production. Everyone was a contractor—the Remingtons themselves were contractors to the governments who ordered their products—and each contractor was assumed to bear responsibility for his or her part of the process.

The contractors' relative independence, I believe, is at the root of a curious local usage: historically and still today, people often call the Remington works, "the shops." Indeed, each contractor's shop had its own style, rules, and rhythm. The larger shops even organized their own benevolent societies. For dues of a few cents a week the mechanics maintained a fund to help out members who got sick or had an accident and to pay the cost of a decent funeral when they died.[4]

But what happened to all these contractors when a contract was fulfilled? Sometimes there was another contract; sometimes there was not. When business was "dull," as it was in the mid-1880s, the shops ran with as few as 150 to 200 mechanics. When the company captured big contracts, as it did during the Civil War and the 1870s, as many as two thousand men and women could find work in the shops. Given the on-again, off-again seasons of nineteenth-century factory work, mechanics could not depend on the company for their entire livelihood. How did they live between contracts?

The short answer is what I call "backyard agriculture." In the nineteenth century (and still visible in some places today) house lots in all the old Northeastern towns were long and narrow. Houses fronted on the street, with ample room for barns, sheds, and gardens behind.

Backyard agriculture, 1856. Looking east from West Hill toward the shops of E. Remington & Sons (Ilion), this photo shows the gardens, sheds, and barns of an extensive domestic subsistence practice. Courtesy, Historical Room, Ilion Free Public Library.

Everyone kept chickens and grew vegetables and fruits—even the Remingtons. Many kept pigs. Several kept cows.

The historical union of agriculture and manufacturing appears to be a largely forgotten chapter in U.S. history. We are typically taught that this country was an agricultural nation that became, largely by way of technological advances, an industrial nation. And from a bird's-eye view, above the ups and downs of everyday life, this is not untrue. But for a century, most industrialization in the United States depended on the agricultural skills of the populace. Manufacturing firms were not typically able to carry all their mechanics between contracts. In the "island communities" of the nineteenth-century United States, agriculture and manufacturing went hand in hand.

And, too, we typically think of factory work as going on in cities, but early industrialization was largely rural. Until the later nineteenth century the United States was not a "developed" country. It lacked developed fuel resources and a large-scale iron and steel industry (Chandler 1972). It would take both of these to urbanize manufacturing with steam power as English manufacturers had done. Early manufactories in the United States ran on water power, and water is at its most powerful in the steep hills and valleys of the countryside, not the safe harbors of the big coastal cities. The factories went up among the farms.

This too had its advantages from the mechanics' point of view. Starving urban "masses" desperate for work, who could be taken on and let go whenever the factory owner wished, were not readily available in the countryside. There was no "labor market" to speak of. People who could do the work were not easy to replace, and wise factory owners treated them well. Workers and owners lived in the same small world and could not easily escape the pressures of each others' needs.

These constraints of capital, power, and labor gave a uniquely rustic character to much of precorporate manufacturing in the United States. The Remington success, from our modern point of view, might be seen as a product of these undeveloped conditions, but people at the time did not see it this way. Indeed, the most influential thinkers of the mid-nineteenth-century United States had made a virtue of necessity, building up, against the bad example of English industrialization, a model of manufacturing that preserved the "gospel of work."

Manufacturing Prosperity

Abraham Lincoln's economic guide, Henry C. Carey, was the most remarkable social thinker of the nineteenth-century United States to be so thoroughly forgotten today.[5] In keeping with the Jeffersonian ideal of broad-based prosperity, Carey's economic policy focused on keeping labor "dear"; that is, keeping wages high. High wages meant a prosperous people and a stable republic.

But Carey was also a capitalist, a big investor in Pennsylvania coal, iron, and steel (Wallace 1978, 1987). One might think that it was in his interest to beat down wages and raise his profit ratio, but Carey did not see it this way. Carey's genius was to envision a new kind of industrialization that not only capitalized (literally and figuratively) on the limitations of U.S. development but also updated the egalitarian ideals of the Jeffersonian revolution for the age of mass production.[6] Carey's American system was intended to produce "a substantial, intelligent and virtuous yeomanry,"[7] not the desperate, propertyless masses of the British system.

Central to the practice of Carey's plan was the imposition of steep tariffs on imported (mostly British) goods so that American labor would not be forced to compete with the downtrodden workers of Europe (Foner 1970:20–21). The virtues of this policy were firmly entrenched in the Valley's political thinking. As the Ilion paper editorialized in 1888, "The Republicans will, as ever, stand firm by protection to American labor and industry—the Democrats for free trade, or in other words, American interests versus English interests."[8]

In addition to the tariff, keeping labor "dear," as Carey analyzed it, meant increasing competition for the *purchase* of labor, not its sale, and this could only happen with "diversification of employments."

> The shoemaker does not need to purchase shoes, nor does the miner need to buy coal, any more than the farmer needs to buy wheat or potatoes. Bring them together [with] the hatter, the tanner, the cotton-spinner, the maker of woollen cloth, and the smelter and roller or iron, and each of them becomes a competitor for the purchase of the labour, or the products of the labour, of all the others, and the wages of all rise. [1856:3–4]

Considering the "tax" of transportation, it should be clear, he continued, that "the nearer the loom and the plough, the hammer and the harrow, the larger would be the reward of labour" (1856:7).

Keeping the hammer near the harrow, of course, was not a recipe for the growth of big cities. On the contrary, Carey argued, great cities centralized political and economic power, tending to generate tyranny and impoverished multitudes.

> Whatever tends to the establishment of decentralization, and to the production of local employment for time and talent, tends to give value to land, to promote its division [i.e., many small holdings rather than large estates], and to enable parents and children to remain in closer connection with each other. [1858:45]

Carey had, he believed, discovered the natural "law of distribution." This is how he stated it: "both capitalist and laborer profited by every measure tending to render labor more, while losing by every one that tended to render it less, productive" (1858:v)—in other words, both labor and capital benefit by rising productivity. Is this reasonable? It may be if we bear in mind that wages at the time were based on the quantity of "pieces" produced, so that if a new machine or a new process resulted in more product per unit of labor, that also meant more pay for the workers. The capitalists would have to pay more in wages, but, in the end, Carey reasoned, they would benefit too by getting a higher return on their capital because there was more product to sell—and more well-paid working people to buy.

Thus, Carey argued, there exists "a perfect harmony of interests" between labor and capital such that, in the long run, labor's share and capital's share would tend to equalize (1858:v–vi). Carey's vision proposed an egalitarian counter to the gloomy predictions of the "classical" economists, especially to the "iron law of wages," a self-fulfilling prophecy that decreed, as a law of nature, that the wages of labor must fall to the minimal amount for maintaining bare subsistence (Galbraith 1960:25–26). According to these economists (and, indeed, to their heirs today), inequality is inevitable—it is *natural*.

It is *not*, Carey vehemently argued in dozens of books and thousands of articles and pamphlets. The true natural way was that the "powers of improvement" grow in tandem "with the growth of wealth and population" (1858:vi).[9] It was a stunning vision. The United States could have all the productive capacity of Europe *and* a happy, comfortable working people! No wonder Lincoln was drawn to it.

Looking back, though, there was an intriguing flaw in Carey's reasoning. If wages were to keep rising with productivity, he evidently expected that capitalists would continue to pay workers a relatively stable price per piece. He did not anticipate, that is, that capitalists would unilaterally push the price down, pay workers less and less per unit, and take more and more for themselves. In Carey's culture that would surely have seemed indecent.

But this little problem remained hidden over the horizon of the future. By the mid-nineteenth century, Carey could have used the enterprises of E. Remington & Sons to demonstrate his momentous "law of distribution." Wages had, in fact, steadily risen with the productivity of labor. In 1850 the Ilion shops produced 5,825 gun barrels and 850 rifles (valued at $26,050), and 50 mechanics made an average of $25 per month. Five years later annual production was up to 10,020 barrels (valued at $42,700) and 50 mechanics averaged $30 per month. In 1860 annual production was 6,000 barrels and 6,000 pistols (valued at $60,000) and 75 mechanics made an average of $40 per month. By 1865, stimulated by the Civil War, annual production figures were off the charts at 15,000 barrels, 12,000 rifles, 80,000 pistols (valued at $1,207,357)—and 600 mechanics averaged $52 per month.[10]

The cancellation of Civil War contracts in 1865 dealt the Valley a sudden and severe economic blow. But Philo Remington and his brothers had been thinking ahead. The future of military arms would belong to the mechanics who could develop reliable "breech-loaders" (as well as come up with a reliable system for converting the Army's "muzzle-loaders" to "breech-loaders").[11] Before the treaty at Appomattox was signed, the Remingtons had brought to Ilion the most accomplished mechanics they could find. In 1867, after a two-year lean period during which they were able to continue only through the generous credit of their friends, the Remingtons got their first major contract for breech-loading rifles, from the government of Denmark, and for the next seven years, the work was ceaseless. When the Franco-Prussian War broke out, Samuel Remington, the family's agent in Europe, negotiated a remarkable contract with the French government—for as many breech-loaders as the shops could produce during the critical period. The Armory ran night and day.

"When he was at the height of his prosperity," a friend of Philo Remington later recalled, "he could have retired from business a wealthy man. But he said: 'Here are all these people depending on this factory for a livelihood; what will they do?' He was continually thinking of the people."[12] Prosperous as things looked at the time, the Remington brothers knew that peace treaties would one day be signed. Philo, at the helm, was approaching his sixtieth year and must surely have been tempted by visions of an easier life. Instead, he committed the family's resources to diversifying the firm's production.

And so the shops machined up for the plethora of products that the *Scientific American* reporter saw in 1872. The following year, the most portentous new product of the lot was introduced by the visit of a delegation from Milwaukee, representing mechanic and inventor Christopher Latham Scholes. Philo and his most trusted mechanics received their guests in the meeting rooms of the Osgood Hotel, across the street from the Armory. With a flourish, one of the Milwaukee men pulled the gadget out of the newspapers in which he had wrapped it and set it on the table (Cent52:25). It was a writing machine, crude but interesting. Philo was intrigued. The spindles on which the type was mounted, though, kept jamming, a problem that the Remington mechanics assured him they could fix. They did, eventually.[13] Three years later, the new "type-writer" made its national debut at the grand

Centennial Exhibition in Philadelphia—the little type-written mes-
sages that fair-goers could dictate at the Remington exhibit became
quite the rage.

The future seemed to hold nothing but promise—local historians
have dubbed the 1870s "the golden age of Ilion." To all appearances
the Valley exemplified the hopes and promises of producerist ideals.
Principled capitalists and skilled mechanics worked together, building a local society that was prosperous for all its members. Walking
down tree-lined streets, stepping into position behind your work-
bench, chatting in the garden after church, enjoying a picnic in the
park as the Municipal Band played on—no one could have imagined
that this way of life would soon be history.

7

The Remington Failure

At first no one had an inkling. Every day but the Sabbath, people poured into the shops, and crates of well-crafted products poured out. There were the usual ups and downs, of course, but nothing seemed different from the way it had been for as long as anyone could remember.

It was early 1886 and the firearms business had been "dull" for the last six or seven years, but with firearms it was always feast or famine. At the end of the Civil War, and again at the end of the Franco-Prussian War, the Remingtons found themselves with tons of sophisticated machinery and more skilled mechanics than ever, but with fewer and fewer contracts. The shops had diversified, though, into iron bridges, street-car engines, cotton gins, sewing machines, threshers, fire engines, velocipedes, and typewriters. A large number of mechanics were employed and the community prospered.

Typewriters were the most commercially promising of all the new undertakings and the Valley was settling into its providential industrial duo—"the Arms" and "the Typewriter," everyone called them. The Valley's hard-working "producers" could hardly have asked for more. Then, unaccountably, in March of 1886 the Remingtons sold off the typewriter—stock, machinery, and rights. Why sell off their most promising venture? In retrospect, the typewriter sale was the first sign of a momentous turn of events: the Remington failure.

What exactly had happened was anything but clear. Philo Remington's death a short time later—from a broken heart, people say—provided the occasion for much reflection on the company's long past. But regarding the Remington failure, the *Citizen* offered only this: The firm "continued until business reverses came in 1886" (4/5/1889). "Business reverses *came*"? Came from where?

An account in the Utica *Daily Press* (UDP) that same day, though, gives a crucial clue: "This firm for years did a most prosperous business. They had *unlimited credit* and an enormous capital at their disposal. Unfortunate business transactions and unwise advisors brought them down to financial ruin in 1886" (4/5/1889, my emphasis).

The problem was not technology, then, nor labor; it was financial. But notice the contradiction. "An enormous capital" could be squandered, as the writer implies it was, but how could a firm with "unlimited credit" be brought "down to financial ruin"? With "unlimited credit" surely they could have gotten a loan to tide them over.

That is exactly what the Remingtons had tried to do. Like any business, they had hit a cash-flow crisis—peace continued in Europe, the Agricultural Works were losing ground to a new Chicago conglomerate, and they lost an expensive lawsuit having to do with sewing machine patents (Russell 1897:14). The Remington brothers contacted a wealthy New York City connection, Marcellus Hartley, to arrange a loan of $500,000, a large sum but not a spectacular one for a firm with, at that time, assets conservatively valued at $2,300,000.

Hartley was a partner in Hartley and Graham, a retail firm that had sold Remington firearms since the late 1860s. Hartley had made them large loans before—Hartley's firm was the Remington's largest secured creditor when the works were sold—but for some undisclosed reason, this loan (as the newspapers anxiously reported for a month) was "delayed."

By April 1886 rumors were flying of an impending crisis, but people were still optimistic: "The loan of $500,000 with Hartley and Graham," the UDP reported, is still under negotiation and "the outlook is encouraging that it will be made" (4/20/1886). Otherwise, the firm's finances appeared to be in excellent shape. At the last annual inventory, the paper noted, the firm's assets totaled $2,336,000, with no mortgages or liens "sufficient to embarrass it" (*ibid.*).

But unbeknownst to the anxious Valley, a shadowy conspiracy was plotting the end of the Remington era. Someone, never named, brought damaging information about the Remingtons' financial condition to the New York State Attorney General. On the basis of that information, the *New York Times* reported, the attorney general applied "for an order dissolving the firm." "The application alleges," the *Times* story continued, "that the firm is, and has been for some time, insolvent" (4/23/1886). On April 22 an Albany court appointed two Ilion men, associates of the Remingtons (and fellow Methodists), as "receivers" of the firm's assets. Just like that, the Remingtons were forced into bankruptcy.

How could the situation have gotten so desperate without anyone knowing about it? Product was being shipped out every day. All those mechanics were getting paid, weren't they? It didn't add up. Information that surfaced at the sale of E. Remington & Sons, nearly two years later, offers some answers—and poses more questions.

The Sale

It has been said that Ilion saved the Union, and now it seems a pity that something could not be done to save Ilion.

Utica *Daily Press* 2/3/1888

The Remington shops were twice sold at auction, both times to the same party. Even before the receivers finished their inventory of Remington assets, a group of some sixty local men—most from Ilion, most longtime associates of the shops—had begun organizing to "save Ilion." The plan was to pool their capital and buy the company. They collected pledges that amounted to a substantial pool of capital, and got scores of sympathetic creditors to sign over to the group their outstanding Remington debts. The day of the auction drew near. The Ilion group was ready.

Mechanics and other townspeople crowded in close as the auctioneer strode toward the podium. But he had barely struck his gavel when a New York City attorney pushed his way to the front of the crowd and made a shocking announcement. He claimed to represent a mystery creditor to whom the Remingtons owed a whopping $750,000. All bids, he warned, would be subject to the claims of his client.

The Ilion group stood by, stunned, while two bidders, Winchester Arms and Hartley and Graham, dominated the bidding—strangely unaffected by the shocking news of the big mystery creditor. After Winchester dropped out at $150,000, Hartley and Graham took the property for the pathetic sum of $152,000.

But *surprise!* After the bidding, the New York City attorney changed his story. The mystery creditor was actually owed $17,500, he said. Well, maybe it wasn't even that much. It was actually nothing. There was no such client (UDP 2/1/1888). The ploy, however, had accomplished its ends.

The Ilion group was in shock, and the village was demoralized. "There is a future," the *Citizen* editors commented—there must be. But "'The Lord help Ilion now' is not an unheard expression today" (2/3/1888:4).

Who really bought the Remington works, though, was not quite clear. It is "currently accepted as truth," the *Citizen* editorialized, that Winchester Arms Company, not Hartley and Graham, is the real buyer. "Monopoly is the order of the day," the editors commented, "and the Winchester Arms Co. are by no means backward in their desire for monopoly" (2/3/1888:4). In fact, as several citizens had noticed, Mr. Reynolds, Hartley and Graham's representative, had conferred throughout the day with the president and vice-president of Winchester Arms. And after the auction, all three returned to New York City together (*ibid.*).

Once it became clear that they had been hoodwinked, the Ilion group brought suit to have the sale voided. Certain other bidders, they argued before the federal district court in Watertown (New York), seemed to be well aware that the New York attorney's claims had no basis in fact. Hartley and Graham's attorney strenuously objected. The Ilionites, he sneeringly alleged, "have not the capital to run it." If the judge granted a resale, he warned ominously, Winchester Arms Company might purchase the works—and dismantle it. A Utica ally agreed. Some of the Ilionites, he scoffed, "could not pay a quarter of the amount they had subscribed." But despite these arguments, the judge ordered the sale "set aside" and fixed a date one month hence for a new auction (*Citizen* 2/17/1888:1).

The *Citizen* was optimistic that in an honest contest the Ilion group would succeed. The newspaper lent its offices to the fund-raising drive, so that the Ilion group could, as the editors put it, "equip themselves and go out on the warpath" (3/2/1888:5). Now led by Philo Remington's son-in-law, W. C. Squire, the group looked to polish their image with a prestigious spokesperson. They were grateful when U.S. Senator Warner Miller (originally of Herkimer) agreed to represent them for the second round of bidding. They had raised subscriptions of $300,000. With the $50,000 of debt that local creditors had assigned to them, they went "on the warpath" with an impressive $350,000, more than double the amount of the previous winning bid (New York *Tribune* 3/8/1888:1).

On the fateful day, "the streets were thronged" and "hundreds of anxious workmen surrounded the works" (UDP 3/7/1888). The bidding was spirited but quickly came down to an apparent contest between Mr. Reynolds, for Hartley and Graham, and Senator Miller for Ilion. Back and forth they went in $100 increments until Senator Miller abruptly left the room and headed for the train station—bound for Chicago, the Valley later learned. Mr. Squire stepped in for the Ilionites. He raised one more increment to $199,800 and then, unaccountably, fell silent (*Citizen* 3/9/1888). Reynolds jumped to $200,000 and—though the auctioneer "dwelt long on this figure"— nobody bid again (UDP 3/7/1888).

"Spoils to the Victors," was the *Citizen*'s bitter headline: "Hartley and Graham Get the Property Again" (3/9/1888:4). "Immediately upon the close of the sale," the paper observed, the town was full of "strange speeches and strange swearings and strange rantings and strange rumors" (*Citizen* 3/9/1888:4). What had gone wrong? The Ilion group could have easily outbid the $200,000. Why didn't they?

They were betrayed, the Utica paper suggested: "the bottom dropped out" and secret "combinations were made" (UDP 3/7/1888). Part of the answer was soon forthcoming. Hartley and Graham, it turned out, had sent a letter to Senator Miller promising—in exchange for what, we don't know—that they would not "dismantle" the shops (*Citizen* 3/9/1888:4). Perhaps the Senator, too, believed that the Ilion group did not have the cash to run the shops. Or maybe he knew that behind the half-hearted show of competition between Winchester Arms and Hartley and Graham lurked an emerging trust. Maybe he thought that the best anyone could realistically hope for was to keep the works in the Valley. Or, maybe, he went over to the trust's side.

"IS IT A GUN TRUST?" the *Citizen* headline asked (3/9/1888, all-caps in the original), already knowing the answer. The trusts were evil, as everyone knew, but suddenly the Valley was in a delicate position. Alienate the new owners and who knew what they would do. The usually forthright *Citizen* was coy: "When it was told here Wednesday after the sale . . . that this was to be a big end in [the gun] trust, it was difficult to find a man who was opposed to trusts. (Do you catch on?)" (*Citizen* 3/9/1888:4). Surely the readers did "catch on," and were careful to watch what they said.

By late May, there was no doubt about trust ownership. The nominal purchasers of the Remington armory, the *Citizen* reported, had legally transferred ownership to "a powerful and wealthy syndicate" that included Winchester Arms, Marcellus Hartley, and unnamed Chicago capitalists. They secured a fifty-year corporate charter for the manufacture of arms, ammunition, sewing machines, and tools. Everyone hoped for the best. Ilion is probably on a firmer foundation today, the paper optimistically editorialized, than it had been "for a dozen or score years" (6/1/1888:5).

Had the Remingtons been in trouble for that long?

Unlimited Credit

We can now safely assume that Hartley's "delay" in getting a loan to the Remingtons was a time of eager planning on the part of the emerging gun trust. Hartley must have contacted the monopolistically inclined Oliver Winchester with news that the Remington's attempt to negotiate a big loan had revealed a fascinating opportunity to crush the competition: E. Remington & Sons was debt-logged, a plum ripe for the picking.

But this leaves a big question still unanswered. How did a supposedly "insolvent" firm keep up all the appearances of success until days before the Remingtons were forced into bankruptcy?

The answer is stunning. In a cabinet at the Ilion Library Historical Room (ILHR) are several shelves of old scrapbooks, among them the scrapbooks of A. N. Russell, one of the two court-appointed receivers of Remington assets. Russell saved every scrap from his active involvement with the Methodist Church, from every local election over his long life in Ilion, and, of course, from the business of the receivership. There, neatly pasted together by the hand of this key participant, was the stuff of revelation.

The firm's finances were extremely complicated. "The works and their fixtures last January [1886] inventoried at $2,000,000," a UDP clipping noted, but outstanding indebtedness is "believed to be" $600,000–$800,000 (UDP 4/22/1886, RS). "Believed to be"? Why didn't they know for sure? As it turned out, the Remingtons' outstanding indebtedness was practically impossible to calculate—precisely because of their "unlimited credit."

Remington mechanics, it turned out, had not been paid *in cash* "for more than ten years." The firm had paid in "orders"—in effect, company scrip. All this time, local merchants had "received Remington

orders *as if they were money*" (UDP 4/20/1886, my emphasis). The
Remingtons got through all those paydays with, in effect, IOUs![1] A
clipping in Russell's scrapbook described this practice in detail.

> The method has been for an employee to give an order on the Rem-
> ington firm for his boots, his coat, his bed, his board, his cigar and his
> minister. These orders after three months, during which they drew no
> interest, were changed for a short time note of the company's, which
> at the end of three or four months, was paid or renewed. Very many of
> the short notes have been changed into long-time notes, . . . so that the
> creditors of the corporation are very many of them the residents of Il-
> ion, most of them, as it is believed. [UDP 4/20/1886, RS]

All of Ilion—barbers, grocers, landlords, and preachers—had, in turn,
taken the Remington notes and "used them to pay their own creditors." And that's not all. "Ilion merchants are not the only ones on the
anxious seat."[2] So are those of Herkimer, Mohawk, and Utica (UDP
4/22/1886, RS). Talk about unlimited credit! Everyone in the Valley
was a Remington creditor.

Why didn't the mechanics complain? In the annals of labor history,
payment in company scrip was one of the most disreputable practices
of early U.S. industrialization. How did the Remingtons get away with
it for more than a decade? Because, evidently, "orders" or not, the
Remingtons saw to it that their mechanics lived well. Here is the im-
pression of a Utica reporter:

> In 1861 the village of Ilion had but 800 inhabitants. Now it has 4,000
> and their houses show that they are a well-to-do class. . . . The chil-
> dren of the Ilion workmen have been brought up under favorable in-
> fluences, and many persons who came to the town as laborers have
> greatly benefited their condition and own neat homes with well-kept,
> attractive surroundings. [UDP 4/20/1886]

If everyone in the Valley had not accepted Remington notes as money,
there surely would have been complaints about payment in scrip.
Since they all did—what was there to complain about?

But *why* did they all accept payment in scrip? Because, apparently,
everyone in the Valley believed in the Remingtons. They had come
through crisis after crisis for three generations, bringing the Valley's
prosperity with them. The Remingtons had unlimited credit because
they had unlimited *credibility*. They had unlimited credibility be-

cause they acted on the egalitarian values that held the moral high-ground in the nineteenth-century United States—everybody works hard and everybody gets the fruits of their labor.

The Remingtons lived in Lincoln's and Carey's culture. Labor and capital, they wished to believe, were in perfect harmony. As the mechanics became increasingly productive, their wages should, *naturally*, increase. When business was "dull"—through no fault of the mechanics—the Remingtons plugged the gap by, in effect, printing their own money.

Remington notes, as local currency, can actually be seen to have enjoyed an important advantage over normal money capital: independence from the ups and downs of the "nonproducer" capitalists' markets. During "the golden age of Ilion" (the 1870s), most of the country was deep in economic recession. The nation's major capitalists had insisted on being repaid in gold for the Civil War loans they had made to the Union in "greenbacks," precipitating a massive and painful currency deflation (Goodwyn 1976). Remington notes, as local currency, had kept the Valley prosperous, insulating its economy from the nationwide contraction.

The Remingtons went deeply into debt, in large part, to uphold the living standards of the Valley. That's taking egalitarian values seriously. The Remingtons failed for the same reason they succeeded—they kept labor "dear."

End of an Era

On every side can be seen some mark or monument which will last for all time connecting the name Remington with this prosperous village. Of the man who has passed away we cannot say one unkind word if we would; his life, acts and deeds have been those of a good, pure, upright, honest man.

Ilion *Citizen* 4/5/1889

Philo Remington's death in April 1889, just months after the gun trust captured the shops, signaled the end of an era in the Valley.[3] After the funeral a huge memorial service was held at the Opera House. As friend after friend stepped up to the podium to praise Mr. Remington's virtues, it seems that they seized the occasion to send a message to the new owners. It was a message about the "gospel of work."

Mr. Remington's "innermost feeling," one eulogist declared, was "that there should be no injustice in the distribution" of wealth.[4] Another eulogist observed that it is "not gold" but a "marked desire for justice" that makes true leaders in "industry and prosperity." Yet another recalled: "I was there when his first reverses began. [Mr. Remington] said the market was dull and didn't pay. But, stopping suddenly, he said[,] that must make no difference. The works must be kept running, even if the firm did lose. The men shouldn't be allowed to suffer."

The Valley had of course expected the worst from the gun trust. In these tributes they pled the moral authority of traditional American values—in which prosperity, business success, prestige, and even wealth itself were embedded in the well-being of the community. But as we'll see, this was a value system that the trusts did not share.

The trusts and their allies would endeavor to establish a new truth in the Valley, predicated on a system of wealth making that was entirely separate from the community. It was based on an impersonal force, "the economy," that moved like the weather from equilibrium to equilibrium. The new owners of the Valley's production would tolerate no interference with the arcane workings of that force—no loyalties, nor ideals, nor sentiments had any proper place in the process. The trust could not do business with traditional American values.

Part III
The Corporate Regime

The ominous sense of a shrinking margin of practical liberties pervaded men, as each successive step in the nation-wide consolidation of the country's resources and means of production brought no tangible gains to the population at large.

MATTHEW JOSEPHSON, *The Robber Barons*

8

Cultural Revolution

The trust owners wasted no time on pleasantries. From day one, the threat of factory closing was the trusts' blunt instrument of political conquest in the Valley. Like their corporate successors today, they demanded special privileges—more space, cheaper utilities, and, most of all, lower taxes. The ink was barely dry on the Remington Armory receivership when the new owners of the Remington Typewriter Company threatened to close the Ilion factory unless the Village gave them the "inducements" they wanted (*Citizen* 12/10/1886).[1]

The Valley went into shock. Nothing in their experience had prepared them to make sense of this. They built that factory and all its machines with their own hands and minds. They struggled for a decade on short rations before the new machine started to sell. It was a joke in the commercial world: "Why buy a $100 writing machine when I can get a pen for $1," the wags laughed. But the mechanics continued to build and improve the typewriter, and now it was a huge success. How could others claim the fruits of all their labor, their own and their childrens' future prosperity?

Close our factory! the *Citizen* exclaimed. Without us to "nurture and develop" it, this "now famous machine" would not exist (11/26/1886). Anxious negotiations ended with the Armory owners offering "the Typewriter" (as local people called the typewriter factory) additional space at its facilities, but less than two years later the new masters of the typewriter again announced that they had been offered "inducements" elsewhere, "in the shape of buildings, land, exemption from taxes and the like."[2]

For all anyone knew at the time, the Remingtons had sold the Typewriter to two Ilion men, Clarence Seamans (son of the Remington brothers' longtime shipping contractor) and Henry H. Benedict (Philo Remington's former personal secretary). Seamans and Benedict had been the Remington's sales agents, and it was known that they had out-of-town partners, but for months these partners kept a low profile.

In July 1888 it was Seamans himself who announced melodramatically, "doubtless we [the Typewriter] will be from among you before snow flies."[3] The rapid response was a citizens' meeting that agreed on a subscription drive "for the purpose of inducing the Standard Typewriter Manufacturing Company to locate their manufactory at Ilion."[4] (The new owners had, unaccountably, renamed the company, a move soon reconsidered—they re-renamed it the Remington Typewriter Company in 1903 to capitalize on the enduring credibility of the Remington name [Cent52:31].) In this remarkable undertaking, at least 165 local people pledged at least $5,082.00, in amounts ranging from a humble $5 to a grand $250, payable to the company "as a consideration for the location of . . . said works at Ilion."[5] Two weeks later, presumably sweetened by this "consideration," the company agreed to stay, taking over the space of the struggling Agricultural Works.

The typewriter company held the Valley hostage. What choice did people have? Already at least three hundred Valley families depended on the Typewriter for their living (Cent52:31), and all signs indicated that the market was burgeoning. The Typewriter was no longer theirs, but they could hardly let it go.

"Cornering" the Community

Trusts had to be secretive. It was not until January 1893, nearly seven years after the Remingtons sold the Typewriter that the Valley began to realize that it had come under trust control (*Citizen* 1/20/1893). In April of that year all was revealed when the typewriter trust incorporated (in New Jersey) as the Union Typewriter Company—with the Ilion factory as its largest single asset.[6]

The typewriter trust-turned-corporation would run the closure-threat tactic whenever the Valley hesitated to grant its every wish, once every decade on average. An Ilion newspaperman joked in the 1950s that "a real old-timer will say: 'Look, son, Remington has been 'moving out of Ilion' since 1900 and they're still here and always will be.'"[7] A decade after this joking comforted a jittery Valley, as we'll see, the company finally made good on its long-standing threat.

The gun trust-turned-corporation tried the closure tactic in 1897.

Marcellus Hartley himself, evidently, was behind the flurry of rumors that he was going to close the factory and move production elsewhere. A citizens' committee quickly organized and went to his office to find out what he wanted. (Surely they guessed, after their experiences with the Typewriter.) True to form, Hartley told them that "excessive" taxation was putting the Armory "at a disadvantage." A few conferences later he agreed to keep the plant open—after a group of anxious employees and citizens paid the company's taxes for that year ($4,500, HCP 1946:34).

Was there any way out from under the heavy hand of the trusts? What about starting up new lines of manufacturing? The Valley was full of hard-working mechanics. You name it, they could make it. Diversification, of course, was not a new strategy in the Valley—and this is where the devastating impact of the trust movement becomes dramatically clear.

The Remington brothers, with characteristic foresight, had tried to diversify their product line since the 1870s. They invested a fortune— that might have bought lives of luxury for generations of the family— in expanding the firm's production and keeping the mechanics gainfully employed. (Imagine a corporate branch office making this decision today!) Remember *Scientific American*'s glowing tribute to Remington industriousness (4/13/1872, quoted in Chapter 6). When arms and ammunition were not in demand, the magazine reporter enthused, the Remington works "burst out" in a dozen other products. The article mentions cotton gins, iron beams, iron bridges, trolley cars, sewing machines, plows, mowers, and reapers.

A manufacturing enterprise, of course, does not simply "burst out" with this variety of goods. Each product involved major commitments of time and money for planning, designing, making new tools and machinery, and learning and teaching new production processes, not to mention the costs of fuel and raw materials. The files of the ILHR are full of colorful ads for these goods, each trading on the Remington reputation for top quality at a fair price—and each one sustaining, for some years, its own crew of mechanics.

But each of these products, by the mid-1880s, had become the target of a trust. By 1883 agricultural machinery was gathered up into the Chicago trust that would later incorporate as International Harvester. That same year the sewing machine trust had conquered New York and New England under the Singer name, and would go national in 1885. The iron trust dates back to 1875, and an iron bridge-builders trust was secured by 1886.[8]

The trusts, just as the critics of incorporation had predicted (Chapter 5), locked up the future of manufacturing, locking out local ventures that had, for a century, supported the autonomy of "island communities." The trusts had "cornered" not only firearms and typewriters but also communities and their citizens throughout the industrialized United States.

The blunt instrument of plant closure would not, in itself, sustain the future of corporate manufacturing. The trusts faced wave after wave of political resistance, across the country. And as long as people continued to expect the rewards of the producerist ideal, that resistance would persist. From the trusts' perspective, the people needed a dose of "re-education." They soon embarked on a long cultural campaign to replace the "gospel of work" with a philosophy more friendly to their way of doing business. Ready-made for their purposes was a new philosophy, the curious perversion of evolution theory that took as its motto "the survival of the fittest"—so-called social Darwinism. It rapidly won a following among "the captains of industry" and their political and academic supporters (Hofstadter 1955b:44–45, 50).

The most important debate of U.S. culture was engaged. What kind of country was this going to be?

Men of Push

An anonymous Utica critic is the first to articulate the new ideal (in the ILHR data)—just as the gun trust was securing ownership of the Ilion shops. The "employes [sic] of the firm," this critic pointed out, "earned big wages and enjoyed prosperity" but "bad management" set the firm on "the sure road to bankruptcy": "Had the Remingtons . . . run their business on business principles as men of business would, the firm to-day would be one of wealth and power."[9]

The Remingtons, of course, had been held in high esteem precisely because, tempered by their interest in local prosperity, they had not single-mindedly pursued "wealth and power" (Chapter 5). On the other hand, according to this critic, the officers of "the Type-writer" were true "men of business." In two short years, he observed, they had turned the company into "one of the leading industries of Central New York." They were "men of push and enterprise" (*ibid.*).

And how had they accomplished this great success? In short, at the expense of their employees. Although the trust had to retain some skilled mechanics, it quickly contracted out all the skilled work it could, including forging and cabinetry (DN:170–171). For the manual labor, it hired women and "foreigners." Women sought work at the Typewriter before marriage or, more desperately, after divorce and widowhood. (Women were 43 percent of the workforce in the early 1930s [ET 5/13/1934; TS34]). The "foreigners" were mostly people of Italian descent who had settled on the fringes of Ilion and Frankfort. The typewriter trust hired people, in other words, that they could get away with working hard and paying badly.[10]

The work was grueling and the hours were long. Among the women of the Typewriter were my maternal grandmother and her youngest sister. An imposing woman who took her respectability seriously, my grandmother was reluctant to tell me about her years at the Type-writer. Finally, at the age of ninety-five, she wrote me a few sentences:

> You asked me what my job was when I worked in the Typewriter . . .
> I never had the Education [but] to work only hard labor. I worked on punch presses, mammoth ones and small ones, and large drill presses, and when we would finish our piece of work, very seldom did we ever have some one to help us. We lifted our own work to our machines.

She worked until she was too pregnant with my mother to continue, and resumed work a couple of years later when my grandfather set off "on the road" in search of work. For full-time work—five 10-hour days and a half day on Saturdays—her wage was so low that she fell behind in her rent payments. "Honey," she closed the letter, "you have my whole History that I want to talk about."

How do "men of push and enterprise" rationalize hard treatment of their employees? In a culture where the pursuit of wealth still smacked of "worshiping Mammon" and labor was a divine calling, they did not have much room to maneuver. They had to change the culture.

The "men of push and enterprise" who stormed into the Valley with the trusts quickly found a few allies among local businessmen. They had big plans. They would bring "progress" to the Valley—and, yes, make a lot of money doing it. Big plans needed organization, coordi-

Women of the Typewriter, 1923. Courtesy, Historical Room, Ilion Free Public Library.

nation, and good press. To these ends, the "men of push" and their local allies founded the Ilion Board of Trade in 1897. But the Board's
meetings would not turn out to be quite the platform its founders intended. In the volatile atmosphere of the late nineteenth-century Valley, the Board of Trade became the stage for a collision of social ideals.

The Board's charter members included corporate officers posted in
the Valley, their local allies, and other local elites, most of whom at
this time—lawyers, doctors, local officials, and businesspeople—were
skilled mechanics or the sons and daughters of skilled mechanics,
men (they were all men) whose esteem in local circles was grounded
in mechanic skills. As leaders of production in the shops, skilled mechanics formed a category of local elites with no equivalent today.
These men (my great-grandfather, a toolmaker, among them) formed
the largest occupational group of the Board's membership. The "men
of push" were a distinct, though pushy, minority.

"Though not yet half a year old," a reporter gushed at its first annual banquet in 1897, the Ilion Board of Trade already "has a membership of 175 *live, pushing, enterprising* business men."[11] At the head table were such dignitaries as Typewriter directors, Seamans and Benedict, and Wilfrid Hartley, brother of Marcellus Hartley and treasurer of Remington Arms. Seated with these dignitaries was the keynote speaker, Lieutenant Governor of New York State Timothy L. Woodruff. (Woodruff was "associated in business," as he put it, with Seamans and Benedict—as an investor and, I presume, political crony).

The meal commenced with oysters on the half shell and baked bluefish, then moved on to stuffed turkey, fillet of beef, and lobster salad, wrapping up with Neapolitan ice cream, charlotte russe, "fancy cakes," bon-bons, nuts, fruits, wafers, and cheese. After this digestive marathon, the gents leaned back and puffed on their fine cigars while the speakers took turns introducing and congratulating each other.

A. D. Morgan, president of the village (and grandson of a one-time Remington partner), outlined ambitious plans for paving and lighting Ilion streets and creating municipal parks. Lieutenant Governor Woodruff went on at great length about his administration's commitment "to keep pace with the progress of the people, and all that makes up this wonderfully *aggressive and progressive* commonwealth."[12] If any of this talk made the mechanics uncomfortable, they kept their doubts to themselves. They were, of course, in favor of progress like everyone else.

The first hint of battles to come surfaced at the Board's third annual banquet in the spring of 1899. "Every progressive movement always meets much opposition on the part of the *dead weights* of the village," Reverend R. E. King of Herkimer remarked in his after-dinner speech. Dead weights? Was he referring to angry working people? No. "The ignorant, self-satisfied, contented spirit is in every village," he declared, "and has to be overcome."[13] "Contented" villagers had to be "overcome"? What was wrong with contentment? The reasons for this mysterious remark would soon burst the thin veil of unity that stretched tighter and tighter across the Board's progressive consensus.

The next two speakers that night came prepared for cultural combat. First to the podium was Chancellor J. H. Day of Syracuse University.[14] "When I accepted this invitation to speak," he began, "I told my friend Seamans I was going to speak against trusts and thus get even with him." The gentlemen chuckled. "This great movement,"

Day continued, was the next great stage of evolution. This "massing of labor and this combination of money forces," as he put it, "fits the niche in this closing century as did the improvements of the last century the niche in their time." "The workingman of to-day," he concluded, "is getting more happiness and morality and blessing in every way because of the trusts." If this comment left the mechanic contingent wondering what planet Day hailed from, the next speaker must have set all that heavy food churning in their bellies.

That was J. H. Holmes, recently brought in to manage the new (and short-lived) Remington bicycle department. Holmes had some tough words on the theme of progress in the Valley's villages: "If the citizens of Ilion wish to see their village progress," he declared, "they must accomplish it through this board; *it cannot be done by politics*" (my emphasis).

What was that? Not by "politics"? What kind of "progress" would take place without the consent of the voters?

But Mr. Holmes was not finished. He concluded with what may have been the most provocative remark of the evening: "Let me say that the success of those two industries [i.e., the Arms and the Typewriter] is due to the energy and push of the men who furnish the capital."

What?! He got that backward, didn't he? Everyone knew that labor creates wealth. Was this man saying that *capital* creates wealth? Yes he was. And this was just the first of many such affirmations that the mechanic contingent would have to sit through over the next few years. The contention that capital, not labor, is the wellspring of national prosperity was at the center of the cultural revolution that the trusts were trying to orchestrate.

Holmes knew that he had dropped a bomb. He concluded with a plea for "faith." "We have faith in our families," he said, and "we have faith in our religious convictions . . . so also should we have faith in our village and its Board of Trade."

The "men of push" may well have believed that capital was superior to labor—they were capitalists, after all. And they certainly recognized that the superiority of labor to capital was at the center of popular beliefs. But they also had a few practical aims in mind. If capital was superior to labor then they, the capitalists, had a natural right to take charge of the conditions under which capital (not labor) produced wealth.

Scientific Management

Philo Remington was never ashamed of being a workingman.
He wanted to be reckoned among them to his latest day. . . . I
cannot conceive of a strike among the workingmen employed
by the Remingtons.

"Ilion's Honored Dead," 1889

The capitalists had a problem. They supplied the money that, in their view, built the machines that produced the goods, but they had no idea *how* the machines were built and the goods produced. And that's just the way the mechanics wanted it. For its first century, the work of manufacturing in the United States was organized by skilled mechanics. Those with less skill contracted to those with more, the most skilled of whom ultimately sold the production of their contractors to the company. In home-grown outfits such as the Remington enterprises, the factory owners knew some of the actual production processes, but they relied on the knowledge and practice of their skilled contractors to get the work done.[15] The new corporate owners, though, had no clue.

Skilled mechanics closely guarded their knowledge of production processes. It was their trade secret—and their job security. As the official history of Remington Arms put it, the skilled mechanics were "set in their secret ways," with their "little black books" of figures and formulas "for their eyes only" (Hatch 1956:203). As long as mechanics, loyal to their fellow mechanics, could keep their secrets, the capitalists were at their mercy.

The new corporate managers determined to wrest those secrets from them. In the name of "scientific management," the companies sought to transform the processes of production with new machines and armies of "efficiency experts," who descended on each department with clipboards and stopwatches.[16] These men timed and noted the mechanics' every move, then compiled their data and reported to the company. The company, then, typically tried to reorganize the work processes with "company men" at the helm. This invasion of their domain deeply offended the mechanics' sense of propriety. They had worked out the innovations, overseen the quality of materials and products, hired the best men and women they could find, trained them, and provided for them. And doing this well earned them the respect of the community.

The "men of push" at the Typewriter were the first in the Valley (and among the first in the nation [Chandler 1977]) to invest in scientific management. It provoked the first strike in Ilion's history.

In the summer of 1909 the Aligners, the mechanics who adjusted the delicate key mechanisms for each character on the typewriter— one of the most highly skilled departments in the factory—left their workbenches to protest the nonproducers' attempt to reorganize their work. Although they were perfectly civilized about it, they brought the production of typewriters to a standstill for three weeks.

The typewriter trust retaliated by locking them out of the shop. The trust was determined to put the Aligners in their place—their *new* place. They were no longer to be independent contractors. They were employees now, dependent on the company, and they had better get used to it. To emphasize their point, the trust rolled out, for (at least) the fourth time, the familiar threat of plant closure: "The Remington works are the largest owned by the Union Typewriter Company and it has been intimated that if no adjustment of difficulties is made that the local works might be transferred elsewhere."[17]

In a bid to divide and conquer—to turn local businesspeople against the Aligners—the trust spelled out the dire consequences of plant closure in the terms of their own cultural values, dollars and cents: "The pay roll of the nearly 2,000 employes [sic] has run from $23,000 to $30,000 weekly, and to have this amount taken from the merchants and businessmen of Ilion and its neighboring villages who depend on Ilion is sure to work much privation and hardship" (*ibid.*).

"Father of the typewriter" W. K. Jenne, the first Aligner, much respected for his mechanic skills and, by this time, a supervisor at the Typewriter, published an "open letter" to "all his friends," urging them to "fully consider what it will mean to us all, to try and enforce an impossible regulation of the business upon such a firm as the Remington Typewriter Company. Such action," he cautiously concluded, "might indeed close the works, might even drive the business to some other place."[18]

The Valley, nevertheless, stubbornly supported the Aligners. They were respectable, skilled, hard-working men, pillars of local society. A number of them were members of the Board of Trade. Two days after it obediently printed the company's threats, the Utica *Daily Press* (UDP) broke ranks, boldly publishing the strikers' carefully worded statement in full.

"We appreciate greatly the almost unanimous support given us by the business men of this place," the Aligners told the community. How could anyone "think for a moment" that they were asking for "anything unreasonable or unjust"? The trust claimed that the Aligners were blocking progress. That was a lie: "We are not now and never have been against mechanical progress." The real issue was naked power. The company's goal, the Aligners argued, was plainly "to reduce the workman to want so as to more easily compel them to do as the company dictates."[19]

The company had tried to slander the Aligners as just the kind of "contented" obstacles to progress that the "men of push" had warned against. They were not. They simply could not consent to a "progress" that had to be achieved at the expense of their dignity and their independence. That was not progress, in their view—it was *regress*.

In the end, though, the trust got its way. The Inspectors, crucial allies of the Aligners, voted to return to work, breaking the strike.[20] The lesson of everyone's dependency on the trust was being learned. Capital could beat labor into subordination. Six years later the Armory's toolmakers, again the most skilled and respected mechanics at the shops, faced the same impasse.

In 1902 Marcellus Hartley, largest shareholder of the Remington Arms Company, died, leaving leadership of the works to his grandson and heir, Marcellus Hartley Dodge. In 1908 Dodge, only twenty-six years old, attempted to use his inheritance to set up a modern corporate empire, combining the Ilion works with the Union Metallic Cartridge Company (UMC) of Bridgeport, Connecticut—he named the new corporation Remington Arms UMC. Dodge's dreams, however, outpaced his abilities.

Inexperienced engineers foisted off bad designs on the mechanics. Inexperienced executives—drawn from the sales staff, not the production staff—pushed hard for higher and higher production numbers. And Dodge enthusiastically pursued "scientific management." Ilion Works Manager C. C. Tyler protested the new management's "false economies" and "interference" with production but to no avail.[21] Tyler, caught between corporate pressure and the indignation of his most skilled men, asked the striking mechanics to return to work and give the new methods "a week's trial." If they could "make the increase" in production numbers, then maybe their jobs would not be "regulated."[22] Speed up, in other words, and perhaps you might retain some control over your work.

The strikers conducted themselves in the democratic manner befit-

Pillars of the community, the toolmakers of E. Remington & Sons (and their "oiler,"
with ladder), c. 1875. A copy of this photograph hangs in the toolroom today. Courtesy, Historical Room, Ilion Free Public Library.

ting their dignified status. "No finer type of the high class American
mechanic can be found than in the armory town," the UDP report concluded (*ibid.*). Still they lost, just as the Aligners had.

For the Valley, a great deal more was at stake in these struggles than
control over production methods. "Scientific management" ushered
in a new social order, drawing a line of social class division through
the egalitarian local society in which mechanic skills and hard work
were the broad highway to esteem, social status, and local leadership.
The mechanics were now to be on the "lower" side of that line, subordinate to the "company men" who upheld the claims of corporate
capital. Never again would mechanics be the pillars of local society.
But the Valley was not ready yet to admit defeat.

Rebellion

[T]he apostles of Big Business, who by tortuous paths and devious methods have wrested great fortunes unearned from pro-

ducer, wage earner and consumer alike, these are the real blots
upon civilization, the real curse to the rising generation, in
whose breasts they generate the desire of emulation and the
spirit of trampling down all humans who stand in their way.

Utica *Daily Press* 12/18/1911

No, these were not the words of a wild-eyed radical on a soapbox.[23]
These were the words of Utica judge James K. O'Connor, guest speaker
at the fifteenth annual banquet of the Ilion Board of Trade in 1911.

Board members were fed up. For years they had listened patiently,
giving the trusts every benefit of a doubt, hoping for the best. They
worked hard to make a go of it. And what had they got in return? Be-
trayal, manipulation, and contempt for their accomplishments, intelligence, and democratic rights.

Corporate contempt for democracy was the topic of attorney W. S.
Mackie's speech that night. A "moderate sized corporation is a benefit," he began, but "the *monster of power and strength*" is "a menace
to our existence as a free people" (my emphasis). A free people chartered the "monster," he argued, and a free people have the right to de-
stroy it "when it interferes with public affairs."

> such a corporate life should be killed, its debts paid, stockholders paid
> par value and the rest of the assets forfeited to the state. There is no
> anarchy about this. It is self-preservation. It is keeping a government
> of the people, by the people and for the people.

Judge O'Connor (cited above) ended his address with a stinging indictment: "Why are politicians corrupt?" he thundered—"Because Big
Business has made them so."

You could hear talk like this all over the United States in these years
as the trusts (still so called by an irate public, though most were
securely incorporated by this time) stepped more boldly into the national public sphere. In the wake of the Panic of 1907, a clear consequence of speculative mania on Wall Street, the "monopolists" had
managed to maintain punishingly high prices for the "necessaries" of
life (discussed more fully in Chapter 9). Business was "dull." Strikes
were rampant.

The trusts' opponents also stepped more boldly into the national
public sphere, with the series of exposés initiated by Ida Tarbell's *His-*

tory of Standard Oil (1902–1904) and rapidly followed by dozens more hard-hitting and carefully researched "muckraker" revelations. Presidents Theodore Roosevelt and William H. Taft rode to victory on "trust-busting" platforms. More and more Americans were looking to the most radical solutions—membership in the American Socialist Party doubled between 1909 and 1911, and rose by another 40 percent the following year (Salvatore 1982:242). From every corner of the land, uneasiness jelled to conviction: The trusts-corporations had usurped government "of the people, by the people and for the people."

Rebellion would ferment at the Ilion Board of Trade for two more years until it was quietly squashed in 1914 when the procorporate faction prevailed and the Board was "federated" with the National Association of Chambers of Commerce. Only nice words about the trusts-turned-corporations would be heard at future meetings. But the broader rebellion against corporate rule would only strengthen as the trusts tightened their grip nationwide, and community after community lost hold of the enterprises they had built for their own prosperity.

9

The Gospel of Wealth

The community was "cornered"—we rule or we leave, said the trusts-corporations, taking your prosperity with us. The mechanics, once the pillars of local society, now chafed at the bit of "scientific management" but still did not release their grip on the traditional American values of the "gospel of work." The corporate cultural revolution had been considerably less than successful.

But the corporate revolution was far from over. The capitalists' insistent claim about the superiority of capital over labor was about to undergo a persuasive transformation: It would be dispatched from the small circle of capitalist interests, bearing no less a burden than the evolution of "advanced" civilization. The "gospel of work" met its match in the "gospel of wealth." Influentially disseminated by steel baron Andrew Carnegie, the most articulate man of the trusts, the new gospel would attract converts from the ranks of new money and old.

"The gospel of wealth" was coined by Carnegie,[1] but the philosophy on which it rested was not his own. It was the work of self-appointed English philosopher and sociologist Herbert Spencer who sought to apply the "new philosophy" of the nineteenth century, evolutionism, to human societies.[2] Charles Darwin had proposed some careful scientific points about how multiple species could arise from a single species as isolated breeding groups adapted to particular environments (1859). But Herbert Spencer, Darwin's younger colleague, left careful science behind to speculate on social evolution as the "natural selection" of rich and poor, speculations that would, by the turn of the twentieth century, exert a powerful influence on the builders of the great trusts.

Carnegie's encounter with Herbert Spencer was virtually a religious experience, Carnegie recalled in his autobiography: "Light came in as a flood and all was clear."[3] Spencer was certainly delighted too—he'd found a rich patron. Under Carnegie's patronage Spencer spread the "light" through speaking tours to the United States and dozens of books (Hofstadter 1955b). What was this "light" that made everything clear?

For Spencer, it all came down to "survival of the fittest." (This sound bite is often wrongly attributed to Darwin.) In human societies, Spencer argued, there were two kinds of people. As he explained it in his book *Social Statics* (1868),

> The poverty of the incapable, the distresses that come on the improv-
> ident, the starvation of the idle, and those shoulderings aside of the
> weak by the strong, which leave so many "in shallows and miseries"
> are the decrees of a large, far-seeing benevolence. . . . Under the nat-
> ural order of things society is constantly excreting its unhealthy, im-
> becile, slow, vacillating faithless members.[4]

In Spencer's view, these "shoulderings aside" of the weak by the strong were not, as religious and humanist thinkers had always maintained, bad. They were, Spencer taught, no less than "natural law": By weeding out the "unfit" the human race moved ever closer to perfection.

Spencer's "doctrine" (as he called the body of "laws" he claimed to discover) left no question about who is "fit" and who is not. The strong, wealthy, and prosperous, are. The poor are not. What could be more obvious? In Spencer's philosophy, it was worse than foolish to be concerned about the condition of the "weak"—such concerns only retarded the progress of the human race. So the "light" flooded in on Carnegie: Be strong, make money, save the human race! Had the trusts been frustrated time and again by the "weak" in this nation of "producers"? No more! If Spencer's law "may be sometimes hard for the individual," Carnegie argued in an article entitled "The Gospel of Wealth," it "is best for the race, because it insures the survival of the fittest in every department" (1889:655).

A number of significant conclusions flowed from this law, as Carnegie interpreted it. Paying high wages, for example, only propped up the "unfit," against nature's design—if wealth were "distributed in small quantities among the people," he argued, much of it would be "wasted in the indulgence of appetite" (1889:660). And what was true of wages was true of "wanton" charity. It simply encouraged "the slothful, the drunken, the unworthy" at the expense of the "prudent"

(1889:662). The "man of wealth," Carnegie argued, with "his superior wisdom, experience, and ability to administer" could do for such people "better than they would or could do for themselves" (1889:662). That is the "gospel of wealth" in a nutshell: since wealth was a mark of superior wisdom and fitness, then it is good for the human race that the nation's wealth should be concentrated in the hands of such worthy custodians.[5]

Spencer dignified capitalists, placing them at the leading edge of human progress, and soon many more of the most active men of the trusts saw Spencer's "light." After Carnegie came John D. Rockefeller, railroad barons James J. Hill and Senator Chauncey Depew, iron "magnate" (and Mayor of New York City) Abram S. Hewitt, and coal baron George Baer, to name just a few.[6] Leading academics signed on too, most prominently, President of Harvard, Charles W. Eliot, and Chair of Sociology at Yale (for thirty years), William Graham Sumner. And so did great men of politics, like Senators Henry Cabot Lodge and Nicholas M. Butler, Secretary of War Elihu Root, and Supreme Court Justice Oliver Wendell Holmes. The lessons that these men drew from Spencer were the intellectual legitimation of an ever-broadening cultural campaign, given increasing urgency by hard times and hardened popular distrust.

Carnegie and his coreligionists also defended the trusts with the now familiar argument of abundance through technological advance. The wondrous new machines that their capital could purchase would, Carnegie argued, "scatter the good things of life . . . among the toiling millions," thus "refining and uplifting a people" (1900b:90–91). How? Through the operation of another "natural law" that tended to lower prices for manufactured goods (1900b:89).

By the turn of the century, however, just the opposite had actually occurred, as the ancient warnings against monopoly predicted—the price of every "necessary" under trust control had risen substantially. Corporate financial scheming had thrown the country into deep recession. The speculative "bubble" that burst into the Panic of 1907 left slashed wages and high unemployment in its wake. But working people had been feeling the pinch of corporate economics since the 1890s. These were the age-old consequences of monopoly: higher prices and lower real wages. Economist Alexander D. Noyes worked out the figures for a dramatic conclusion to his *Forty Years of American Finance* (1909).

The average price of commodities increased 13.38 percent between 1897 and mid-1904, by Noyes's calculations (315). That was bad enough, but it was modest in comparison to what happened over the next two and a half years. From mid-1904 to 1907 the average price of commodities rose a further 21.75 percent (315). That was a 35 percent increase in one decade! And, Noyes pointed out, these price increases took place during a period of exceptionally abundant production, both of manufactured and agricultural goods (314–315).

According to economic theory, of course, the greater the supply, the *lower* the price. Why didn't prices fall? The answer was clear. The "great corporations" were holding prices at "artificially" high levels (Noyes 1909:316,333). There was no doubt, Noyes concluded, that a "large section of the community" was being "steadily forced back to a lower scale of living" (318). Industrialization certainly was not, as Carnegie had asserted, lowering the prices for manufactured goods.

Working people were angry. With their support the states and the federal government had thrown up law after strongly worded law to stop the trusts. That is what the Interstate Commerce Act of 1887 was supposed to do, and when it did not, the Sherman Anti-Trust Act of 1890 was passed to penalize any corporation that joined a trust with confiscation of its property. But somehow the trust lawyers found a way around every prosecution. Labor unions offered working people one line of defense. Union membership doubled between 1896 and 1900 to about 900,000 (Ginger 1949:217), and doubled again between 1900 and 1904 to about 2,000,000 (Foner 1965:27).

It was the largest labor union in the world at that time, the United Mineworkers of America, that galvanized the White House into action. When the coal trust refused to negotiate with striking miners in 1902, President Roosevelt, fearing revolution, made secret plans to nationalize the coal mines and the railroads that monopolized them (Roosevelt 1913; Doukas 1997). And he would have had not Secretary of War (and Spencer convert) Elihu Root convinced J. P. Morgan, the real boss of the railroads, to get his men to the bargaining table (Cornell 1957). Two years later Roosevelt's Department of Justice successfully prosecuted Northern Securities, a cartel of the wealthiest men in the country who were plotting to, in effect, monopolize the entire rail system of the United States.[7] The second Roosevelt administration prosecuted John D. Rockefeller's monumental Standard Oil.

But somehow, none of this broke the grip of the trusts. Northern Se-

curities was forced to dissolve, but its constituent capitalists lost none
of their vast holdings. (The dissolution liberated a financial windfall,
Noyes noted, much of which was poured into further stock speculation [1909:356].) The Standard Oil trust was reorganized on paper, but
nothing prevented the formally separate parts from coordinating their
management and lobbying efforts. But then the fine points of legality
had never much preoccupied the highly evolved men of the trusts.

The "gospel of work," with its moral claim to the dignity of all work
and to a decent living for anyone willing to do it, had never set well
with the trusts. Now they thought they had the ultimate rebuttal: The
magic potency of capital was now scientifically confirmed. Those who
controlled it were the finest specimens of the human race, the most
evolved beings on earth. The "gospel of wealth" exerted a strong at-
traction on the minds of the trust movement and filtered into the
ranks of employees newly dependent on them. "Make" more money
than your neighbors and you will prove your superior fitness.

Boomtown

In the Valley the Ilion Board of Trade, liberated from its antitrust element, was alive with big plans. With control of the workplace and
local government virtually in hand, the "men of push" turned their
attention to the supply of a key "necessary," housing. Turning the
homes of the Valley into real estate would be a real money-maker, but
(as we'll soon see) at the working people's expense. The Valley split,
along the social fault line that early Board of Trade meetings predicted:
the mechanics and the capitalists—the "producers" who lived off
their own work and the "nonproducers" who lived off the work of others. The latter had the trusts on their side. The mechanics were clearly
losing ground.

In 1900 the Board of Trade members could all agree on the wisdom
of attracting new capital to the area, if only to offset their humiliating
dependency on the trusts. That year the Board produced the first in a
series of brochures that were intended to advertise the region's charms
to "outside capital." They entitled it, "The Typewriter Town—Birth
Place of Some of the Largest Enterprises on the Face of the Earth." The
first header was the come-on: "The Fortunes that have been made
here, and the Fortunes that can be made yet!" (Ilion Board of Trade
1900, ILHR). It promised that "every inducement that can tend to the

success of your enterprises will be extended to you"—"Seldom if ever," it claimed, "has such an earnest feeling existed toward outside capital in any community" (*ibid.*).

The hand of the mechanic contingent, however, is evident in another key selling point. Local society, the brochure enthused, "is what might be expected from the high degree of intelligence possessed by mechanics able to turn out the famous Remington gun, the unrivalled Remington bicycle, the celebrated Remington typewriter" (*ibid.*). The mechanics' "high degree of intelligence" would be "expected" to generate a fine "society" where the "gospel of work" still retained public currency.

By the year of the Board's purge, however, the hand of the intelligent mechanics was gone. The 1914 Chamber of Commerce booklet reflects a new era in which the "men of push" could imagine the mechanics as a "lower class," not cocreators of the world they all shared but social inferiors, subjects to be managed, no less in the community than in the corporate workplace.[8]

The 1914 booklet makes a statement, though, that will soon reveal to the "men of push" the limits of their influence. Ilion, it promises, "will be a city in a short time."

It is reasonably clear why these men wished to turn the Valley villages into cities. What capitalist wants to invest in a village? Capitalists are attracted to *growth*. The plans of the "men of push" were as simple as they were bold—create a boomtown. All the progressive towns were doing it. More capital meant more enterprises. More enterprises meant more jobs. More jobs meant more residents. More residents meant rising land values. Rising land values meant profitable real estate speculation *and* higher tax revenues—for the kind of improvements that attracted more capital!

By 1917 the campaign to turn the Valley villages into cities was heating up. "Ilion and Herkimer–A Great City of the Future," was the featured piece in a Syracuse *Herald* Sunday supplement, complete with clever caricatures of Valley businessmen and politicians. "Frankfort and Ilion and Mohawk and Herkimer will be merged into one vast municipality in the future," the article confidently claimed (Syracuse *Herald* 11/18/1917).

The Valley's workforce was still a selling point, but they were no longer "mechanics." They showed up in their new, reduced status as simply "working men," not "intelligent" anymore but stable, "content," and "sturdy": "[M]ost of the working men and their families have been in the valley for generations. The workingman has come from a good and sturdy ancestor. His father and his forefather worked in the several industries, and they own their homes and are content to remain" (*ibid.*).

Much had changed in the Valley's industrial center. In 1914 "not a wheel turned in Ilion" (Remington Centennial Transcript [RCT], Schmidt speech 1916), but a year later the long recession was giving way to the stimulus of war—the United States was entering the war in Europe that would later be called World War I. For Remington Arms UMC, war in Europe looked like salvation. Marcellus Hartley Dodge borrowed heavily from his grandfather, William Rockefeller (John D. Rockefeller's brother), and from the Rockefeller banks, to expand production capacity at the Ilion and Bridgeport factories.[9] Construction began in the winter of 1914, shrouded in secrecy behind a massive stockade.

The new Ilion works would be a showplace of the "gospel of wealth"—Dodge built a monument to the productivity of capital. In its honor, the Ilion Chamber of Commerce (the former Board of Trade) proposed a huge, three-day celebration, and they had the perfect occasion. 1916 would be the centennial of Eliphalet Remington's first enterprise, the forge on Steele's Creek.

War contracts had pushed the Arms into high gear. Employment swelled to a record eleven thousand. The factory hummed around the clock, and every spare room in Ilion was let to the mechanics who poured into town. Elder Ilionites remember their elders joking about the "hot beds" the war workers slept in—so called because one tired shift would roust the next from bed and climb right in after them.

Corporate Americanism

In this heady atmosphere, the Remington Centennial celebration commenced in August 1916. The decorations committee had been at work for two weeks decking every building in town with red, white, and blue bunting. Suspended on wires that stretched across Main Street at twenty-foot intervals, hundreds of American flags waved in the summer breeze. At the "court of honor," erected in front of the new Masonic Hall, three thousand incandescent lights formed a

The Remington shops, 1875. From the south, looking toward the Erie Canal, this mechanic's-eye-view shows the enterprise as a cluster of separate, cooperating workplaces. Courtesy, Historical Room, Ilion Free Public Library.

Showplace of the "gospel of wealth," Remington Arms UMC, 1915 (Erie Canal in foreground). This artist's rendering of Dodge's World War I reconstruction projects, in striking contrast to Figure 6, the monumentality and uniformity of the corporate imperial vision. Courtesy, Historical Room, Ilion Free Public Library.

canopy "that paint[ed] in light the American flag."[10] Corporate capital, still the object of popular suspicion, even hatred, was "wrapping itself in the flag" on a grand scale. Just as capital, in the capitalists' view, had bested labor in the production of prosperity, the corporate elite, it seemed, meant to best the working people in the production of patriotism.

From the Centennial's first moments, the uneasy truce between the corporate and the mechanic contingents showed through the festive surface. The opening exercises in the "court of honor" became the site of contest, albeit a polite one, between the relative merits of capital and labor.

O. B. Rudd (cofounder of the Ilion Board of Trade) gave the welcoming address—complete with his version of the Remington myth. "One hundred years ago, within a short distance from where we are now assembled," he began, "Eliphalet Remington, a young man of skill and perseverance[,] made a gun for his personal use, little realizing that he was starting an enterprise that within a century would make his name famous throughout the world" (RCT1).[11]

Judge Charles Bell of Herkimer stepped up next to set the record straight for the capitalists: "Let us not forget," he declared, "the debt of gratitude we owe to the men, past and present, who *with their money* and by their business energy, industry and skill, have *made* this thriving, industrial valley" (RCT1, my emphasis). There it is again, the key idea of the corporate cultural revolution: capital, not labor, produces prosperity.

"Captain" Tom Marshall, Western sales representative for Remington Arms UMC (Dodge's conglomerate), next to speak, was more specific. "[T]he growth and prosperity of the Remington U.M.C.," he insisted, "is due to the dynamic force of Marcellus Hartley Dodge. . . . Then comes the part you people play so efficiently, that is, loyalty to the U.M.C. people and the assistance you render" (RCT1). (Tact, evidently, was not much prized in the Dodge organization.) Clearly, the mechanics played no part in the trusts' version of the Valley's industries.

One suspects that Frank A. Schmidt was steaming when he stepped up to the podium, and not only from the August heat. Schmidt was an attorney, but he spoke as the son of a respected Ilion mechanic, for whom he had worked before and during his legal studies. Schmidt tried to put the mechanics back into the story.

"Our town has grown and depends upon the product of the skilled mind *and* skilled hand," he announced, following this claim by naming off each local invention and innovation. And he had a cautionary tale for Dodge's men in these days of wartime boom. The Remingtons, he reminded his listeners, had "unselfishly" invested in the development of dozens of new products after the Civil War to "replace the guns with which our country had been saved." He named them. "We are proud of it," he declared—"we have a right to be proud of it" (RCT1).

Were Schmidt's remarks a welcome relief to the working people who stood patiently through these long-winded speeches? No. The mechanics had not been invited. A Utica reporter informs us that behind the speeches "the clang of the forges . . . resounded in the distance" as "the war in Europe permits no delay."[12]

But that afternoon the mechanics were let out of the shops to form up into the "Remington industrial army." Behind what promoters billed as the largest American flag in the world (seventy-five feet long by sixty feet wide)—carried by seventy-five mechanics dressed all in white—"the ranks of the Remington army of industry" marched past the reviewing stand.[13] Nine bands and four drum corps marched with them. "It was an all-American parade," said the newspapers (*ibid.*).

The corporate cultural campaigners saved the best for last. For the third and last day of the Centennial, the organizers had engaged a famous speaker, Senator Warren G. Harding. (People in the know were already whispering about him as the next Republican candidate for president.) Harding had a few words for the mechanics, and corporate managers obliged him by letting them out early to hear his message.

"I don't know how many of you boys in the shops want to become capitalists," he began, "but I can tell you how to do it, and you can start on the next pay day. You see that a part of your earnings go into the Savings Bank and you become a capitalist from that day on" (RCT 3).

Was this intended to be egalitarian? Harding certainly knew that the mechanics were suspicious of capitalists. In fact, he had hatched a clever argument.

"I heard a man say the other day," he said, "that no human being could honestly earn $50,000 a year." But what about our adorable moving-picture star, Mary Pickford?, he asked—she gets a million and

Corporate Americanism, the "Remington army of industry," Remington Centennial, 1916. The mechanics were released from the shops and formed up in ranks to parade before the assembled dignitaries. Courtesy, Historical Room, Ilion Free Public Library.

a half a year. "I only speak of it, men," he concluded, "to show you that great earnings and great fortunes are not wrung from the oppression of those who toil—they are the results of genius and industry and saving" (RCT3). Clever but hardly convincing. Mary Pickford was not a capitalist. Harding's dissembling equation of capitalists with "the rich" missed a crucial point (cf. Zweig 2000:75): Mary Pickford did not live off the work of others.

Harding had nothing to say about "the oppression of those who toil," and this proved to be an incorrigible problem for the gospel of wealth, from the mechanics' point of view. The work of skilled hands had no respected place in it.

Contented Villagers

Dodge's man "Captain" Marshall had some rather rough words for local converts to the gospel of wealth. "They tell me your city is a *village*," he remarked at a Centennial ceremony. "I am really surprised at that," he said—"You should be a city" (RCT 1, my emphasis). The "men of push" looked down at their shoes. They had been trying to turn the villages into cities for at least a decade. City-dom was key to their dreams of wealth, but it seemed that there were a few tenacious problems.

As a city, an Ilion official enthused to the Syracuse *Herald* in 1917, we could "centralize all of our municipal departments," and "induce manufacturers from other parts of the country to come and look [us] over." We'll build "modern up-to-date apartments" with "all of the latest sanitary plans," a Herkimer businessman added. An Ilion bank officer commented, "[W]e must get away from the small village idea, and operate on broader lines."[14]

Three years later the "men of push" finally managed to bring their city initiative to the people of Ilion. The people of Ilion dealt them a resounding defeat, voting the measure down by a majority of *five to one* (VBM 1/22/1920). Once again, the movers certainly thought, the villagers had demonstrated the "ignorant, self-satisfied, contented spirit" that had annoyed the old Board of Trade for more than a decade.

Perhaps the majority was sick and tired of being "pushed." What the Ilion bank officer had looked down on as "the small village idea" was a way of life that the mechanics were not prepared to give up. Why should they? They had lost the battle for control of the factory workplace, but they were people with skills and land. They still had their backyard agriculture and the kin and neighbors they "looked out for" and could count on. They wouldn't have it any other way.

"You didn't need money to have fun in those days," Valley elders often told me. In the winters the young people spruced up their "bobs"— bobsleds—and raced at breakneck speed down the Valley's steep, icy roads to much acclaim and party-making. Two or three times a week in the summers everybody brought picnics to Russell Park or the band shell on Armory Hill to enjoy free concerts by the Municipal Band, or the Typewriter Band, or the Beethoven Choir. Young marrieds formed "social clubs." Six or seven couples would meet at one or another's home, hire a fiddler, eat a potluck supper, and dance the night away while their children romped in the yard. "We'd have the time of our life," one woman recalled.[15]

Hers was the first family in the neighborhood to get a Victrola, another woman, in her nineties, told me. "Jean," her mother would call her after supper—"go open up all the windows!" She knew what that meant. Mom would then put a record on the Victrola "and put it up *loud*." And out the neighbors would come with a cold drink to sit on their front porches and enjoy the music.

People knew each other, looked after each other, had a good time together, felt safe. What had they to gain by "growing" into a city?

Clearly, from the perspective of their would-be social betters the working people were not getting the message. In 1923 the Typewriter, not to be outdone by the Arms, put on its own gala, its semi-centennial, and the Valley was treated to another brilliant cultural campaigner for the gospel of wealth, Illinois governor Frank Lowden.

Lowden, a Spencer convert, argued that capital is more *highly evolved* than labor. "Without capital," he declared, "we would sink back into barbarism from which the race painfully has emerged." How was that? "Our own Indian tribes," he argued, "nationalized their wealth" and look at what it got them. The moral of the story: "private property must remain if civilization is to go on." "Today," he concluded (Carnegie had made exactly the same argument [1900b]), "the working man lives in greater comfort than the king of a few centuries ago," and this great boon, "would have been impossible in any other than a capitalistic state of society."[16]

Ill-conceived as it was for the purpose of converting the mechanics to the gospel of wealth, this crude rhetoric was surely intended to soften their resistance. The converts' big plans were taking shape and only the "villagers'" contented stubbornness stood in their way. They planned to turn this valley into a real estate gold mine.

The Plan

A modern real estate market is based on certain premises. For one thing, creditors and insurers want guarantees that "unsightly" land use will not mar the peaceful residential areas they invest in. The Valley's would-be real-estate tycoons would have to do what their colleagues across the country were doing. They would have to bring in zoning. It was the modern way. The people would have to accept it.

In Ilion the Chamber of Commerce took the initiative, appointing five men to the new Planning Commission, charged with developing the zoning plan. The Village Board quickly endorsed them, and the commissioners set about preparing their "study and survey." They knew perfectly well that this work would be less than welcome by the Village majority and set out to circumvent their resistance, taking the high road of advance publicity. Planning would be "to the benefit of all property owners," they insisted—it "gives to the poor man the same protection it gives to the rich man."[17]

And what protection was that? the Village asked. The commissioners were stumped. The Chamber of Commerce brought in an expert, one Alvin Burger of Ohio, who soon took charge of selling the zoning campaign to the village.[18] Say a workingman "just bought some land" to build "a cozy home," a Chamber PR piece explained, and there are vacant lots to either side of it. Zoning would keep someone from using the vacant lots for "a large apartment house," a "giant airless hive" that would soon be "stealing his sunshine"—or "a noisy, evil-smelling public garage," or "such things as fly-by-night stores or junk yards." "When a town is zoned," the piece concluded, "property values become stable, mortgage companies are more ready to lend money, and more homes can be built."[19]

Now most Ilion working people already owned their homes, without mortgages (RCT1, Schmidt speech). They, most of them, expected to live out their lives in these houses and pass them on to their children after they were gone. This was the "value" of their property. Why would more mortgages and the construction of more houses be of interest to them?

Mr. Burger and the Chamber had made a fateful miscalculation. They did not bother to find out who they were dealing with. Who was it that might "blight" a fine residential area with "unsightly" auto shops, workshops, and second-hand stores and, yes, what might look like "junk" to "men of push and enterprise"? They *were* the working people, the voting majority. When business was "dull," as it had been for much of the 1920s, and would be for all of the 1930s, the voters used their land to make their living in no end of "unsightly" ways.

The zoning enthusiasts, nevertheless, pressed on with the same line of reasoning as the Special Election on the zoning plan (set for May Day 1926) drew near. Zoning, they argued, protects "the workingman" from "a selfish and greedy neighbor," from "an unsightly building," from having "factories or garages as his next door neighbors."[20] The Chamber assembled these selling points into a brochure, in question and answer format, and distributed it first to the newspapers (the Utica *Daily Press, Observer-Dispatch,* and *Community Review* all carried it), then to the Foremen's Association at Remington Typewriter,[21] and, finally, to every home in Ilion.[22] The zoning proposition, supporters said, was "receiving more favorable comment each day."[23]

A group of citizens buttonholed M. E. Conklin, chairman of the zoning commission, after a Conversation Club meeting. Conklin had said that zoning would not raise taxes. How could that be true? the citizens wanted to know. Cornered, Conklin admitted that the plan, "with all of the technicalities and legal intricacies involved," would require "the services of experts" at taxpayer expense.[24] In fact, the Village Board had already quietly appropriated $4,800 (a lot of money in a total annual budget of $164,000) for "professional services" (4/14/ 26 VBM).

On the eve of the election, one Colonel House, a longtime thorn in the side of pushy "progress," gave voice to the majority's reservations. Did we need outside "experts" to tell us how to run the village? House had read the proposal and pointed out that the plan included expert "recommendations" to "our Board of Water Commissioners, Sewer Commissioners and Electric Light Commissioners." Why? Was anyone worried that our Water Commissioners, for example, "will lay a two-inch service main where the needs are for a four-inch main"? No. We should place our trust, he counseled, in "members of our own Ilion family, with years of local experience."[25]

The zoning plan, like the city plan before it, was soundly defeated, nearly three to one.[26] Interestingly, voter turnout was quite low (only 796, compared with 2,264 against the city charter). Despite the media blitz, it seems, people did not take this issue seriously.

They should have. A huge gap had opened up between the interests of the "men of push" and those of the working majority—and the Chamber of Commerce was not giving up. Mr. Burger vowed to "continue all the more steadfastly" to convince the locals of "the common-sense purpose of zoning."[27] His arguments for zoning, though, added up to common sense only for converts to the gospel of wealth.

10

Learning to Expect Hard Times

The Valley's remembered past can be read as a long story of hopes raised and hopes dashed. By the late 1920s working people had dealt the "gospel of wealth" a series of political defeats, and it would have been possible to imagine that, thanks to the democratic process, they had preserved some semblance of the good life as they envisioned it, despite the trusts' interference at the shops. But the upcoming decades had hard lessons to teach. The terrain of local sovereignty would be dramatically eroded from both ends—work and home.

Emboldened by New Deal legitimation of labor unions, the mechanics would mount two major strikes against their corporate masters. One was a humiliating disaster, the other a Pyrrhic victory. The lesson was plain: Corporate capital could still maneuver around the law. On the home front the "men of push" began to take J. H. Holmes's dictum—that "progress" cannot be accomplished by politics (Chapter 8)—to heart, finding ways to circumvent the vote and carry through a radical and demoralizing transformation of the local landscape. The lesson was clear, and I heard it often: "There's just a few people around here who control things, and they do whatever they want."

In stories and documents, though, the Valley tells an unexpected history of the Great Depression, World War II, and the decade of post-war prosperity. It is not a story of dark age and deliverance. It is a story of return to and reenvisioning of "old values."

Wage work, sporadic since the end of World War I, got considerably more so in the 1930s, but it is not the privation that Valley elders today wish to discuss. The Great Depression gave the Valley a measure of relief from "push," as capitalists, fearful of losses, held onto what they had. Elders want to tell about the renewal of and new challenges to, the practice of neighborliness.

In 1974 Ilion High School history teacher Francis Cunningham gave his eleventh graders an oral history assignment—to conduct tape-recorded interviews of local elders. Two boys chose to interview their grandmothers about life in the Great Depression.[1] Both grandmothers had been young women in the 1930s, and both describe a life poor in cash but rich in the things that, to them, mattered more.

> People weren't buying typewriters and I guess that, and the Arms . . . didn't employ an awful lot of people, but I wouldn't say Ilion was too terribly hard hit, not like a city. In a village like this everyone helps everyone else. In a city, people are thinking just of themselves. [Mrs. Lester 1974]

Mrs. Lester was the daughter of a toolmaker at the Arms. His pay had fallen to two dollars a day—when he worked, and "sometimes he wouldn't work maybe for three weeks." (For comparison, in 1916 *average* daily pay at the Arms was three dollars [RCT1, Schmidt speech], and toolmakers were always paid more than the average.) Her parents kept chickens and exchanged with her grandparents for vegetables from their garden.

Food prices were high, Mrs. Lester remembered, but grocers were generous with credit. "You know, we didn't have to have supermarkets," she told her grandson. "We had little stores around the village," and if grocers "knew that you were fair," you could get what you needed, or else you could "go to your Welfare." But what she most wished to say Mrs. Lester found hard to put into words. Everything seemed so different in the 1970s. "You had so little," she said thoughtfully, "well, not really so little—you had a lot."

Mrs. Entwhistle was the young wife of a toolmaker in the 1930s. "Were like any of your friends or neighbors, were they hurt badly, that you can recollect?," her grandson, Bill, asked her.

> Mrs. Entwhistle: I don't recollect that they were, no, no.
> Bill: Were they all basically the same off as you?
> Mrs. Entwhistle: I'm trying to think—I think they were pretty well off as we were at that time but not *well off*, nobody was.

Factory work was so unreliable that the Entwhistles rented a small dairy farm. The whole family pitched in, and they did "pretty well" on the butter, milk, chickens, and Thanksgiving turkeys they produced together.

For Valley elders the Depression still carries lessons of neighborliness. "I was born in the Depression and I think we were better off then," a retiree and poet told me—"there's too much difference between the classes now, and those that *got* have no sympathy for those that *ain't got*." "You know, it's worse now than it was in the Depression," a library patron and retired factory worker observed to an elderly woman friend in my earshot—"we didn't have anything, but back then people cared about each other."

Nobody had quite enough, but that was not the most important thing. What was important when nobody is "well off," was that everybody "helps everybody else."

Why, asks a remarkable essay of the 1930s, couldn't the capitalists understand this? In "Controlled Capitalism: A Cure and Prevention of Depressions" (1935), C. J. Diss, a medical doctor and the son, grandson, and brother of Ilion mechanics, argued—in classic producerist style—that "moderate wealth" is "good for a country, while excessive wealth is bad for a country."[2] The problem was, in his view, that capitalists and government officials had forgotten the basic principles of political economy, the most basic being that "all wealth is due to labor."

Capital, he continued—clearly not under the spell of the "gospel of wealth"—only "receives an income when labor is using the capital." The income of capital is simply "a rake-off from what labor produces," the *rent*, in fact, that labor pays for its use. With these principles in mind, he reasoned, the cause of depressions is obvious: *hoarding* capital drives the rent up too high for labor to afford. Prevent hoarding and there will be enough for everyone. Among the prescriptions of Dr. Diss's "cure": tax away "the reward of selfishness."

But of course the capitalists and their friends had not "forgotten" the basic principles of political economy. They had *rejected* them in favor of the modern, advanced principles of the gospel of wealth.

The "Mohawk Valley Formula"

Such were the principles behind James H. Rand Jr.'s final solution to the problem of disobedient working people. In 1927 Remington Typewriter came under the ownership of the huge office-products empire that Rand, a fanatical enemy of labor unions (Kolopsky 1986), had put together out of the old typewriter trust and ran with an iron fist.[3] When the National Recovery Act guaranteed the right of labor to organize, unhappy Typewriter workers joined the American Federation of Labor (AFL) in droves. Along with millions of working people across the country, they were ready to fight for respect and a living wage.

Rand's managers ignored their grievances. Why should they coddle workers? It's survival of the fittest! At a time of massive unemployment, they reasoned, if some workers didn't like the company's terms, too bad. There were plenty to replace them.

But the law was on the workers' side now, many working people believed, and all across the Rand empire, they went out on strike. Valley officials, at first, supported them. The strikers had "won the respect and admiration of the townspeople."[4] A businessmen's group, calling itself the Ilion Merchants' Bureau, sent a telegram to President Roosevelt: They knew, it read, that Typewriter workers have gotten "miserable returns" for their labor. "Big businessmen" were wrong, they told the local newspapers—the return to prosperity depended on workers' receiving a living wage.[5]

Both sides backed down to an uneasy peace, but both planned for a showdown. In early 1936 it came. Rand moved quickly to head off community sympathy. He personally called a meeting at the Union Club in New York City for the local officials and businessmen of the nine towns where his corporate empire owned factories. Predictably, he told them: We'll close the factories if you don't follow our instructions. And they could begin to demonstrate their appreciation for the corporation immediately, by organizing "special police" to "keep order" in their towns.[6]

Ilion was full of strangers. Some, claiming to be workingmen, went door to door talking up a "back-to-work movement." A "rumor mill" ran overtime, spreading fears of factory shutdown. Strikers' wives were treated to frightening tales of imminent disaster. A team of movers began packing up factory machinery and loading it into trucks.

A small "back-to-work movement" sent word to Rand "that the majority of the workers" were "more than pleased with the pay and working conditions." If Rand would please let the factory stay, they said, they would leave the union. Rand called off the movers, and the majority of Ilion workers, broke and intimidated, returned to work. But a few union men smelled a rat and brought suit through the new National Labor Relations Board (NLRB), charging the company with numerous violations of labor law.[7] The NLRB agreed to hear the charges.

An amazing story came out at the NLRB hearings. The Valley had been manipulated by a carefully orchestrated "formula." The "special police," the rumors whispered to strikers' wives, the "back-to-work movement," the move, the plea to Rand—it was all in the formula. And those strangers who said they were Typewriter workers? They were employees of a professional strike-breaking agency. Rand called it "the Mohawk Valley Formula." It was the plan that "business has hoped for, dreamed of, and prayed for," he had bragged, before the strike, to the National Association of Manufacturers (NAM).[8]

As the NLRB analyzed it, the Mohawk Valley Formula was a multipronged "strategy that combined police intimidation and court injunctions with propaganda campaigns" (Fones-Wolf 1994:138–139). In April 1937 the NLRB ruled in favor of the strikers. Rand was enjoined to cease interfering with union organizing and to rehire the still-unemployed strikers (Herkimer County Historical Society 1992:185). But the great Rand, a man of superior "fitness," was not about to be intimidated by a government bureau. The corporation refused. When the NLRB repeated the order a year later (July 1938), the corporation got vindictive, shifting product lines from factory to factory across the empire.[9] Familiar work groups were broken up. Everybody had to start from scratch, learning new skills under new supervisors. Rand showed them who was boss.

The mechanics were bitter—"humiliated," as they said later. The company with its endless resources had outmaneuvered them, but something else disturbed local people nearly as much, because it divided mechanic against mechanic. An anonymous poet, a striker's wife, called it "keeping up with the Jones's."

> There are a lot of people, who never save a cent,
> To help out on a rainy day, or even pay their rent.
> They must keep up with the Jones's and put on lots of style.
> When they know they are getting in debt, deeper all the while.
> They must drive a little better car, than their neighbor next door,
> Better furniture in their homes, better rugs upon their floors.
> So when a case comes up just like this strike,
> They haven't any money, or any spirit left to fight.
> [from "Remington-Rand Co.," flier, 1936]

It was the lesson of the times.

One after another, the old mechanics were dying. Would the "old values" die with them? An Ilion historian started a scrapbook of obituaries.[10]

L. B. Walrath, died March 7, 1936, "one of the oldest living former associates of the Remingtons"—worked for the Remington Arms Co. "more than 50 years."

Edmond E. Wakelee, died February 12, 1941, "lone survivor of a group of men who helped develop the first Remington typewriter."

James C. Hamilton, died February 6, 1942, "one of the original 13 aligners for the E. Remington & Sons typewriter works."

But soon there was no time to think about that. Everybody back to the factories! There was a new war to win.

Fighting Totalitarianism at Home

"Old values" and old skills brought people through the 1930s. The better you were at making things and fixing things—helping your neighbor when you could—the better you lived. "Waste not, want not," Grandma and Grandpa used to say, and it looked like they were right after all.

The Valley went to war not as conquerors of the world but as skilled producers of wealth, who could work together to make more arms and ammunition than the enemy—and who could fight together. It was fighting together, some elders told me, that buried the old hostilities between native and "foreigner," Protestant and Catholic. And they came out of that war brimming with confidence that democracy and equality had been vindicated as the true destiny of humankind. The soldiers came home in 1945 to the world-renowned heartland of democracy and equality: They had won the future.

But there was trouble in paradise right away. Under pressure from corporate lobbyists, wartime price regulations were lifted and the cost of everything soared. Well, not everything. The corporations were determined to push down the cost of labor. Good wages were fine as long as guaranteed wartime profits were flowing in. But back in the competitive world of peacetime, well, the needs of capital were naturally superior to those of labor.

The country was still burying its dead and figuring out what "normal life" was supposed to be when the cultural combat commenced anew. The corporations were ready to claim for themselves the victory of production that had out-gunned the forces of totalitarianism. Now they were ready to dedicate enormous resources to the claim that they, not working people, were the creators of "the American way of life."

In January 1946, Remington Rand argued this view to the readers of its new company newsletter. "Close to 3,000 men and women" worked in the Ilion plants alone, a lead article in the first volume of *Remington Rand INK* asserted, and "through the production facilities afforded them by *the capital* invested by this company's 26,000 stockholders, earn the livelihood which enables them to give their children the advantages of the American way of life" (1(8):5, my emphasis). There it was, back from the 1920s in updated form. The company's capital, not labor, produces prosperity.

The locals were still not buying it. Something had been "generally overlooked in the telling of the Remington story," a local writer insisted, and that was "the contributions made to industrial progress by the *craftsmen* of the Remington Arms Company." The company's achievements, the article noted, were not based on "organization or system or supervision," but on something "more exacting" and "infinitely more creditable to the humanity of labor"—"earnest, individual cooperation."[11]

By 1947 it was time to fight again. Was the "American way" to be corporate dictatorship or democracy? The corporation had "more than doubled its profits during the past year," said the United Electrical Radio and Machine Workers of America (UE/CIO), the union that had gained the loyalty of Typewriter workers during the war.[12] But the company "arrogantly refused" a modest fifteen-cent-per-hour raise, the very least that could be expected to cover the runaway inflation of the postwar years—seven cents, the company said, take it or leave it.[13]

Five thousand Typewriter workers walked out. At a "giant rally" in Russell Park, UE district officials presented the Ilion locals with their first check from the national union's strike fund (OD 6/24/47:1–A). "We are fighting for more than just money," said the president of Local 315. We are fighting for "honest-to-goodness collective bargaining *in the American way*," the picket chairman of Ilion Local 334 added.[14] Rand responded with a lockout—a "vacation shutdown," the corporate spokesman said. A violation of contract, the union spokesman said.[15]

The CIO, whose successes had attracted intense red-baiting, was careful to identify its goals with traditional American values.[16] And, indeed, it had worked hard to reinforce those values against the escalating corporate campaign (Fones-Wolf 1994). In 1947, so soon after the war, the enemy of American values was clear—totalitarianism. And James H. Rand Jr. was typecast for the role of dictator.

Ilion's fight against Rand for the American way made a two-page spread in the union's paper, the *UE News*, under the headline, "Rem Rand Strikers Vow—No Mohawk Valley Formula This Time." This time, they were standing up to Rand "dictatorship." This time, when undercover agents tried to start a "back-to-work" movement, Ilion workers "answer[ed] with a picket line stretching to the thousands." And when the corporation put up "smear sheets" denouncing union leaders as "communists," Ilion workers "tore [them] down."[17] No greedy corporation was going to tell *them* what was American.

War veterans were prominent among the strikers. Along with the "veterans of the '36 strike," the *UE News* noted, they "form the fighting core of the strike." "Vets who fought against Hitler," the paper commented, "couldn't see living under dictatorship in . . . America."[18]

But the corporation was not about to let the strikers' definition of the American way go unchallenged. It got its own war veteran, the

"Fighting totalitarianism at home," pickets at the Typewriter strike of 1947. Under UE/CIO leadership, the strike was a success, provoking the wrath of the rabidly antiunion James H. Rand Jr., head of the Remington Rand corporation. Courtesy, Historical Room, Ilion Free Public Library.

hapless John O'Connor of Herkimer, to lead the predictable "back-to-work" movement—setting off the most notorious event of the strike. On the morning of July 14, O'Connor went to his appointed spot, across the street from a line of pickets. He carried a large American flag (loaned to him by the Kiwanis Club). As the pickets walked toward him, O'Connor hastily leaned the flag against a railing. It slid toward the ground. An older man rushed at O'Connor, shouting that "his son had died for that flag." He demanded that O'Connor pick it up. O'Connor refused, and the old man reportedly grabbed at him, tearing his shirt.[19] What gave O'Connor, a traitor to American labor, the right to carry the flag of this country?

Two pickets filed a complaint against him at the Ilion Police Court for violating paragraph 16–D, section 1425 of the Penal Code: "Displaying contempt for the U.S. flag." The CIO national jumped into the fray, sending an attorney from New York City to try the case. Contempt for the flag was contempt for the nation, the attorney argued before a packed courtroom—the American flag was "the symbol of its existence." O'Connor was acquitted when five defense witnesses testified that the flag did not actually touch the ground. But the strikers won the symbolic case—the corporation *did* show contempt for the nation.

Rand bowed to public pressure. The corporation agreed to the raise. But two years later, when the glare of publicity had faded, the corporation followed the same vindictive strategy as in 1936. This time they called it a "consolidation." Out went the few typewriter jobs that remained after 1936. In came high-tech—the new punch-card machines.[20] "The manufacture of the new and more complicated machine required new skills, new personnel and a whole new inventory," a local reporter obediently commented.[21] It was the Old Deal of corporate domination all over again, but now, at least, it paid better.

The New Good Life

The corporations were feeling the pressure of organized "working-class Americanism" (Gerstle 1989) from every part of the country. Cornered, they could make no other convincing demonstration of their patriotism than by paying a living wage for a steady work year.[22] Under wartime regulations, wages and the work year had got steadier, and the unions were not about to let the corporations regress to their

old ways. The public backed them. A 1947 poll asked high school social science teachers if organized labor or "business" had "done more
to improve living standards." Organized labor, they said, by a margin
of two to one (Fones-Wolf 1994:192). A 1951 poll found that only 39
percent of high school seniors "believed that keeping the profit incentive alive was essential to the survival of the American business
system," and 66 percent favored "stiff progressive taxation" (Fones-
Wolf 1994:192–193).

The corporate regime was on the defensive. Alarmed by such widespread "socialism," it spent lavishly on a new campaign to educate
the public or, rather, as C. S. Allyn of National Cash Register put it
bluntly: to "indoctrinate citizens with the capitalist story."[23] Standard
Oil Chair Frank W. Abrams was a bit more circumspect. The goal was
"genuine public acceptance" of corporate leadership—"we must," he
said, "reappear in the role of warm-hearted human beings."[24]

The Remingtons became grist for the mills of the corporate cultural
campaign, through the devious minds of Batten, Barton, Durstine &
Osborn, Inc., the DuPont Corporation's ad agency. What was the
DuPont connection? Marcellus Hartley Dodge, staggering under the
burden of his debts, sold Remington Arms to DuPont in 1933.

A major DuPont contribution to the corporate campaign was the radio program, "Cavalcade of America," a showcase for the corporation's version of "our national heritage." The problem, of course, was
that actual history did not readily lend itself to the campaign's goal of
winning "genuine public acceptance" for corporate rule. But this was
not a major problem for Batten, Barton, Durstine & Osborn. Their
Remington story did not have to worry about history.

The Forge, starring Ronald Reagan as Eliphalet Remington, was first
broadcast in October 1947 (original script at ILHR, Remington Arms
File). Eliphalet (actually the second Eliphalet) and his wife are living—
where else?—in a log cabin. (Everyone in the Valley knows the two-
story stone house near Steele's Creek where the Remington's lived before they moved down next to the Canal.) The family's "little lambs"
are under attack by wild bears. (Is this Davy Crockett?) Eliphalet tries
to shoot them but has trouble with the shotgun. He decides to make a
better one. A kindly older man intervenes—"son . . . a man's life in a
wilderness depends on his rifle . . . You've got the skill, Eliphalet—the
skill and the brains—to help your country." Gee, Sir, "I didn't think of
it that way," says Eliphalet. And the rest is, so to speak, history.

There are no skilled mechanics in this story. There is no bankruptcy or gun trust. There is no corporation.

And so it would be in the company's official history, *Remington Arms in American History* (Hatch 1956), where fatherly Eliphalet read stories to his children before an open fire—in their log cabin of course (23). In the corporations' version of the past, the corporation itself faded from view, disappearing as a target of public discontent, and leaving in sight only the good life it provided.

But provide a good life it must, or "genuine public acceptance" would never be forthcoming. By the early 1950s, work at the Arms and the Typewriter, as at major corporations across the country, earned good steady wages and paid vacations, medical programs, and pensions. Never before had manufacturing work been so steady and paid so well. But never had producers worked so hard for it.

Under the regime of "scientific management," the producers had to continually produce more or lose their jobs. If the men with the stop-watches and clipboards happened to come into your department on a good day, Remington workers learned the hard way, their base production figures—the quota—would get set at a higher level. That meant that you had to push ever harder to qualify for the incentive pay that made the difference between getting by and living decently.[25]

Did greater productivity actually lead to better pay? It should, of course, according to the producerist "gospel of work" (see Chapter 5): if pay did not rise with productivity then working people were being cheated of the fruits of their labor. To this extent the corporations themselves can be said to have returned to "old values," because, evidently, pay and production did rise, nationwide, though productivity rose more steeply than real wages—until the early 1970s (Zweig 2000:64–65). For a while the corporations would act like the "warm-hearted" custodians of national wealth their propaganda pictured them to be.

So both DuPont and Rand gladly lent their support when the Ilion Centennial Committee approached them in 1951. It would be week-long celebration of the new good life, nothing like the Remington Centennial of 1916. Gone were the ranks upon ranks of the "Remington industrial army." Gone were the aggressive sermons about capital's superiority over labor. The Ilion Centennial of 1952 was a producers' celebration. Quietly financed by corporate sponsors, it stood nonetheless as testimony to the persistence of producerist "old values."

Capital and labor presented themselves as "harmonious." In the thumbnail history that DuPont provided for the inside cover of the souvenir *Centennial Book*, the company "took pride" in the "far-seeing research" that produced Remington firearms (capital produces goods), but it acknowledged as "equally important . . . the skill and painstaking craftsmanship that has been passed from father to son for generations. Ilion has a right to be proud of the part these generations of native sons have played in bringing fame to Remington firearms . . . the world over."

The AFL Polisher's Local 46 (Ilion's oldest labor union) returned the compliment: "Local 46 has the best relations with management, its other unions and with all concerned. The members are 100% union in their room and work like one big family" (Cent52:36). Labor and capital could get along just fine.

The week's events included the "Remington Whisker Contest" ("Men! Stop Shaving! Emulate the old time Remington dignity by growing a Remington beard!" the promotion read); a pageant, *Highlights of Local History*; a performance of Thornton Wilder's *Our Town*; high school graduation; Strawberry Festival at the Presbyterian Church; an open-air dance on Morgan Street; an ice-cream social at the Methodist Church; picnics, athletic competitions, parades, and fireworks.[26]

The Valley was ready to bury its dead and enjoy the sweetness of life. Finally, it seemed, they could. When the Centennial Committee put together its promotional brochure, it painted the Village as a working people's paradise:

> Ilion's residents are friendly . . . good providers . . .
> master craftsmen . . .
> governed by a group of their own fellow workers who have
> given us . . .
> A large and modern
> FIRE DEPARTMENT
> A most efficient
> POLICE DEPARTMENT
> A modern and economical
> MUNICIPAL ELECTRIC DEPARTMENT
> An ultra modern
> WATER WORKS
> PLAN NOW TO ATTEND OUR
> CELEBRATION!

Distributed to local officials and businesses, and enclosed in out-of-town correspondence, this invitation was credited with bringing some ten thousand visitors to Ilion for the Centennial.[27] An "ultra modern" town of "master craftsmen," governed well by "their own fellow workers" was an image with a lot of appeal.

But just backstage, the indomitable "men of push" were preparing to overcome the villagers' "contented spirit" once and for all. Three days before the opening of the Ilion Centennial, the Village Board quietly held a hearing on a new zoning ordinance. Zoning had been a hot-button issue in the Valley since the 1920s, and, aside from the practical problems it posed for self-reliant villagers, the issue had come to symbolize a "progress" in which working people had no voice. Since many politically active villagers were feverishly engaged in Centennial preparations, as the zoning proponents surely calculated, no one in attendance voiced opposition to the new ordinance, and it was adopted *effective midnight that very day*. (The late Barry Wilson, master craftsman, teacher, and Concerned Citizen, who generously helped me with village records, was shocked—"It had to be an old boys' network!" he exclaimed.)

The last time the Village Board had tried to sell the citizens on zoning, working people denounced them as "robbers" (IHC 1947:243) because among the "unsightly" land uses that the zoning ordinance prohibited was the keeping of small livestock, an essential part of the backyard agriculture that villagers had always relied on to meet the difference between their wages and their needs. Now the safety net of backyard agriculture was gone. Just like that. No doubt the zoning proponents regarded this experiment in vote-free governing as a success. It would be an important strategy in the years to come.

"Our prosperity ended when UNIVAC pulled out."

Just ten years after the Ilion Centennial, the Rand corporation would make good on the last of its many threats to leave the Valley, but, in the fall of 1952 the news was of a glorious, high-tech future. James Rand, with General George MacArthur (newly recruited to Rand's board of directors) at his side, personally delivered the big news: "Here in Ilion," Rand announced, you will "shortly witness the birth . . . of a great new industry: that is, the electronics industry."[28] It was the dawn of the computer age, and Ilion had been chosen to produce the "baby brain," a small UNIVAC computer. Employment would rise. Real estate prices would rise (thus the urgency of a zoning ordinance). It would be a bright, bright future.

The signs above the factory buildings were changed from REM-INGTON TYPEWRITER to UNIVAC in the fall of 1956,[29] barely a year before the round of layoffs that were the first signal of major problems to come.[30] Under Rand's leadership, UNIVAC had fallen behind an aggressive new competitor, IBM. A new management team was easing James Rand out and desperately reorganizing to catch up (Kolopsky 1986).

The shop floor grapevine saw it as the beginning of the end. Company officials denied that any major changes were afoot right up to the moment that they announced, in July 1962, that the Ilion plants would be "consolidated" into the Utica (New York) works. "People were just standing in the streets as if they were thunderstruck," one woman remembers. As many as seven thousand people stood to lose their jobs.[31]

The works were shut down bit by bit—corporate officials giving as little advance notice as possible. Management left first. The "general offices" moved to Utica in the early spring of 1963. Some managers went with it and others accepted transfers to new Rand sites in the South (OD 4/2/79 HS). Production work moved more slowly, department by department, beginning a few months later. Management showed less tender loving care toward the production staff. A few were offered transfers to the Utica works; most were not (OD 8/23/62 HS). By the late 1960s only a small "customer engineering" department remained in Ilion. That went in August 1976 when the corporation shut down its Utica works, its last site in the region. It was "UNIVAC's darkest hour in the Mohawk Valley."[32] All told, that was nearly two decades of pink slips and/or the constant fear of them.

Demolishing the Past

It would get worse. Little did they know, those stunned crowds on the streets of Ilion in 1962, that just out of sight in the offices of local government, the "men of push" were plotting to demolish the landscape of their past, the busy red-brick downtown that had been the center of village life for a century.

Urban planners had been stalking the Valley's villages for years, a

former mayor remembers. Across the country, the planners were offering a deal that local governments found hard to refuse. "Modern-
ize," they urged. You can double your assessed valuation (the dollar
assessment of aggregate property value on which municipal property
taxes are computed) and it won't cost you a dime—it's *federal* money!
They called it "Urban Renewal" (UR), a complex of government
programs that were funneling federal tax moneys to state and local
governments.[33] Nelson Rockefeller, grandson of "the father of the
trusts," sat in the governor's office, with a fistful of aggressive new
plans to "rebuild" New York. Out with the old. In with the new. There
was money to be made!

Carefully conceived to avoid the consent of the governed, UR demolished town centers across the country and in the process generated a windfall of government jobs. In the Valley, UR drove a wedge of
distrust between citizens and local government that endures to this
day.

I heard about it before I began my fieldwork, riding in on the bus
from the Utica train station. There were only a few passengers, and
the bus driver was happy to chat and show me the sights. "Don't know
if you ever saw how it used to be here, before they changed everything
around," he said, as we turned off the highway onto Main Street—
"most of us liked it better the way it was." I didn't know what to say.
He pressed on. "And it's too bad, too," he said, "most of us really miss
it." But people must have voted for it, I said. "Nah," he exclaimed.
"Way it is around here, just a handful of people control things."

The UR process began with the Village Board's commissioning a
study from Russell D. Bailey and Associates, a Utica urban planning
firm. *The Master Plan: Village of Ilion, NY* laid out the "programs necessary for the Village to remain a modern progressive village" (Bailey
& Assoc. 1965:36). The plan was to "rejuvenate" what the planners
called the central business district by replacing "blighted" and "obsolete structures" with "sound, tax producing property" (Bailey & Assoc. 1965:28–29, 37).

There were problems from the outset. For one, it was hard to find
"blight" in Ilion's tidy downtown. Urban renewal proponents took
thousands of photos (now in the ILHR collection), but to get shots of
"blighted and obsolete" structures, they had to step into the back al-
leys where they could achieve a certain *West Side Story* look with
shots of fire escapes, garbage cans, and laundry hanging out to dry from

second-story apartments. For most local people there was no "blight" in their town. "Blight!" an indignant library patron exploded (at a slide show I put together of "old Ilion")—"What *blight*? Why, we were in and out of those buildings every day."

Nevertheless, in May 1966 the planners reported to the village's newly founded Urban Renewal Agency that more than 75 percent of the ninety-four buildings in the "project area" were "sub-standard" and "surrounded on all four directions by substantial blight."[34] What about all the people who lived in those buildings? The people who "live above the commercial uses" will be "relocated," the *Master Plan* explained (Bailey & Assoc. 1965:28–29). What about the people who owned small businesses there?

"We realize," a planner told the Kiwanis Club, "that some businessmen will not be able to come back into the scheme" and that "some will go out of business," but "if you weigh the advantages to the community against the disadvantages for certain individuals, and the advantages win, then it would be wise to pursue urban renewal" (OD 10/5/66 HS). But don't make the mistake of bringing it to a vote, he warned. A public referendum would be "foolish" and "inappropriate" because of "a lack of information on the part of those who would be voting." And decide soon, he urged, "Ilion is falling behind" (*ibid.*).

A citizens' group was already agitating for a referendum, but a vote was not legally required, the Village Board insisted, unless the village was issuing bonds.[35] Well, of course they were not issuing bonds— they were going for federal grant money. But what kind of an answer is that? Was the town theirs to do with as they pleased?

Desperate for some good PR to disarm the clamor for a vote that they clearly could not win, UR proponents in the business community hastily organized themselves into a so-called Citizens Advisory Committee. The Committee leapt on the clever idea of a real estate investor and cochair: How about a "shoe-box survey"? Selected businesses would ask their patrons to answer a short questionnaire and stuff it into a shoe box.

Three hundred people filled out questionnaires (in a village of about eleven thousand). The Committee tallied them up. On Question #1, "Do you understand UR?" 77 percent said yes. On Question #2, "Is the present business district 'satisfactory'?" 71 percent *abstained*. Question #3, "Will UR raise your taxes?," 82 percent said yes.

The cochair was annoyed. The tax question, he insisted, "has been

explained over and over." If local taxes go up, he said, it will be by a
"negligible" amount, and the increased revenue from the new development *may* even reduce taxes.[36] For reasons unclear, the Committee
interpreted the "shoe-box survey" results as "indicating" that Ilionites wanted UR and were anxious for the village to take advantage of
the federal money. The money's there, said a Committee member, and
"Ilion might as well use it" (*ibid.*).

That was too much. An Ilion attorney, representing a "Voters Committee," the names of which he would not reveal, demanded a referendum. There's no way, the spokesman charged, that three hundred
responses, in a village of over ten thousand, could be called "ap-
proval." As far as the Voters Committee was concerned, the Citizens
Advisory Committee's "Shoe Box Surveys and Tin Box Projects" were
an insult to the voters.[37] The mayor coolly responded to the group's
charges, telling a reporter that he "refuse[d] to be drawn into a controversy over the project" (*ibid.*).

It became dramatically clear that the Valley's last remaining large
employer, Remington Arms/DuPont, had thrown its considerable
weight to the side of UR. The Arms announced its intention to *buy*
the section of Main Street that had run between two factory buildings
(once the Armory and the Agricultural Works) since the Canal era. A
team of surveyors, in fact, was already at work to determine the exact
boundaries.[38] The sale, an obedient local paper reported, was "key" to
the company's new plans for expanding the works. The company
needed "additional space," a spokesman announced, a need that
"could be met if Ilion's proposed Urban Renewal project is approved"
(*ibid.*).

My elderly predecessor at the Historical Room, Mrs. Pearl Wheeler,
recalled the local shock. "They bought Main Street and closed it off,"
she told me—"*We* didn't know it was for sale!" Come to think of it,
though, two of the four original members of the Village Planning
Board, one the chair, were Arms managers. (The other two were a bank
officer and the chief of the fire department.)

Proponents of UR stonewalled the citizens time and again. There
was protest after protest, a local DAR (Daughters of the American Revolution) officer told me—the DAR led anti-UR protests across the
country—"but it didn't do any good—they were determined to do
it."[39] So they were. And their "progress" was too important for the
uncertainties of democratic process. Demolition of the village center

finally commenced in August 1972. Before it was through, 113 buildings had been reduced to rubble.

The demolitions were big events. Girls and boys on their bicycles and adults on foot and in cars flocked to the demolition sites to watch their town come tumbling down. A UR defender told me that he saw "rats and cockroaches running all over the place" when one old building came down. But that is not what most people remember. A Vietnam veteran "wept," he told me, when they demolished the landmarks of his childhood. "They" were telling everybody that the buildings were not "structurally sound," but that, he said, was a lie. He and his sister watched, and counted. The wrecking ball hit one building twenty-seven times before it "even dented that old brick."

A Concerned Citizen drove her elderly father-in-law to a demolition. They watched in horrified fascination from the front seat of her car. "The wrecking balls weren't doing *any* damage to it," she recalled—"it was *so well built*, it wouldn't go down."

"It breaks my heart," a library patron told me. "They took away a part of my life I'll never get back."

The coffers of local officialdom filled to overflowing with federal funds. And of course there were lots of contracts to hand out for demolition and construction. For people in the right place at the right time, with the right friends, the UR process was a windfall. Canny businessmen, too, stood to collect. The federal grants included funds to compensate business owners in the "project area" for lost trade. How much? Well, however much the businessmen thought they would have made, one told me. People still talk about one man who owned a few stores and dozens of apartments and "made out like a bandit."

"The only people who don't hate it [UR]," said the Vietnam vet who told me his demolition story, "are the people who made money off it." But even some people who made money off it have had second thoughts. One contractor who made his fortune in UR work now admits that it "didn't do anything for the Village—in fact, it did it harm."

Only a few people still defend UR, mostly officials and former officials. The massive artist's rendering of a glamorous modernized Ilion—a future that would never be—still covers a wall in the mayor's office. One defender still insists, "we had to *progress*—it was a matter of going ahead or losing business." Losing business? The "men of push" looked out on a different world than everybody else did: "Two

Main Street, Ilion, N.Y., c. 1900. Looking west down the tracks of the trolley that brought mechanics and shoppers to the busy little downtown. Postcard in author's collection.

Main Street, Ilion, N.Y., 1972. Courtesy, Historical Room, Ilion Free Public Library.

Wrecking the past, Main Street, Ilion, N.Y., 1974. "Urban renewal" not only demolished the busy downtown that had been the center of local life for generations, but it also pulled down local trust in government. Courtesy, Historical Room, Ilion Free Public Library.

years after HUD rebuilt Ilion," an Arms mechanic told me angrily, "half the businesses in Ilion were gone."

Did UR really result in loss of business? I made a study, tabulating local business as listed in city directories, taking 1952, the prosperous centennial year, as my starting point. The 1952 directory lists 270 businesses.[40] By 1970, after the Typewriter/Rand/UNIVAC was gone but before the demolition of "old Ilion," I count 199 businesses—74 percent of the early 1950s total, a quarter lost with the Rand closure. By 1994, 112 businesses remained in the village—56 percent of the 1970 total. The village lost close to half of its business establishments since the "rejuvenation" of the central business district. Urban Renewal was decidedly not good for business.

After the demolitions, things did not go according to plan. Space in the "rejuvenated" downtown was hard to sell.[41] Today a supermarket and a discount store hold down opposite ends of a strip mall on the site. These, along with a couple of professional offices and retail outlets, do business around a modernistic concrete structure, complete with a dry and rusting would-have-been fountain. Some people call it "the monstrosity," some, more colorfully, "the Berlin wall."

The ILHR's huge collection of Old Ilion photos drew a steady stream of library patrons upstairs to the cozy Historical Room where I was, for a happy year, Village Historian. Most were looking for dear old places they had "lost." Finding them among the photo files was often an emotional moment. One burly man poured over file after file in complete silence. After the better part of an hour he fished a handkerchief out of his pocket, pulled up his glasses, and wiped his eyes. "If my Dad was up here," he said, head still bent over the photo files, "he'd be in tears."

The decade and a half after World War II was the longest period of prosperity the Valley had known since the dawn of the corporate era. Looking back over these years, and the war and depression that preceded them, my fatherly friend, the late Mr. Paul Kinney, grew pensive. In his eighties then, he had been a mechanic at both the Typewriter and the Arms. It was a sweet September afternoon, and we were out in his garden, quiet in the beauty of it. "It's pretty much always been hard times," he mused, "except for those few years after the war when they filled us full of false hopes."

11

Wealth against Commonwealth

The world, enriched by thousands of generations of toilers and thinkers, has reached a fertility which can give every human being a plenty undreamed of even in the Utopias. But between this plenty ripening on the boughs of our civilization and the people hungering for it step the "cornerers," the syndicates, trusts, combinations . . .

HENRY DEMAREST LLOYD, *Wealth Against Commonwealth*

Old Ilion is a dreamscape today. People live their daily lives alongside the "Berlin wall" and drive to Herkimer or Utica to buy what they need. You seldom hear them drift off in nostalgic reverie, though. There is little time for that. They are running too hard to stay ahead of the bill collectors and the tax man. What you hear, especially when local elections roll around in the springtime, is hard-bitten distrust of the "in-crowd" who thwart the processes of local democracy. No matter what we do, one citizen noted at a public hearing, "they're gonna do what they want to anyway." "People have been so abused," another commented, "most people have given up hope."

Gone are the days when the prosperity that most local people wish for loomed large on the agendas of local government. They try, many of them, but under present conditions, local government has little room to maneuver. Paradoxically, though, while the decisions that determine local prosperity are no longer within the scope of local government, it takes more government to run the Valley. The legacy of UR and other Great Society programs made local government a well-paid career at a time when the corporations were rushing to the exit, on their way to the reservoirs of "cheap labor" in the South and abroad. This dual movement has transformed social life in the Valley and in the many places that share its "postindustrial" predicament.

"I always told my kids," a former mayor told me, "to get in with the State." Why? Because government jobs are the only secure jobs in the region. For the majority of the Valley's population, working insecure, temporary, and part-time jobs, or holding onto small businesses that their neighbors can barely afford to patronize, the disparity between their insecurity and the security of public employment presents a serious moral problem—serious, anyway, for a people whose moral imagination was shaped historically by "the gospel of work," and who live in a place where, as recently as the 1950s, self-governing workers held the moral and political high-ground (Ilion Centennial invitation, Chapter 10).

The problem is not simply that the tax-funded commonwealth pays for public-sector employment, and that public-sector employment continues to "grow" at a time when Valley people, as the Concerned Citizens often noted, are losing their homes, farms, and businesses because they are unable to keep up with their tax bills.[1] The Concerned Citizen's comment about so-called "public servants" "feeding off us" (Chapter 3) is an assessment with which most of the Valley would agree. The moral problem for Valley working people is that public officials are taking their money but they are not *working for them!*

At a 1994 meeting of the Concerned Citizens, their darkest suspicions were confirmed by an explosive "anonymous tip." They had received proof that a number of well-positioned but officially part-time public employees were claiming full-time status in order to receive luxurious state health and pension benefits, far beyond the compensation available to those who struggle to make a living in the private sector. Heads together over the conference table, the Concerned Citizens went down the list of "respectable" offenders:

_____ is a retiree of New York Telephone. He's already got a big pension!
_____ is [State Assemblyman]'s full-time assistant.
_____ teaches at the High School.
_____ is "the last one to let you down" [an undertaker].
_____ works for NiMo [Niagara Mohawk, the local public utility]—he's got big benefits already.
_____ owns his own agency for real estate and insurance.

(I have shortened the list.) It was an outrage. People like themselves who had worked hard and contributed to the community could barely make ends meet while a handful of already wealthy people (by local standards, anyway) got wealthier by taking more than they gave from the commonwealth that all rely on. Like the aristocracy of old, these officials were stealing a (relatively) luxurious life from the fruits of others' labor.

What officials should have been doing in these hard times became clear at an explosive county hearing about a budget that included substantial pay raises for staff and department heads. The indignation of Ilion's Concerned Citizens was shared by like-minded folk throughout the county—the hearing room was packed. Jim, the Concerned Citizens' most visible spokesperson, was in position near the public microphone when the County legislators finished their introductory remarks.

"Don't tell us you're 'scrimping and saving,'" he said, "People can't pay their taxes already and now some people who are getting forty to fifty thousand a year vote themselves raises. This is *unacceptable* and we're not going to take it anymore!"

The crowd cheered him on. The chairman gaveled for order.

The county legislators surely expected as much from this notorious "troublemaker," but the following, from a county employee, had the force of a body blow: "No one should be getting a raise at this point," she said. "It's not a question of deserving or not. I work for one of the best department heads in the county. I'm willing to give up my raise. I know I'm lucky I've *got a job.*"

The assembled citizens erupted in applause, quieting only at the chairman's threat to adjourn the meeting. "The point is," the heretical county employee said in the crowded hallway after the hearing, *"we should all be pulling together."*

This comment and its cognate, "we should all be in the same boat," can be heard daily in the Valley. They represent a belief that is foundational to the perspective of the Valley's working people, as it is to the traditional American values they have conserved. In it lies the practical meaning of "equality" and the hidden message of U.S. cultural aversion to the idea of social class divisions. It is not that everyone is supposed to be equal in the quantitative sense. Everyone is supposed to be equal in the *moral* sense, to be one people, such that, in hard times, the better-off are obligated to "pull together" with the worse-off for the well-being of the whole community. This is the lesson of the long past that has shaped the Valley's material life and cultural expectations.

That's what the Remingtons did. The Valley's former prosperity, the legacy of which still supports an exceptional standard of living on low-end paychecks, exists only because local leaders did not abstract themselves from the well-being of the community. But such is not the case for their successors today, and this is a consequential difference between the locally owned manufacturing of the nineteenth century and corporate capitalism. The corporate successors to the enterprises that the Remingtons founded take their orders "from above," and hold the threat of deindustrialization over the heads of any local official whose loyalties stray too far from corporate plans. The networks of wealth and political influence that consolidated in the years around the turn of the twentieth century—they can fairly be called, in aggregate, the "corporate regime"—reach into every corner of this country. The corporate regime has made the ideal of "pulling together" difficult to practice in any community.

A January 1994 Ilion public hearing demonstrates this difficulty in microcosm. It was called by the Ilion Board of Light to address the subject of a proposed increase in the cost of electricity. The Board of Light had been an exemplary public agency. Chartered in 1899 by popular vote to supply the village's electricity, it had done, by all accounts, an impressive job. Under its auspices, the village invested, early in the twentieth century, in the development of hydroelectricity from the area's abundant streams and rivers. Not only were Ilion's utility rates among the lowest in the New York State, but the agency had also generated surpluses and reinvested them in the village—free streetlights and free power to run them, a public park and playground, and in 1927 it donated the funds to construct the handsome Municipal Building that houses village offices and the spacious village auditorium. Light Board members serve without pay.

In recent decades, however, rates have inched steadily upward as one of the largest "authorities" in the state, the New York Power Authority (NYPA), steadily gnawed away at the autonomy of local providers like the Ilion Board of Light. Less well-known than, for example, the depredations of corporate campaign contributions, the authorities have played a central part in subordinating democratic government to the corporate regime. They are the "shadow government," as a carefully researched exposé puts it (Axelrod 1992). Also called "commissions," "corporations," "districts," "boards," and "agencies," the authorities are "quasi-public corporations"[2] that manage everything from garbage disposal to highways, airports, subways, prisons, water, gas, and electricity—without the risk and bother of democratic process.

The legal line that divides the authorities from government proper makes them a useful tool for "men of push" on both sides, corporate and political. Without a doubt, many fine people do good work at the authorities, but these organizations have also become a Pandora's box of patronage jobs, sweetheart deals, and hidden public debt—off the books of official state and local government accounting. Through the authorities, politicians can maintain "the appearance of fiscal conservatism" (Axelrod 1992:9) while taking care of their cronies with well-paid jobs and lucrative contracts. The authorities have enmeshed state and local governments in a web of interests that tie politicians and administrators to corporate officers, bankers, investors, and bond traders.

The Ilion Board of Light hearing was occasioned by NYPA's latest rate schedule, and it was one of the best attended public meetings of my research period. NYPA claims, a Light Board member explained, that commercial users are paying more than 100 percent for their electricity and that residential users are paying less than 100 percent. In the interest of "fairness and equity," NYPA was demanding a "rate equalization" that would raise residential rates and lower commercial rates.

An angry citizen took the floor as soon as it was opened to public comment. "They can write off their expenses," he said—"I can't write mine off." "What's 'fair and equity' about that?" The board member at the podium was stumped. All he could manage to say was, "the Power Authority is insisting we come to 100 percent."

"They [commercial users] get all the tax breaks and we pay for 'em," the citizen shot back, looking around the auditorium for support. Murmurs of agreement rose up from the assembled citizens. The citizens understood the situation perfectly well. Householders would pay more so large corporate users, with all the privileges to which that status entitled them, could pay less.

"We're trying to be fair," the board member replied defensively. The Light Board, he said, had worked out an alternate rate schedule that would meet NYPA's demands but soften the blow to village households.

The angry citizen was not satisfied. "They can't just do the figures any way they want," he said, more to the visibly sympathetic audience than to the Board. "This has nothing to do with the cost of living in this Valley!"

So that was what bothered him. Public service policy, in his view, ought to take into account the conditions of the public: We ought to "pull together."

Another Light Board member, a respected elder man, stepped up to the podium. As he explained it, the issue was simple: NYPA was trying to force its rate schedule on the village, the Light Board was trying to get NYPA to accept a fairer schedule, its own, and it needed the citizens' support.

It's not that simple, said a Concerned Citizen. He paid both commercial and residential rates, and his residential was already higher than his commercial. NYPA was "correcting" a condition that did not exist, he argued. It only wanted to lower the rates for its corporate cronies.

The Light Board member tried to steer him back to the question of NYPA's plan versus the Board of Light's plan. "That's not my question," the Concerned Citizen pressed: "Couldn't you *make a decision in Ilion* to give a rebate to homeowners? The homeowners are suffering the most."

The auditorium went quiet. The Board Member took a long, deep breath and spoke carefully. "Look, I worked for the Board in 1939," he said—"in those days we used to give December for free." (Free power in December was for decades the Light Board's annual Christmas present to the villagers). "It's not like that now," he said—"*NYPA overruled all existing charters.*"

The Board of Light is no longer empowered to make decisions about local electricity (despite its having funded the power development), any more than the Village Board is empowered to make decisions about local work. Both, like other agencies of local government, are practically required to administer corporate decisions in which they have no voice. "Pulling together" as a community becomes extremely challenging when communities have no say over decisions about their own resources.

The corporate regime has room for the people of the Valley as consumers and low-wage workers, but not as political actors. As much could be said of most people in the United States. It's "one dollar, one vote," the Concerned Citizens say—"the upper-class people," one observed, "don't care one bit about us working people." This is not just polemic, it is grounded in astute analysis. The corporate regime was founded on the principle of, in Janet Siskind's words, "distancing production"; that is, the physical, ideological, and political separation of production from consumption, owners from workers, capitalists from the people whose labor produces the stuff of profits (Siskind 2002:145–153).

The cultural campaign that the corporations waged in the Valley, and across the United States, presented the rationale for this distancing in its central claim that capital, not labor, is responsible for the American standard of living. This claim rationalized the practical disenfranchisement of "the producing classes." A democracy in which any producer counted as much as any capitalist would not have given its blessings to a political order in which corporate wealth could rearrange the resources of the nation to prioritize corporate "growth"— at the cost of pushing back the unprecedented triumph of the mechanics' long struggle for respect.

The Social Production of the Past

Exhausted from their many campaigns to democratize Valley politics, the Concerned Citizens have retrenched. Now meeting only once a month, they are less confrontational but have not given up. They have shifted focus to working with young people, in the hope that the "old values" they cherish will not pass entirely from the place they love. Though I have not been able to attend personally, I am confident that the Concerned Citizens' promising new projects are surrounded fore and aft with storytelling of the remembered past and the past before memory (Chapters 3 and 4).

Through these stories, they drive another channel through the mainstream American culture of individualism, optimism, and upward mobility. Thus they add a new venue for the ideals and warnings, meanings and etiquette, practicalities and satisfactions of the Valley's producerist "old values," increasing the chances that these values can pass to the next generation. When elders worry that there will be "nothing left" for their children and grandchildren, they do not mean only the places they built and the skills they learned, they also mean appreciation of the spirit that built and learned, that dignified their efforts not by superior wealth but by superior community, where the measure of respect, of social capital, was *work*—and that respect was available to anyone. This is the legacy of their past.

We may imagine that the past is stored somewhere for all time, but the past actually does not exist on its own. To be a factor in the cultural life of the present, it must be told, "produced," by living persons who had it told to them, and communicated to living persons who find meaning in it. This is the cultural work that goes on in the storytelling that is such a striking feature of social life in the Valley. The social production of the Valley's past, in turn, produces social persons who imbibe the values that past has come to encode and learn the neighborly reciprocity and pride in hard work well done that those values promote.

"Traditional American values" have not yet disappeared. They have changed, yes. The Valley does not live in the nineteenth century. It lives in a present that continually updates "old values," producing the egalitarian ideal that is the necessary precondition of neighborliness (Chapter 3), and producing, too, stubborn distrust of the "hustlers" and "go-getters" who wish to "think that they are better than us" and that they can "tell us what to think." They cannot, evidently. More than a century of corporate-sponsored cultural revolution has not succeeded in that.

And it has not, in part, because the "gospel of wealth," by the same kinds of social productive processes, legitimates precisely the conditions of degraded work that produce social persons like the Valley's working people, for whom the gospel of wealth offers no promise. The Valley's working people, like working people across the industrialized world, are not invited to the great feast of corporate affluence. The feast, in fact, depends on the work of the many who are not invited, whose work—systematically hidden in the core belief of the gospel of wealth, the magical productivity of capital—must be undercompensated for the feast to go on. It *is* a feast on the fruits of others' labor.

Thus the gospel of wealth still depends on Herbert Spencer's influential coinage: "survival of the fittest." The many who cannot partake in the promise of great wealth—*so that such wealth can exist*—must be comprehended as lesser persons, as morally *unequal*, or else the gospel of wealth itself will be revealed in the nakedness of the systemic abuse it justifies. This moral inequality is, we could say, a structural predicament that afflicts corporate capitalism across the globe.

But there is (to borrow a key insight from anthropologist Clifford Geertz [1972]) "excess meaning" in the "old values" that Valley working people continue to produce. That is, there is meaning that the basic structural predicament of corporate capitalism cannot account for, that comes from the particular historical contingencies of the United States' past, and that shows up in a stubborn unwillingness to give up on a particular vision of democracy.

The Original American Dream

The social production of the past among the working people of the Valley (and surely elsewhere in the larger region of which it is a part) has persisted in reproducing a distinctive egalitarian culture in opposition to the "survival of the fittest" logic that is embedded in the mainstream American culture of individualism and upward mobility. That past, the Valley's legacy from the Remington era, was embedded in what used to be, before the cultural revolution of corporate capitalism, the dominant culture of the United States. The Remingtons were not unique. They exemplified an egalitarian vision that was the historical product of a particular moment in the social history of the human condition. The Valley's past, I wish to suggest, is one instance of a larger legacy, the legacy of the *original* American dream.

"The American dream" is a phrase with a historical past. Its author was Yale historian James Truslow Adams, who dreamed it up for his book, *The Epic of America*, first published in 1931.[3] Adams' "epic" was a retelling of American history, with a moral. Like many other thinkers of this time, Adams saw the Great Depression as a moral failure and coined the now-famous phrase to symbolize just how this country had gone wrong. He first mentions it in his preface, noting that the book would trace the origins of American distinctiveness, especially, "that American dream of a better, richer, and happier life for all our citizens of every rank which is the greatest contribution we have as yet made to the thought and welfare of the world" (vi).

"The American dream" appears throughout *The Epic of America* as a guiding ideal, with an enlightened "common man" steadily insisting on it "from below" and a responsible leadership negotiating among competing interests to secure it. This was in no way radical thinking for Adams's time. "The rise of the common man" and the benevolent leadership that supported it had become important themes in U.S. public discourse (Fish 1929). But this is not, clearly, the American Dream we know about, the "rags to riches" story of individual wealth.

The original, as Adams introduced it, was a vision of the good *society*, one that provided well for all its members. Since then, evidently, the American Dream has been subjected to considerable "spin."

But what about Horatio Alger, the thoughtful reader might ask. Weren't his hugely popular stories about the "rags to riches" promise of the American dream? They were not, as some important but neglected historical works demonstrate (Cawelti 1965, Grimstead 1971). Alger's heroes did not seek riches. They sought a respectable "competence" (the nineteenth-century term for a modest, independent livelihood), and they achieved it through fidelity to the principles of the *original* American dream: hard work, honesty, generosity, loyalty. Alger's stories are morality plays in which good triumphs, and hustlers, deceivers, and manipulators meet the evil ends to which their infidelity destines them (Grimstead 1971). The rags-to-riches "Alger hero" of modern myth took off just as the books themselves were being pulled from library shelves, dismissed in the 1920s as old-fashioned moralizing (Cawelti 1965:103).[4]

Adams's definition of the American dream as "a better, richer, and happier life for all our citizens of every rank" would have enjoyed agreement among the mechanics of the nineteenth-century Valley (and their descendants today, for that matter). What it lacks in producerist specifics—notably the foundation: living off the fruits of one's own labor, not the labor of others—it makes up for in political savvy. As Adams told it, in every generation, "ordinary Americans" had risen up "to save [the American] dream from the forces which appeared to be overwhelming and dispelling it." And, he added ominously, "possibly the greatest of these struggles lies just ahead of us at this present time" (1931:viii). What was threatening to overwhelm "the American dream" in his generation? It was, in his words, "our modern economic monsters," "dinosaurs" of immense bulk but little "brain power" (1931:343)—the corporate giants.

Adams's American dream caught on because it encapsulated something many people valued and saw as threatened by the extent of corporate power that the Great Depression revealed. The original American dream was that this country would be (at least after the "Jeffersonian revolution" of 1800) the land where everyone could live decently. It was an original ideal, indeed it may well be the United States's greatest contribution "to the thought and welfare of the world" (Adams 1931:vi).

It rang true in the 1930s to see the original American dream under siege by the "economic monsters" because at that time everyone could still remember the trusts' stunning rise to power. Many of Adams's readers were surely of the old "middle classes" who, like the Remingtons, lost to the corporate empire-builders the mines, mills, and manufactories on which their communities had thrived. It was Adams's generation's agitation for legal limits to corporate autocracy that opened the door to post–World War II prosperity.

Today we have forgotten the rise of the economic monsters, and, as Adams feared, they have overwhelmed the original American dream. The rules of the corporate regime are largely taken for granted. Corporations construct the ladders of upward mobility that the privileged among us are educated to climb. They police the entrances to a decent life. And if the better-off among us latch onto the idea of our superior "fitness" to explain our achievements, this is not difficult to understand in a world where opportunities for living well are strictly limited.

It is interesting, though, that we seek explanation for living well, that we cannot quite take for granted the many who do not live well among us. This is the persistent "excess meaning" of the original American dream—it lingers among the resources of mainstream American culture as a discomfort with and need to explain the vast disparities of wealth that, we somehow know, our society was not supposed to generate. But it does not take the "survival of the fittest" to explain the limitations that the corporate regime enforces on the opportunities for a decent life.

The Postindustrial Dream

Under the guise of social Darwinist "science," the gospel of wealth smuggled back into American culture the most basic assumption of aristocracy: that there are two kinds of people. In classic aristocracies there were "gentle folk," the few, and "common folk," the many. In the social Darwinist version, there are the strong and the weak, the fit and the unfit. The strong are few. The weak are many. The strong should rule. Behind the backs of working people, the trusts and their cronies in politics (and allies in the academy) quietly rejected the proposition that all people are created equal.

The corporate cultural revolution was not successful in the Valley.

The corporate regime might well "scatter the good things of life," as Carnegie put it (1900b:90–91), among its professional cadres (though even the ranks of middle and upper management have been decimated in the economic recessions of the late twentieth and early twenty-first centuries). But for the working majority—taking Michael Zweig's 62 percent as a useful rule of thumb (2000)—the corporate regime has proliferated the kinds of bad jobs that most people in the Valley work.

The bus driver who first told me about the heartbreak of urban renewal is not untypical. He "really" worked at Remington Arms, he said, but he had been laid off three times over the last nine years. Twice he had been recalled, and rumor had it that they were planning another recall. He would not quit "driving bus" though. At this point he didn't dare. He has a family.

Someone has to drive the busses in this society. Someone has to operate the machines, grease the gears, polish the gadgets that the machines turn out, assemble them into finished products, pack them up, transport them. It's work that gets dirt under the fingernails, as does packing the meat and poultry and fish that we place on our tables, and picking the fruits and vegetables that, even in the winter, we can serve with it (if we can afford them).

You can keep your fingernails cleaner in another huge domain of work that the corporate regime proliferates, selling, stuffing envelopes, answering phones, "telemarketing," or plugging names, addresses, and numbers into computers. "It's clean work, honey," my grandmother might have said, but it will not pay a living wage and, no matter how well you do it, the job can vanish in an instant when corporate headquarters decides to reorganize.

In the last decades of the twentieth century a curious fantasy arose and gained exceptional currency in policy-making circles. The United States would take its place in an emerging global society as specialists in the "information economy" (Bell 1973). No dirty work here. The "knowledge workers" of this "postindustrial" economy would blaze new trails in a sparkling wonderland of computing and automated manufacturing. The information economy dream enchanted echelons of the "highly evolved," *as if* garbage no longer needed dumping, messes no longer needed cleaning, or envelopes stuffing, or meat butchering, or vegetables picking—as if hard work were a thing of the past.

The mechanics' ideal was that all work, *because a morally equal human performed it*, should be decently paid. The corporate regime, on the other hand, is bound to feed off the labor of the weak, the "un-fit," in order to support the work of the strong, the "fit." Under the protective cover of the postindustrial dream, the corporate regime exported manufacturing from the land of the original American dream to lands across the planet—the very places that anthropologists have historically studied—where desperate peoples, dislodged from ways of life that the "highly evolved" considered backward, would do hard, dirty (and often toxic) work for pennies because their worlds offered no other hopeful choice (Korten 2001, Nash 1981, Nash and Fernandez-Kelly 1983, Ong 1991). Whatever egalitarian-minded mechanics these so-called developing nations might have developed were preempted by an international division of labor that cast their people for the grunt work of our "information economy."

The unforeseen consequence is that they hate us. The corporate regime, by the ubiquity of its material success, has seeded a global *anti-American dream* that lays all blame at our doorstep. Sadly, because most people of the United States have not been consulted in the decision making of the corporate regime, much blame belongs at our doorstep.

They do not really know us, of course. They do not know that many of us, maybe most of us, live in desperation too, albeit a desperation cushioned by the things that they make for us, the nice-looking clothes, the athletic shoes, the CD players, and what-not that they will never make enough money to buy. They know us through movies and television, and the hard task-masters who push them to meet extravagant production quotas under conditions that U.S. labor law would condemn.

This book has sought to reveal a cultural boundary of which the dominant American culture is little aware, on the other side of which a subordinate American culture, with its dream of a respectable, modest prosperity in which *all people* can partake, preserves the long-germinating seeds of liberatory vision "from below." It is not the vision of socialism, in any form yet attempted or described,[5] though it does project relative equality in the distribution of wealth—"what's good for the little guy is good for the big guy," as one Concerned Citizen used to say. Their American culture envisions universal *autonomy*, universal social and political adulthood, without slaves or masters—the original American dream.

The problem with socialism as we know it, from this point of view, is exactly the problem of autonomy: It would leave the determination of the working people's portion to the tender mercies of "people who think they're better than us." The people I worked with in the Valley believe, I think, that they have a better idea: "pulling together" in a democracy of working people. The liberatory vision "from below" and its visionaries have something significant to contribute to the most important question of our time: How are we to have a sustainable future?

Rebuilding Democracy

Something new happened in 1998. Young people, old 60s radicals, faith-based activists, and labor unionists looked down at their feet and thought about the desperate people in "developing" countries who made their sneakers—and showed up that November in Seattle to protest corporate "globalization." Dodging clubs and tear gas, they have continued to show up wherever the leaders of the corporate regime meet to divide the world's wealth, raising awareness throughout the world of the inequities of the corporate regime and the possibilities for finding a better, fairer way to produce and distribute the things we want. These are brave people, but their efforts have little impeded the course of the corporate regime. This book would like to suggest that the conditions exist in the United States—headquarters, tax haven, and, arguably, birthplace of the modern transnational corporation—for a movement with more clout.

No people better knows the excesses of corporate power than the working majority of the United States who have lived on the front lines of the corporate regime for more than a century. They do not need a lengthy education. A potentially huge constituency of U.S. working people might lend their vision—and their votes—to a well-conceived plan for the democratization of the corporate regime. But conceiving it well enough will require finding our way out of some basic assumptions of mainstream American culture.

We will have to reclaim the social relationships of production from their thralldom to the magical productivity of capital, an ideology that acts to devalue the contribution of labor to the production of wealth. We will have to thoroughly divest ourselves of the social Darwinist corollary to the magical productivity of capital: the moral inequality, the "unfitness," of working people. Only by reclaiming the human relations of production and distribution *as our own social capital*, that is, by politicizing them, can a broad-based movement rein in the freedom of capital—a freedom gained at the expense of our democracy. Working people are there already, with cultural resources equal to the task. They never bought into the magical productivity of capital.

One night after a Concerned Citizens meeting five or six of us lingered on the steps of the library. The library had closed but the group had not finished pondering its latest defeat at the hands of an "in-crowd" who just could not seem to understand their arguments. It is "because of their limited world view," one Concerned Citizen suggested. "They just don't realize that most people don't think the way they do," Jim added pensively. "They can't see through their own screen," said Hilda.

Most people do *not* think like the powerful. If we can see through the cultural screen that divides this society, it is just possible that millions of people could join together in rethinking and rebuilding democracy. At the center of global empire, that would resonate around the world.

Appendix 1

Theoretical and Methodological Orientations

Broad reading in late nineteenth-century popular sources set me on the chain of questions that led to the research and analysis presented in this book.[1] The range of concerns around "the trusts" and the indignation in which these concerns were couched suggested to me a cultural borderland not unlike those that anthropologists have encountered across the world where colonization and/or "modernization" have precipitated the category of "tradition," an emotion-charged resituation of "our ways" as against the designs and impositions of powerful others. During my resident fieldwork I was surprised to discover just this sort of cultural borderline in the everyday interactions of the Valley's working people. It does not ride on the surface of casual contacts. I first became aware of it in the contentious village meeting I recount in Chapter 3, and, as my personal relationships warmed, I was increasingly exposed to working people's critique of the dominant American culture.

Anthropologists have so thoroughly embraced the need to historicize that it is hardly necessary to argue the case (Siskind 2002:157, note 1). The overweening theoretical ambition of the present study, however, is to knit together history and ethnography, collective memory and interpretations of the present, if not seamlessly, at least more tightly than our conventional cultural distinction between past and present typically intimates. Indeed, the challenges are substantial because the data of history and ethnography are substantially different in character.

Historical data come to us through the seductive factuality of the written word but need to be carefully situated in the multiple contexts of their production and consumption (Trouillot 1995). Ethnographic data come to us so embedded in context that prying them loose can disfigure them. Mediating between these two categories of data are two others: Oral histories and storytelling represent the past as it "lives" in the ethnographic present, while the work of professional historians fills gaps in the "circumstantial picture" (as Clifford Geertz put it in *Negara* [1980:7–8]) that informs and contextualizes my reconstruction of tradition, and thus understanding of the present.[2] In what follows I wish to discuss the ethnographic approach, historical sources, and theoretical frames that undergird the work presented in this book.

I conducted my ethnographic fieldwork with the conviction that, as Faye Ginsburg has noted, good ethnography requires a sympathetic approach to the people one studies, perhaps most poignantly when those people are "close but controversial neighbors" (1993:175). Suspicious that the people I wished to study would be suspicious of me, I entered the region as unobtrusively as possible and let my circle of acquaintances expand in ways that would be available to any "newcomer" (Chapter 2), provisioning myself at garage sales and the local supermarket, joining a church and the county Historical Society, attending public meetings, and working at the local library and the Remington Arms Archives.

The acquaintances on whose knowledge and interpretations I most relied came to number about fifty people in five somewhat overlapping social networks, roughly equal numbers of men and women, roughly proportionate, ethnically and socioeconomically, to the Valley's population. I had important ethnographic contacts, however, with many times this number. I conducted formal interviews with public officials (not included in my social networks) only toward the end of my resident fieldwork, guided in my preference for spontaneous interactions by a provocative idea from anthropologist Sally Falk Moore: "events that are in no sense staged for the sake of the anthropologist," she suggested, are "the preferred form of raw data" (1987:730).

My main source of historical documents reflects the region I studied (I will discuss regionalization shortly): a center for artisans, not literary folk. Even local notables generally rose to prominence through their "mechanic" skills. The most notable of all, the Remington family, left only a few of their own words—a key figure, Eliphalet II, was famously impatient with paperwork, keeping his office, people say, in his stovepipe hat. My interest, however, did not center on the notables but on the local majority.

Recovering the perspectives of the nonnotable majority is notoriously challenging. In this challenge I have been especially fortunate. The Remingtons sponsored a newspaper that took especial pride in its "mechanic" readership and published a wide variety of local opinion more or less verbatim. More generally, I was fortunate in the strong historical consciousness that is prized cultural capital in the region, among elites and non-elites alike. (One of my best "informants," a retired mechanic, was quite shocked when I mentioned the social science truism that American culture is supposed to be "ahistorical.") As discussed in Chapters 2 and 3, local culture maintains and transmits a rich lore of oral and artifactual history.

The documentary sources with which I worked are located in three local historical collections, those of the Ilion Library Historical Room (ILHR), the Herkimer County Historical Society (HCHS, perhaps most important to me as a gathering place for local historians), and the archives of Remington Arms. A serendipity of ethnographic work put me in intimate contact with the ILHR collection, a huge repository of documents, photos, and memorabilia that generations of local residents saved because they held significance for them.[3] Seven months into my resident fieldwork the elderly curator of the ILHR suddenly died, and I was asked to step in as Village Historian (at minimum wage). In this capacity I had unmediated access to the collection.

By archivists' standards, the Historical Room would probably look like unrelieved chaos,[4] but this is not without a certain advantage. As anthropologist Michel-Rolph Trouillot analyzes the production of history, issues of power intervene at every step in a dialectic of "mentions and silences" that creates the historical record (1995:26,53), not least in archive-making, where materials are thematized on the basis of judgments about significance that may hide as much as they reveal (1995:48). My investigations were little obstructed by this process.[5] Like the collection of the Herkimer County Historical Society (HCHS) with which I worked less extensively, the ILHR is largely organized for genealogical research, a systematicity that allowed me to identify the major collectors and the persons they referenced at each temporal stratum.

The ILHR is complexly sedimented. Most of the materials come from personal collections, the oldest stratum dating to the 1860s. Especially useful were the ILHR's large collection of scrapbooks. The "scrapbook historians" turned out to be unexpectedly good informants. Six scrapbooks were the work of surely the most conscientious Village Historian in local history, Mrs. Ella Dimock, who was active from the 1940s through the mid-1960s. (The ILHR collection was originally organized largely through her efforts.) Others are the work of a spectrum of local personages, elite and non-elite. Each scrapbook is a microcosm. In addition to clippings, letters, notices, and handwritten comments that might not otherwise have survived the press of time, they allow reconstruction of the compiler's social networks, public and private affairs, political perspective, and, of course, the local events that each considered important.

But in none of this, of course, do the facts simply speak for themselves. Interpreting the past "from below"—and the present, for that matter—requires much judicious thought about questions of cultural hegemony. The late, great anthropologist Eric Wolf was fond of quoting to his students a saying of anthropological ancestor Franz Boas: "What people tell you they think is what they think they ought to think." There is much wisdom in this for both ethnographers and historians. In the end, no Rosetta stone liberates us from the necessity of critical, informed judgment. Mine has been aided by James C. Scott's distinction of "official transcripts" and "hidden transcripts" (1990), both in its inculcating suspicion about formal representations of the social whole and in its helpful examples of how to recognize the "hidden."[6]

Scott's good advice, like Boas's, is about thinking through the multiple perspectives from which our data come to us. Mexican anthropologist and historian Claudio Lomnitz-Adler's approach to regional culture, a synthesis of geography, history, and cultural anthropology, provides the framework I have relied on for constellating the multiplicity of perspectives that research in complex modern nation-states necessarily involves.[7] My interpretation of historical and ethnographic data, and the generalizations I propose from them, are heavily indebted to this framework. Taking "a systematic and an actor-centered view simultaneously," the regional culture framework provides analytical tools for understanding "the spatial system of mediating structures" through which particular locales articulate to superordinate nexuses of cultural production and political power (Lomnitz-Adler 1992:41–42).

Regional culture analysis offers a satisfying solution to a perennially vexing issue of ethnographic research, the problem of localized "units of analysis" and how to generalize from them (Myers 1988; Wolf 1988; Marcus and Fisher 1986). By problematizing "mediating structures," the regional framework takes the ethnographic site as the locus of analytical perspectives on the other possible sites with which it connects. Through this framework, researchers can avoid both microcosmic isolation, which represents the ethnographic site as too autonomous, and rabid generalization, which "imagines" the entire nation-state in the research site's image.[8]

The regional culture approach, then, can breathe new life into the venerable holistic genre of "community studies." Community studies lost face when their proponents could not respond to a barrage of criticism, well aimed at the fuzzy concept of "community." Innovated in a fertile but impulsive leap from supposedly "primitive" villages to the bustling cities of Muncie, Indiana (the "Middletown" of Lynd and Lynd 1957 [1929], 1937), and Newburyport, Massachusetts (the "Yankee City" of Warner, et al. 1941–1963), community studies could not analyze the implications of the community's status in the political, economic, ethnic, and cultural hierarchies of the nation-state (Arensberg 1955, 1961; Kimball 1955; Steward 1950), not to mention the global hierarchies among nation-states (Nash 1981; Roseberry 1988; Wallerstein 1974; Wolf 1982). The regional culture model places the research site in the context of the various hierarchies that impinge on it, providing arguable parameters for comparisons among and generalizations from local data.

Approached through the regional culture framework, spatial boundaries suggest struggles between local cultures whose differences were resolved territorially. One generation's struggle became the next generation's structure, so that the spatial order, as Thomas Beidelman suggests, comes to condition cognitive and moral space (1993).[9] The smallest cultural region of my research site is locally known as "the Valley" and has been called that, as far as I can determine, for generations. I discuss its cultural borders in Chapter 2. The Valley is located at the geographic center of a larger region, Central New York. Roughly synonymous with what southern New Yorkers call "upstate New York," these two regions have been cultural adversaries at least since the Duke of York's men renamed the city of New Amsterdam after him.

Central New York, I would like to suggest, is located in a larger-still cultural region that stretches from Albany, New York (perhaps even

Western Massachusetts), to Buffalo, New York, the first inland "boom-town" in U.S. history (Johnson 1978), and beyond, through the trade routes of the Great Lakes, including the Canadian commercial centers on their northern shores.[10] Historically articulated by the Erie Canal, this region shared population and, thus, cultural flows, and was at the forefront of nineteenth-century commercial and cultural innovation (Ryan 1981).

The Valley, along with other small manufacturing centers in this larger region, shares a history of locally owned, artisan-based manu-factures, and a similar sequence of "ethnic succession" in the rela-tively autonomous regions of the old, decentralized United States. Each lost autonomy when it was integrated into the corporate-medi-ated national system around the turn of the twentieth century, and each suffered the late twentieth-century fate of deindustrialization (Bluestone and Harrison 1982, Bluestone 1984). These factors, taken together, permit some measure of generalization from my Valley data. While more precise claims will have to await further research, it is possible to hypothesize within the regional culture framework that el-ements of the Valley's past and present may be "diagnostic" (Moore 1987) of broader patterns.

The pattern that most engages my attention is that of social-class culture. Unlike the seacoast cities, dominated by merchant elites, the prestige of manufacturing in the hinterlands dignified the social sta-tus of skilled mechanics and the broadly producerist ideology that they professed (see discussions in Chapters 5 and 6). As the trust movement consolidated into a centralized order of translocal corpora-tions, the mechanics lost control of manufacturing, and most were, so my data suggests, pushed "underneath" a new class boundary that classified them with the masses of labor, in uneasy subservience to corporate capital and its allies. It is this move that, I propose, drove the egalitarian premises of producerism to the terrain of "hidden tran-script," where they still ferment. My claim is that those premises ac-count for the distinctiveness of working-class culture in the larger cultural region that the Valley's historical trajectory exemplifies.

A number of scholars capture this social, political, economic, and cultural transformation in the dialectics of producerist *versus* con-sumerist culture, concerned with how proletarianization and the mass production of commodities under corporate auspices wrought a "cultural revolution" in subjectivity or selfhood (Fox and Lears 1983, and their contributors; Lears 1994; Livingston 1994). Departing from C. B. Macpherson's notion of "possessive individualism" (1962), they propose that the crux of the problem is how the inaccessibility of private property (for working people) and the severance of ownership from control (for the middle class)—both connected to the rise of corporate capitalism—pushed the foundations of identity away from property ownership and toward the consumption of commodities.

This is an important thesis with a wide range of implications, but the cultural revolution my study tracks is quite a different thing. It is a revolution in the dominant *national* culture, a rather abrupt reorientation from Jeffersonian-Jacksonian-Lincolnian commitment to "the common man" as an "intelligent yeomanry"[11] toward Labor as a "mass."[12] The early twentieth-century disillusionment between the Progressives and the working class, I suggest (Chapter 1), was mutual, clearly readable in the Valley's rejection of procorporate elites' self-serving "progress" (see Chapters 9 and 10).

Equally problematic, in my view, the consumer society theorists address the concerns of middle-class property owners, displaced by corporate capital accumulation from the ownership of local production, as though the same range of concerns can characterize working-class attachment to property. The view "from below" suggests to the contrary that these theorists have conflated two different modes of constructing identity through property. The kind of identity these theorists focus on, which can be constructed with commodities like fashion, mouthwash, psychoanalysis, or (as Theodore Roosevelt put in) "the vigorous life," is *personal*. The kind of identity that the people I studied construct with their property is *political*. Property is a hedge against tyranny—its borders keep integrity within by keeping out "people who think they're better than us." As such, it is the mark of "independence," as opposed to the "servile dependency" against which the republican discourse of liberation was constructed. "Free men" had property, and the "unfree" sought it and still seek it. It is, in other words, a social rather than an individual property.

And for that matter, so is the identity that persons construct with consumables, in anthropological perspective. Social persons use commodities to position themselves in the social networks where personal identity ultimately "dwells"—property, landed or consumable, is the price of admission to social relationships, to respect, to the esteem of peers. As anthropologists have long argued, the metabolism of human social relations is the continual exchange of "substances"—things, people, and representations—that engage us in ongoing, reciprocal social interaction (Beidelman 1993, Bourdieu 1977, Fajans 1997, Mauss 1967 [1925], Polanyi 1944, Weiner 1992). In this light, any "substances"—manufactured or homemade—can be brought to serve the purposes of social capital, our most valuable asset.

How we do it, what particular "substances" are currency in which particular social networks, is, as anthropologists say, culture specific, but what we mean by *culture* is a topic of much debate within the discipline. Cultural anthropology is arguably the most contentious of social sciences—indeed, its claim to science is itself hotly disputed. There is no single theory, no "big bang," that unites anthropologists in one approach to understanding human social life, and this is, in part, an artifact of what we study—human cultures. In our warrant to understand the world as the people we study understand it, our own perspectives are affected, so much so that many among us claim that there is no truth across cultures (or within them), such that a juxtaposition of conflicting perspectives is as close to truth as we can get.

This study does not toss out the possibility of discovering social truths. It aligns with one of the most robust strands in recent social thought, social production theory (Bourdieu 1977, 1990; Fajans 1997; Sangren 2000; Turner 1986). The force of thinking in terms of social production dissolves the strong line that much social theory draws between the individual and the social, seeing social life "in the round" as a complex commingling of persons, things, and thinking.

All of us are products of particular cultures in that how we name and categorize things, what we expect from each other, and what we aspire to are all conditioned by the culture into which we were socialized. We are users of our cultures, capable of original innovation with its resources, at the same time that we are dependent on relatively stable cultural conventions in order to make sense of each other. Our culture, that is, is not outside of who we are, a set of rules that we can choose to enact or rebel against. Rather, as we produce our cultures, we produce our selves and, as we produce our selves, we reproduce our cultures, not as exact copies but as emergent inventions that, nonetheless, observably reference the distinctive, analyzable cultural logics that our ability to communicate requires.

The cultural transformation on which this study pivots is no exception. The centralization of material resources and productive technologies that the trust movement achieved was outside the prevailing political consensus of its time, but it drew on a culture of European, particularly British, capitalists that the then-prevailing U.S. culture had suppressed. The priorities of capitalism, it can be said, were driven into the "hidden transcript" in the public discourse of much of the nineteenth-century United States, and for understandable political reasons. In a nation-state that repudiated special privilege, grants of privilege for the profitable reproduction of capital would always be liable to criticism. But capitalists quietly continued to do what capitalists do.

In the space left by the public suppression of capitalist priorities, working people's ideals could flower, emerging from the distinctive cultural logic that I trace in Chapters 5 and 6. The successful capital accumulation of the trust movement, however, thrust capitalist culture into renewed prominence. And Progressives made sense of this, as Daniel Rogers has demonstrated (1998), by reinterpreting European experiments in the mediation of interests between social classes long defined by privileges that the United States had abjured.

Progressivism came to define a U.S. cultural adaptation to capitalist economic centralization that opposed the historical producerist U.S. culture as unprogressive, but the working "masses" that Progressives bid to manage had vested interests in that historical culture. Rather than a total cultural revolution, my reading of the data suggests cultural bifurcation. From the perspective of the Valley (and, I suggest, other places that share its historical trajectory), U.S. culture as a whole takes a shape similar to what Lomnitz-Adler finds in Mexico—two poles of cultural "coherence" (1992), dominant and nondominant, with a very complex terrain of mixed loyalties in between.

This bifurcation does not map tidily onto the major dichotomies of social thought, not left and right nor capitalist and non- or pre-capitalist. The long past of the Valley paints a picture of local people taking advantage of market relationships for the achievement of household and community ends—and, indeed, the political ideals of Valley working people today follow this model—in high contrast to the scholarly model that paints the nineteenth-century United States in the dichotomous terms of a monolithic market economy, threatening and eventually destroying diverse subsistence economies (e.g., Sellers 1991).

This is not how it happened. Producing, selling, and buying were,

and still are, constituted not by abstract forces but by networks of relationships through which social actors secured the things (and future
relationships) they wanted. Among those "things" are the community
itself, the place and persons that must persist with some integrity in
order for members' social and cultural capital to retain its value. As
economic anthropologist Stephen Gudeman suggests, this community "thing" constitutes a material and cultural *commons* (or "base")
that, across all known cultures, social actors act to maintain, allocate,
and augment through whatever means their circumstances provide,
including market transactions (2001).

Gudeman's model offers a means for distinguishing two very different productive systems that have been unhelpfully lumped together
into a unitary "capitalism": *locally owned manufacturing*, like the
Remington enterprises, and *corporate capitalism*. With the former,
communities can strategize to augment and apportion the commons,
producing and selling goods in order to acquire goods that can be applied to the social purposes of community members (Marx's C-M-C[13]).
With the latter, the community is only a raw material on which non-
members (or, as Gudeman might say, the members of another community with its own commons to augment) apply capital to extract
capital (Marx's M-C-M'[14]). And how they got the right to do that, we
should remember, was a political matter, not the outcome of abstract
forces.

This is not, I wish to suggest, an arcane point. One system works
for the broad producing majority. The other does not. Lumping these
different systems together in one "capitalism" obscures what could be
a fruitful line of inquiry into an important problem. Unless we wish
to return to the Stone Age, any vision of a just future must include
manufactured goods. The lessons of the Remingtons' success and the
contingent, political nature of their failure suggest that manufacture
can be undertaken in such a way that all involved live decent, dignified lives.

Appendix 2

Local Historical Sources and Abbreviations

Ilion Library Historical Room (ILHR)

Cent52 Ilion Centennial Book. The paper-bound local history produced for the Ilion Centennial of 1952.

CS Centennial Scrapbook. A clippings scrapbook kept by the chair of the 1952 Ilion Centennial Committee.

DN Dimock Notebook. Ella Dimock's 1940s gleanings from the old Ilion *Citizen*, some two hundred pages, typed single-space, in a three-ring binder.

HS "Historian's Scrapbooks." Ella Dimock's extensive clippings files for the 1950s and 1960s.

IHC Ilion Historical Club. A collection of typed research papers by IHC members, dating from 1946 to 1949, the result of extensive work with village government records, church records, and nineteenth-century newspapers.

IP Ingersoll Papers. A collection from one of the first Yankee families to settle in Herkimer County. It includes letters, legal documents, and memorabilia dating from the 1840s.

RCB *Remington Centennial Book*, 1916. Illustrated local history booklet, prepared for the 1916 Centennial, descriptively subtitled, "Some Historical and Human Facts about the Birth and Growth of the Firearms Industry at Ilion, New York."

RCHSP Remington Centennial Historical Souvenir Program. The daily schedule for the 1916 Centennial, including a detailed, anonymous local history written for the occasion.

RCT Remington Centennial Transcripts. Transcripts of the major speeches presented at the 1916 Centennial, carbon typescript on legal-size onionskin, enumerated from 1 to 3 for the three days of the celebration.

RS Russell Scrapbook. Notes, clippings, ephemera, and texts of his many public speeches, collected by Albert N. Russell, millwright, building contractor for the Remingtons, lumber and office furnishings entrepreneur, and court-appointed receiver of Remington assets, from the mid-1860s into the 1910s.

TS34, TS36, TS47   Typewriter Strike files, organized by years, 1934, 1936, 1947, including scrapbooks, kept by an unnamed union official, probably of the Polisher's Union.

WRS   Walter Rix Scrapbook. Annotated clippings and ephemera collected by Walter Rix, jewcler, bicycle enthusiast, and charter member of the Ilion Board of Trade, from the mid-1890s to early 1940s.

Municipal Records

VBM   Village Board Minutes. Ilion Municipal Building.
ZCF   Zoning Commission Files. Ilion Municipal Building.

Remington Arms Archives

A/G   Alvis/Goodstall Records, Box 1. Papers regarding the organization of the Remington Arms Archive.

Articles of Incorporation Box. Various legal documents pertaining to the business affairs of Marcellus Hartley Dodge over the first two decades of the twentieth century, including several agreements restructuring the monumental debt from Dodge's pre–World War I expansion of Remington Arms UMC.

MFC   "Minutes of the First Convention of the M. Hartley Co. succeeded by Remington Arms-Union Metallic Cartridge Co.," 1911 (taken by two court stenographers hired for the purpose).

Newspapers

ET   Herkimer *Evening Telegram*. Daily, currently published.
Ilion *Citizen*. 1855–1919 Weekly. Incomplete collection on microfilm, ILHR (dates include its forerunners the Ilion *Independent* and the Ilion *Loyal Citizen*); renamed Ilion *News* 1909–1916; briefly succeeded by the Ilion *Community Review* 1921–1933, not microfilmed and largely lost today.
Ilion *Sentinel*. 1934–1955 Weekly. Widely collected in the files and scrapbooks of ILHR.
OD   Utica *Observer-Dispatch*. Daily, currently published.
UDP   Utica *Daily Press*. Longtime daily, now defunct.

Notes

Chapter 1. Introduction: The Other American Culture

1. Credit for this observation goes to the 2000 Green Party presidential campaign. Behind it, of course, are the statistics: With rare exceptions, national elections have brought a voter turnout of 50 percent or less since 1920 (see Piven and Cloward 1988). Turnout for state and local elections is considerably lower.

2. There are many histories of the corporate ascendancy at the national level, dating from the first indignant exposé, Henry D. Lloyd's *Wealth Against Commonwealth* (1894). William Roy's *Socializing Capital* (1997) is, in this scholar's view, the best recent study.

3. I use the expression "working people" because, in situations of political conflict, the people who are the focus of this study use it to distinguish themselves from the "people who think they're better than us" (also termed "higher-ups" and the "big guys"). Cognate expressions are "average Americans," "the little guy" and, simply, "the people." The working people distinguished in this way are a diverse lot. They are factory workers and former factory workers (laid-off or retired) and so-called service workers of all kinds—people who could be included in classic definitions of the working class—but they are also improvisors in the region's large "informal" economic sector (e.g., regular "garage" sellers and other off-the-books service providers), small-time farmers and "half-ass" farmers (as one of my associates in Central New York put it), and a handful of professionals. Their empirical alliance in local conflict and shared perceptions of systemic unfairness suggest a changing landscape of social class that is a central problem for this study.

4. See Appendix 1 for a discussion of the regionalization on which this statement is based.

5. My characterization of "traditional" U.S. culture, dating, arguably, to the "Jeffersonian Revolution" of 1800 (Appleby 1984), is drawn from my own findings (see Parts II and III) and a great many historical sources. Among the most influential for my conception have been Appleby's work on the "Jeffersonian Revolution" (1984, 1992), Faler's work on early industrial Massachusetts (1981), Foner's study of the Party of Lincoln, the early Republican Party (1970), Fink's work on the Knights of Labor (1983), Goodwyn's study of the People's Party (1976), and Lazerow's study of religious reasoning in the making of the U.S. working class (1995).

6. *United Mine Workers Journal* 7/10/1902:1, 8/15/1901:4.

7. These thoughts were penned by the editors of *McClure's Magazine* in their 1902 introduction to Ida Tarbell's ground-breaking "History of Standard Oil" (19(6):589, 592).

8. From David Graham Phillips' *The Treason of the Senate*, first published in 1906 (1964:82–83, emphasis in the original).

9. According to the World Bank's 2001 *World Development Report*, the Scandina-

vian countries are most equal, with a Gini coefficient (a measure of income inequality) of .25. The United Kingdom, by comparison, clocks in at .36. The United States leads the pack at .41 (Thornbecke and Charumilind 2002:8).

10. The Gini coefficient for Brazil, for example, tops the charts at .60, with South Africa close behind at .59 (see note 9, Thornbecke and Charumilind 2002:9).

11. The recent anthropological studies of the United States that have most influenced mine are Blu (1980), di Leonardo (1984, 1985, 1987), Ginsburg (1989), Goldschmidt (1978), Greenhouse (1986), Gregory (1998), Krasniewicz (1992), Lamphere (1986), Nash (1989), Newman (1985), Pappas (1989), Peacock and Tyson (1989), Rapp (1982), Stack (1974), Susser (1982), and Wallace (1978, 1987).

12. Cold War social scientists sought the causes of "extremism," both left and right, in family "pathology," notably among the families of the working class and "lower" middle class. Among the most influential of these studies are Adorno et al. (1950), Bell, ed. (1971 [1963, 1955]), Hofstadter (1955a), Lipset (1959), Riesman and Glazer (1952), and Warren (1976). This work has cast a long shadow over social research on the United States. The idea that "lower" classes were responsible for fascism and McCarthyism has been strongly challenged by sociologist Richard Hamilton (1996). Barbara Ehrenreich's caricature of this literature is a pointed and witty antidote (1989).

13. The present study could be placed in the venerable social science genre of "community studies," ethnographic projects that take as their unit of analysis a single community in a complex, modern society. It is more precisely, though, a *regional analysis;* that is, it lays claim to the body of thought that sought to address cogent criticisms of the community studies tradition. Appendix 1 discusses the critique, the distinction, and the regional analysis remedy.

14. The important observation of the Palatine's "buffer zone" function for the English colony of New York is the insight of James L. Parker, a local historian of Palatine descent.

15. The vast estate of Sir William Johnson, British superintendent of Indian affairs in New York for much of the eighteenth century, neighbored the Palatines to the east. Adopted into the Mohawk Nation, married to a Mohawk woman of rank, and designated a chief, Johnson's leadership is credited with securing Mohawk (and other Iroquois) allegiance to the British cause (Pound and Day 1930).

16. The county is named for a Palatine hero of the Revolution, General Nicholas Herkimer who, despite a mortal wound, as local historians proudly tell, held off British forces at the Battle of Oriskany (1777) long enough for Patriot forces to regroup.

17. As discussed in Appendix 1, I used three local historical collections: the Ilion Free Public Library Historical Room (ILHR), the Herkimer County Historical Society, and the Remington Arms Archives. Appendix 2 gives abbreviations and descriptions of sources in these collections.

18. We tend to associate manufacturing with urban areas, but early U.S. manufacturing was water powered. Hilly, well-watered terrain like the Mohawk Valley was ideal, unlike the kind of geography that made good harbors for the big commercial cities. It was not until the mid-nineteenth century, when exploitation of anthracite coal began to fuel substantial iron and steel production, that U.S. manufacturing could take advantage of steam power (Chandler 1972).

Chapter 2. The Valley

1. Yes, in New York State we have full-blown legislatures at the county level.

2. It is possible that had I been African American rather than Greek/Yankee American, a different vista of racial consciousness might have unfolded before me. Ethno-

graphic research is unavoidably a matter of personal contact. My extensive social networks in the Valley did not connect me to any African Americans, a fact that is surely related to the recency of African American residence there, but that may also suggest hidden constructions of racial difference. In recent years, however, it is common to see mixed-race groups of children and adolescents in the Valley.

3. The concept of "marking" is an important insight from linguistic anthropology. Where, for example, bears are assumed to be brown, marked categories will emerge to specify the unassumed kind, and we'll get, say, "bear" and "black bear." Or, in other domains, we'll get "bass" and "sea bass," or "religion" and "Eastern religion," or "bread" and "whole-wheat bread." The process of marking is a historical process. Marked categories emerge out of prior generalizations on an "as needed" basis.

4. And, short of home ownership, extensive kin connections can also amount to a higher standard of living than available cash could buy by way of helpful connections to housing suppliers, low and in-kind rents, and the "safety net" of safe places to stay in intervals of life transitions and crises.

Chapter 3. Local Knowledge

1. With a few notable exceptions, including Ginsburg (1989), Lynd and Lynd (1957 [1929], 1937), Pappas (1989), Susser (1982).

2. I asked for and graciously received permission to take notes during Concerned Citizens meetings, on the condition (at my suggestion) that I not include members' names. My "scribbling" was the source of some humorous comment but was also a resource for members who occasionally asked me to check my notes for detail on particular happenings.

3. The Concerned Citizens kept no membership list because association with the group was likely to provoke retribution. One member ceased coming to meetings after taking a new job, when his superior obliquely noted that his position was at stake. Others experienced late-night visitations from police officers. Most common, however, were visits from the "codes enforcer," who inspected the homes and businesses of known Concerned Citizens with extraordinary care, invariably finding violations that would require expensive repairs to bring the buildings "up to code."

4. Wachtel 1986; Bozon and Thiesse 1986:241; Connerton 1989:37; Debouzy 1986:269; Tonkin 1992:136.

5. Throughout these examples, I have hidden the identities of storytellers and listeners by changing names and altering certain biographical and geographic details.

6. I say "not wishing to" because, when the reciprocal favor does not come close to matching the original, we may very well calculate equivalency. We do not wish to make the calculation because we do not wish for the problem to arise—we wish for mutual respect. The hidden complexity of calculation in "gift" exchanges, contrary to some anthropologists' tendency to romanticize them, is brilliantly explored in the first chapter of Bourdieu (1977).

Chapter 4. Local History

1. This account of Walter C. Green and his stories is drawn from two newspaper articles, "Early History in Ilion" (Ilion *Citizen* 3/3/1916, Rix Scrapbook, ILHR, also the source of this chapter's epigraph) and "Ilion 89 Years Ago" (Ilion *Citizen* 9/18/1919,

Ilion-History file, ILHR), and a manuscript, c. 1940, "Reminiscences of Old Ilion Residents," by Mrs. Jane Miller (Ilion-History file, ILHR).

2. I summarize from the *Papers of the Herkimer County Historical Society, 1896–1920,* the Society's journal, *Legacy* (1985 to the present), and its county history (HCHS 1992). Other key sources are three histories of the county (Benton 1856; Beers et al. 1879; Hardin and Willard 1893) and one of the region (Greene 1925). Oriskany was the first of some ten battles that took place in the Mohawk Valley between 1777 and 1782, by which year the region had lost more than a third of its population (Franz 1987).

3. *Legacy* histories, like the county history (HCHS 1992), are primarily concerned with the founders and builders of venerable local institutions. Recently, the HCHS has made efforts to ferret out the accomplishments of the region's Irish, Italian, and Eastern European settlers, to examine the question of slavery in the county, and to devote attention to the county's working-class history. The Society's journal, however, remains avowedly elite: "What kind of people read *Legacy?*" an editorial asks potential advertisers; "In a nutshell our audience is very *upscale* with far above average *disposable income*" (1(3):17, emphasis in original).

Chapter 5. The Remingtons of Ilion

1. My sources for the Remington's early years are largely local histories (see Appendix 2), especially the Remington Centennial History Souvenir Program (RCHSP, 1916) and the work of the Ilion Historical Club that went into the *Ilion Centennial Book* (1952, abbreviated as Cent52). The papers of the Ingersoll family (IP, ILHR), close friends and creditors of the Remingtons, were important for contextualization.

2. When the original contractor, John Griffiths of Cincinnati, defaulted, Remington successfully bid on the contract. Jenks had set up shop in Springfield, Mass., where the N.P. Ames Company had begun manufacture of his invention, one of the earliest successful breach-loaders. Remington bought the patent and all of the machinery Ames had commissioned for the project (Peterson 1966:33–36).

3. This was Fordyce Beals, whose improvements had to await the expiration of Sam Colt's 1836 patent. During the Civil War the Remingtons' production of revolvers was second only to Colt's (Peterson 1966:45, 50).

4. The reference is biblical: "Ye cannot worship God and Mammon [i.e., riches]" (Matthew 6:24) (see Lazerow 1995:32–33).

5. How the numbers shake out depends on how you define a city. The Census Bureau declared the United States to be urbanized in 1920 when, by its definition, just over half of the population (51.1%) lived in cities. But to make this determination, they defined places with a population of *2,500* or more as urban (U.S. Bureau of the Census 1975:2). By this definition, small towns vanish. A place was either rural or urban. With a little calculation, however, we might restore small towns to the statistical picture. If we set the bar of cityhood at, say, a population of 25,000, then 17.2% of the 1880 population lived in cities. Too low? If we raise it to 50,000, the urban percentage drops to 14.3. If we raise it to 100,000 (there were only twenty cities of 100,000 or more in 1880), the percentage drops to 12.5. Any way we cut it, the vast majority of the population lived in small towns and farming communities (83% in 1880, with the city bar set at 25,000). And, by the way, they still did in 1920 (64.3%). Figures are taken from the Census Bureau's *Historical Statistics of the United States* (1975:11–12).

6. An interesting case in point is Thomas Paine's *Common Sense* (1776). For the

purpose of rallying popular support for the American Revolution, Paine, a Deist, constructed a long, complicated biblical argument to the point that monarchy was idolatry, an arrogant affront to God's rule over the faithful.

7. My understanding of democratization in the early Republic is much indebted to the work of historian Joyce Appleby (1984, 1992).

8. Cited in Jama Lazerow's *Religion and the Working Class in Antebellum America* (1995:157), a study that aims to correct the widespread neglect of religion in U.S. labor history.

9. The biblical reference is to Genesis 3:19.

10. It is important to recognize that religion did not simply legitimate popular struggles against the ambitions of the new elites. Reason may persuade, but religion, where it reigns as shared culture, *compels*. Labor historians typically contend that religion was the means through which capitalists sought to control labor (e.g., Johnson 1978; Ryan 1981; Wilentz 1984), but the "social control thesis" (Sutton 1995) cuts both ways. Religion could also give workers compelling cultural weapons against employers' mistreatment.

11. At this time "capitalist" tended to refer to people who dealt in lending and borrowing money, rather than the extended range of meaning it has acquired today.

12. See Livingston (1994), chapter 2, and Roy (1997), especially chapters 4 and 5.

13. The vast majority of industrial establishments in the 1880s were family partnerships located in small industrial centers like Ilion, in part because these enterprises still depended on water power (Chandler 1972). The local dynamics at play in the Remington case, notably gospel of work ideology and undeveloped labor markets, would suggest similar relationships in cases like the Cornings of Corning, N.Y., the Parker Brothers of Meriden, Conn. (Parker n/d), and the Rands of Tonawanda, N.Y. (Kolopsky 1986); in the mill villages of Chester Creek, Pa., the Crozers of Crozerville, the Lammots of Lenni, the Riddles of Penn's Grove (Wallace 1978); in the manufacturing villages of Berkshire County, Mass., the Stearns of Stearnsville, the Barkers of Barkerville, the Colts of Coltsville, the Shaws of Pontoosuc (Nash 1989:38–39); even, at one time, the DuPonts of the Brandywine Valley (Wallace 1978) and the old "anthracite aristocracy" of northeastern Pennsylvania (Davies 1985; Wallace 1987).

14. The restless Samuel Remington, Philo's next younger brother, may be an exception to this generalization. As the family's most productive sales agent in Europe and the Middle East, Samuel showed a marked taste for elegance.

15. The Ilion *Citizen* was, according to its masthead, "A Republican Journal Devoted to the Best Interests of the Community." It was devoted, clearly, to what the Remingtons believed were the best interests of the community; they founded it in 1855 (as the Ilion *Independent*) and "patronized" it for decades. Like other papers of its day, it is a compendium of contemporary culture, publishing legal notices, pending legislation, speeches, and sermons verbatim, in addition to "news," opinion, farm-market reports, gossip, fiction, poetry, and "sketches" (today's "features"). It had a wide readership throughout the area, including among the factory workers (*Citizen* 4/14/1865).

16. "Explanation" of the Remington failure by their excessive virtue was first suggested soon after the event by a former employee and one-time family friend (Russell 1897). It is arguable that this man, a "receiver" of Remington assets in bankruptcy proceedings and later a bit of a trust-builder himself, shared the gun trust's motive in painting the family as "too good" for business success.

17. Thomas Jefferson was a committed opponent. He wrote James Madison in 1788 that he wanted the Bill of Rights to include a strict prohibition of monopolies "in all

cases" (Jefferson to Madison 7/31/1788 [Jefferson 1944:450–451], and see also Jefferson to Hopkinson 3/13/1789 [1944:460]). In the end, the Constitution left the issue of corporations, without comment, to the states.

18. These critics' positions are nicely exemplified and summarized in Pauline Maier's study of corporations in the early United States (1993).

19. Jackson, of course, had complex motives, among them, strengthening the state banks of the West against the financial power of the East, but these motives should not detract from the significance of the Jacksonian commitment to promoting democratic politics by limiting the concentration of capital (see Sellers 1991:325,363).

20. In *Jackson versus Biddle: The Struggle for the Second Bank of the United States* (1949:20).

21. Exceptions to the public benefit rule were those harbingers of mass production, the textile manufacturers. In general, manufacturers did not qualify for protections against risk as did the great infrastructure projects. Where was the risk? If they produced useful items at fair prices, they should prosper—if not, it was their own, not the people's, responsibility. Textile manufacturing (and a few other concerns), however, depended on massive credit to set up tons of machinery before any useful items could be produced. Bankers, often linked to political elites, tended to require incorporation to protect their own investment. (See Licht 1995, Roy 1997, Siskind 2002.)

22. The following account of the trusts is based on a large number of sources, including both recent scholarship and writings contemporary to the trust movement. Most influential have been Chandler (1977), Destler (1944), George (1979 [1879]), Horwitz (1992), Josephson (1934), Livingston (1987), Lloyd (1894), Phillips (1964 [1906]), Roy (1997), Tarbell (1966 [1902–1904]).

23. Using the common trust as a device for pooling corporate stocks was the innovation of Samuel C. T. Dodd, John D. Rockefeller's lawyer (Josephson 1934:277; Licht 1995:141).

24. According to Matthew Josephson, journalist author of the last great trust exposé, *The Robber Barons* (1934), the "industrial combination" was invented by a group of Michigan salt and railroad "barons" who banded together in 1868, took control of salt production, and maintained high prices for many years (1934:115).

Chapter 6. The Remington Success

1. Ilion *Citizen* 2/24/1888:4, 3/23/1888:4.

2. In some trades, anyway, the ability to control output, and thus wages—and thus be able to take time off as need be—was understood as a freedom, not an abuse (cf. Cooper 1987:41).

3. Buttrick (1952) is the classic study.

4. The ILHR holds (in the Remington Arms File) a well-worn, pocket-size booklet from one such benevolent society, entitled *Rules and Regulations of the Mutual Benefit Society of Ringwood's Department of Remington Armory* (dated November 18, 1881). It is my assumption that Ringwood was not alone in offering this benefit.

5. Wilentz calls Carey "economist-in-residence" of the "party of Lincoln" (1984:271), and Foner notes that he was "economic advisor" to Horace Greeley, important Lincoln ally and publisher of the New York *Tribune* (1970:19).

6. Carey saw himself as a true disciple of Adam Smith, whose most important ideas, he believed, the British "classical" political economists had practically repudiated. Indeed, in *The Wealth of Nations* (1776) Smith envisioned a world of local pro-

ducers in which the satisfaction of the community's needs was in the self-interest of each producer. It is high wages or, as Smith put it, the "liberal reward of labor," that "increases the industry of the common people" (Smith 1982 [1776]:184).

7. The characterization is Horace Greeley's from an 1850 editorial (cited in Foner 1970:21).

8. "The Tariff Question," Ilion *Citizen* 5/18/1888:4.

9. Carey fought, in particular, the reasoning of Reverend Thomas Malthus that population tends to outgrow nature's capacity to support it and, thus, that the afflictions of the poor were nature's way of rebalancing population and resources. In Carey's view, just the opposite was true: the greater the population, the greater the productivity of nature (as long as production was "diversified"). Carey's was, arguably, a uniquely New World perspective (Marx 1976 [1866]:705; 1971 [1858]:49). Compared to Europe, where population densities exerted visible pressure on the land, the New World, with its countless "unimproved" acres, sought immigration.

10. This point relies on the painstaking work of Jerrold Swinney in culling these figures for the period 1850–1865 (1987:18, 20, 22).

11. At stake is the ability to load ammunition quickly at the "breech" between the barrel and the stock, rather than the slow process of ramming it down the "muzzle" of the barrel. Breech-loading was not a novel idea—pistols had used it for years—but in larger weapons, dangerous explosions at the breech were frequent occurrences.

12. "Ilion's Honored Dead," Ilion *Citizen* 4/12/1889.

13. The solution, in part, involved the invention of the "QWERTY" keyboard, the credit for which local history gives to the "father of the typewriter," Remington mechanic W. K. Jenne.

Chapter 7. The Remington Failure

1. In 1886 the receivers estimated that some $200,000 to $300,000 in Remington notes was still outstanding from company employees ("Industries of Ilion/Receivers Appointed by the Court," N/D, RS).

2. The "anxious seat" is an interesting metaphor. The phrase comes out of the religious revivals that gave Central New York its nineteenth-century nickname—the "burned-over district," burned by the fires Divine. The "anxious seat," or "anxious bench," was at the front of the congregation, nearest to the preacher, on which sat the most notorious sinners, come at last to repent (Cross 1950).

3. "Death of Philo Remington," Ilion *Citizen* 4/5/1889, from which article also comes the epigraph for this section.

4. This and subsequent quotes are from "Ilion's Honored Dead," Ilion *Citizen* 4/12/1889.

Chapter 8. Cultural Revolution

1. The trusts' threats were carefully tracked in the "Historian's Scrapbooks" of Village Historian Ella Dimock (abbreviated HS; see Appendix 2). Dimock, wife of a toolmaker and amateur historian who worked for both the Armory and the Typewriter, was president of the Ilion Historical Club for many years. Also interesting, though the language is much sweetened, is the history of Ilion industries compiled for the Ilion Centennial of 1952 (Cent52; see Appendix 2).

2. "An Effort Necessary," Ilion *Citizen* 7/6/1888:5.

3. "Our Interests at Stake," Ilion *Citizen* 7/13/1888.

4. From the subscription documents (held at ILHR, Typewriter File), dated July 26, 1888. (See note 5.)

5. I say "at least" because there are two subscription documents, one of two pages, the other of six pages, with identical, typewritten explanatory paragraphs and attached pages of different signatures and amounts pledged. The amounts listed on both of these documents sum to $5,082.00. It is possible that other documents once existed that would raise the number of subscribers and the total amount.

6. DN 4/14/1893:191; "Typewriter Works to Close" UDP 6/29/1909.

7. Ernest Sitts, "It's Been 'Leaving' for 57 Years But It's Still Entrenched in Ilion," Herkimer *Evening Telegram (ET)* 10/20/57.

8. Henry Demarest Lloyd's brilliant exposé, *Wealth Against Commonwealth* (1894), has a very useful Appendix, "A partial list of trade combinations, or trusts, achieved or attempted" by the time his book went to press (pp. 537–544). Some, as he notes, were not successful but "these attempts are repeated again and again until success is reached" (4). The attempt alone, however, could ruin small-scale manufacturers. With masses of capital behind them, the trusts could flood the market with goods priced below the cost of production.

9. "Sold for $200,000: Second Sale of the Remington Property," UDP 3/7/1888.

10. We can glean something of the typewriter trust's workforce, and their view of it, from a well-publicized feature of the new buildings they constructed in 1889. They installed "ten of the best porcelain lined tubs to be had for money," in which "workmen have the privilege of bathing at any time before or after working hours" ("Ilion Board of Trade Held Its First Annual Banquet." UDP n/d 1897, WRS).

11. "Ilion Board of Trade Held Its First Annual Banquet," WRS 1897 (my emphasis). The Ilion Board of Trade was big news from the moment of its debut. No detail of its venues, menus, and speech making was too insignificant to be reported. My major source is the scrapbook of Walter C. Rix (WRS). Rix was the son of an English immigrant mechanic who entered the business of O. B. Rudd, Ilion's largest jeweler, and was a charter member of the Board of Trade. Much of the scrapbook reflects his consuming interests in bicycle racing and in the Remington Jollier's Club, an amateur theatrical group, but every several pages he neatly pasted in long newspaper accounts of the Board's activities.

12. "Ilion Board of Trade Held Its First Annual Banquet" UDP, WRS 1897 (my emphasis). The early newspaper accounts published all speeches in their entirety.

13. "Ilionites Enjoy a Banquet: Board of Trade's Annual Dinner," UDP, WRS 1899 (my emphasis). The quotes from Day and Holmes are also from this source.

14. The Remingtons generously contributed to Syracuse University, founded as a Methodist institution. As Day put it earlier in this speech: "There sits almost within my reach the man who more than any other man founded Syracuse University." He referred to Eliphalet Remington III, the last surviving Remington brother (UDP, WRS 1899).

15. The Remingtons identified with their contractors, as Rev. Elija Horr notes in the epigraph to this section (Ilion *Citizen* 4/12/1889).

16. There is a huge literature on the subject of "scientific management." Harry Braverman (1974), in perhaps the most important single work on the subject, argues, as strikers in the Valley did (below), that capitalists used their power to "degrade" work and subordinate workers. The work of Daniel Nelson (1979, 1980, 1992) follows in this analytical path, adding important ideological and practical detail.

17. "Typewriter Works to Close," UDP 6/29/1909.
18. "An Open Letter. Written by the Father of Typewriters—Full of Good Suggestions," Ilion *News*, 7/1/1909:4. Jenne chose his words carefully, no doubt with trust help. His warning about the folly of enforcing "regulation" upon the company through a strike echoes typical claims to autocracy on the part of factory owners, at the same time it clues the mechanics in on the company's perspective and intractability.
19. "Aligner's Statement," UDP 7/1/1909.
20. "The Strike Is Broken," Ilion *News*, 7/22/1909:5.
21. MCF, Remington Arms Archives; for Tyler's protest see MCF:325–326.
22. "No Change in Ilion Strike," UDP 8/5/1915. The *Press* reported a "misunderstanding between employes [sic] and firm." Evidence is fragmentary for the Ilion mechanics' role in the strike, which consumed the Bridgeport works as well. None of the strikers is quoted in the UDP report, and the official company history pretends that this strike never occurred (Hatch 1956). Bucki (1987) describes the strike from the Bridgeport perspective.
23. The section epigraph is from "Ilion Board of Trade Dinner: Annual Banquet Last Evening," UDP 2/18/1911, WRS. The quotes from Judge O'Connor and W. S. Mackie are also from this source.

Chapter 9. The Gospel of Wealth

1. The coinage took place by way of Carnegie's immediately famous 1889 essay in *North American Review*, entitled "Wealth." In it Carnegie concludes that his prescriptions (discussed below) are, in his opinion "the true Gospel concerning Wealth" (1889:664), and so the piece got nicknamed. When Carnegie republished it in a collection of his essays (1900) he renamed it "The Gospel of Wealth."
2. The idea of evolution had been in the intellectual air for decades before 1859, when Charles Darwin published his careful studies on the continuous adaptation of animal species to their environments. Geologists had shaken up the religious world with estimates of the age of earth that contradicted prevailing interpretations of the Bible, and Spencer had already embarked on his speculations.
3. Carnegie (1920), cited in Hofstadter 1955b:45.
4. Cited in Wiltshire 1978:154–155.
5. It is only fair to note that Carnegie tried to live the benevolent ideals he espoused. In later life he devoted himself to the cause of world peace, spoke out against racism, and donated some two thousand libraries to cities and towns across the United States.
6. This list of Spencer "converts" is drawn from Hofstadter (1955b:44–50).
7. But Justice Holmes, a Spencer convert, dissented to the Supreme Court's order of dissolution against Northern Securities. A great deal has been written on this case. Josephson (1934:442–451) is informative, as is Noyes (1909:346–350). Roosevelt himself (1913) is an interesting source.
8. "Ilion: Acquaintance Trip of the Buffalo Wholesale Business Men, June 4, 1914," ILHR. The booklet is not paginated.
9. According to the 1916 "Funding Agreement" that refinanced the firm's prewar debt (in the Articles of Incorporation Box at Remington Arms Archives), Dodge issued company notes totaling $17,000,000, most of which were held by City Company, a City Bank subsidiary, with Remington Arms UMC preferred stock as collateral. In addition, Dodge was personally indebted to City Company for $9,000,000 and to William Rockefeller for $4,000,000.

10. "Centennial Opens Today," UDP 8/29/1916, WRS.

11. The Remington Centennial Transcript (in the Remington Centennial file at ILHR) consists of three typed carbon copies, bound in the style of the era's legal documents, one bound set for each of the Centennial's three days, to which I refer as RCT1, RCT2, and RCT3. Evidently, the Centennial organizers had secured the services of a stenographer in order to preserve the great moment for posterity. Pages are numbered per speaker, so are not particularly useful, and have not been cited here.

12. "Remington Centennial Interests Whole Mohawk Valley" Utica *Herald-Dispatch* 8/29/1916.

13. "State Day at the Centennial," WRS (probably UDP), 8/31/1916.

14. "Ilion and Herkimer—A Great City of the Future" 11/18/1917, WRS.

15. Mrs. Lester, audiotaped oral history, 1974, Francis Cunningham's history class, Ilion High School, at ILHR.

16. "Scholes Ended Drudgery Says Gov. F. Lowden," 9/12/1923, WRS.

17. "Zoning and Planning Survey for Ilion Is Nearing Completion," UDP 1/19/1925, ZCF.

18. "Manager of Ilion Chamber Replies to Insinuations of H.A. House in Recent Letter," UDP 5/7/1926.

19. "City Planning and Zones Eliminate Property Loss, Says Committee in Ilion," 1/30/1926, ZCF.

20. "Zoning and Planning Are Explained for Benefit of Property Owners of Ilion," 4/19/1926, ZCF.

21. "Band Music and Boxing Are Foremen's Dinner Features," 4/22/1926, ZCF.

22. "Zoning Questionnaires Will Be Sent Out In Ilion," OD 4/23/26, ZCF.

23. "Comment Favorable to Zoning Ordinance," 4/25/1926 ZCF.

24. "Ilion Taxpayers to Cast Vote Saturday," UDP 4/28/1926, ZCF.

25. "House Doubts Enforcement of Zone Plan," OD 4/30/1926; "Questions Wisdom of Ilion's Zoning Plan," UDP 5/1/1926, both in ZCF.

26. "Ilion Voters Beat Zoning Project by 566 Ballots to 231," OD 5/2/26, ZCF.

27. "Ilion Taxpayers Defeat Zoning by Big Majority," UDP 5/3/26, ZCF.

Chapter 10. Learning to Expect Hard Times

1. The cassette tapes are in the ILHR collection.

2. Booklet at ILHR. I thank Elaine Griswold for bringing it to my attention.

3. In the early 1920s James H. Rand Jr. aggressively expanded from the base of his family's Rand Ledger Company in North Tonawanda, New York (near Buffalo), to dominate national production of office products. In 1927 Rand's American Kardex Company acquired Remington Typewriter Company—the resulting corporation, Remington Rand, Inc., eventually operated twenty factories in nine towns across the Northeast (Kolopsky 1986).

4. Herkimer *Evening Telegram* (ET) 5/12/1934, TS34. My major source for the Typewriter strikes is the Typewriter Strike scrapbooks (TS), a huge compilation of strike-related clippings from newspapers around the country between 1934 and 1948, referenced by "TS" and the year. The ILHR holds a photocopy in its Typewriter Strike files. The original, evidently, had been kept by a local union official.

5. ET 5/19/1934, TS34.

6. "Moves Behind Scenes In Strike Told By Ilion Mayor," 11/13/1936, TS36.

7. "Rand Workers May Ballot to Fix Bargaining Agency As Court Upholds NLRB," 2/15/1938, TS38.

8. "Rands 'Mohawk Valley Formula' for Breaking Strikes," 3/22/1937, TS36.

9. It moved most typewriter departments out of the Valley and moved in, from Norwood, Ohio, the manufacture of tabulating machines (Herkimer County Historical Society 1992:185, and see Kolopsky 1986).

10. The historian is probably Mrs. Ella Dimock, then president of the Ilion Historical Club (scrapbook at ILHR).

11. "Remington Through the Years," UDP n/d 1946, ILHR Remington Arms file, my emphasis.

12. The UE may have been in Ilion as early as 1941. This was the year that they successfully organized the Rand factories in Tonawanda, New York (Kolopsky 1986). The first evidence of UE organizing in the ILHR files is the fourteenth number of the *UE-CIO Rem Rambler* (dated 3/30/1945), "published by Remington Rand Organizing Committee, UE-CIO," which had taken offices in the Capitol Theater building. By the spring of 1947 Ilion hosted two thriving UE locals.

13. *UE News* IX(27):7, 7/5/1947; "Strike Ties Up Six Upstate Rem Rand Plants," LFT, 6/18/47.

14. "Strike Leader Scores Secret Negotiations," 7/2/47 TS47, my emphasis.

15. "Union Criticizes Rand for Vacation Pay Policy," OD 6/25/47, TS47.

16. The CIO's organizing success was in large part a product of its organizers' skills in linking its labor agenda to popular patriotic symbols, such as Washington, Lincoln, Uncle Sam, and Thanksgiving. Strategists called it "the popular front." My research suggests that for many working people the "labor agenda," in the broadest sense, was already encoded in key patriotic symbols—the corporate cultural campaign, in other words, was not as successful as many scholars believe in emptying them of their original content. See Cohen (1990), Fones-Wolf (1994), Gerstle (1989).

17. *UE News* IX:27. 7/5/1947:6–7, TS47.

18. *Ibid.*

19. I draw on four accounts from testimony at the subsequent trial (all in TS47): "Highlights of Back-to-Work Move That Failed at Plant 1" (7/14/1947); "Counsel Clash as O'Connor Flag Trial Continues" (OD 7/23/1947); "O'Connor Cleared; Says Majority Want To Go Back to Work" (OD 7/24/1947); and "Week's Events Climaxed by 2–Day O'Connor Trial" (Ilion *Sentinel* 7/24/1947).

20. "Plant 1 Will Be Reopened for Norwalk, Tonawanda Work," *Sentinel* 4/3/1952:1.

21. E. Sitts, "'The Typewriter's Reward," ET 6/9/1957.

22. The idea of stabilizing work schedules was prominent in the rhetoric of 1920s "welfare capitalism," but only thirteen companies actually tried out plans for a guaranteed work year, and none of these plans survived the Depression (Brody 1980:71). For many Remington Arms workers, the work year had begun in late summer and ended at Christmas (Baum 1991).

23. Speech to the 53rd Annual Congress of American Industries, entitled "Industry as a Good Neighbor," 12/1/1948, cited in Fones-Wolf (1994:177).

24. 1950, cited in Fones-Wolf (1994:170).

25. Production groups, I am told, developed a keen look-out system. At the first glimpse of the "scientific managers," word passed quickly through the shops to slow down. If you didn't get the word, your competence, in effect, would be penalized.

26. A Saturday night Centennial Dinner was the occasion for the single reference to McCarthyism in the ILHR data. Corporate managers and local notables were

treated to the rabid anti-Communism of Cold Warrior, and wartime director of the Manhattan Project, General Leslie Groves, who attacked the United Nations and warned of an impending world war between the forces of freedom and the global Communist menace ("Groves Charges 'Fumbling' in Waging of War in Korea" OD 6/29/52).

27. "Practical Steps in the Planning of a Successful Centennial Celebration" by Genevieve E. Swarthout, *The American City*, October 1952:100–102 (ellipses in the original).

28. "Ilion to Become Great Electronics Center," OD 11/12/1952, HS.

29. H. Whittemore, "Ilion to Lose Famed 'Typewriter' Sign," OD 9/26/1956:1.

30. "It's Been 'Leaving' for 57 Years But It's Still Entrenched in Ilion," E. Sitts, ET 10/20/1957.

31. Rand/UNIVAC local employment figures are hard to come by. A lot of the work was not full-time, and the company left the Valley over an agonizingly long period of time. Four thousand were more or less steadily employed at the time of the 1952 Ilion Centennial. In the five or six years during which Rand brought electronics manufacture to the Village, employment was locally estimated to increase by two thousand. At its peak the corporation operated three huge factories in Ilion. Six thousand is probably too conservative; seven thousand is the confident estimate of the former official who was mayor during this period.

32. H. Whittemore, "Shortcut to Jimmie Rand's," ET 8/15/1976.

33. The Federal Housing Act of 1949 laid the foundations for federal Urban Renewal grants, but the idea was so unpopular that even where "redevelopment" was aggressively pursued by a coherent political elite, as in Robert Dahl's well-known study of New Haven (Connecticut), it took the better part of a decade for local elites to line up sufficient strength to actually begin demolition (1961:119–122).

34. "Many Buildings in Ilion 'Substandard,' Agency Hears," OD 5/12/1966, HS.

35. "Public UR Referendum Urged by Ilion Group," OD 11/22/1966, HS.

36. "Funds Available, UR Parley Told," OD 11/16/1966, HS.

37. "Public UR Referendum Urged by Ilion Group," OD 11/22/1966, HS.

38. "Main St. Closing Key to Arms Co. Expansion," OD 1/6/1967, HS.

39. The DAR's National Defense Committee published a strongly worded indictment of the whole UR scheme, *Urban Renewal—Its Failures and Follies*, that rapidly circulated through the Valley ("DAR Votes to Release Anti-Renewal Books," 6/11/1966, HS).

40. What counts as a business? I included all retailers, banks, contractors, manufacturers, and such service providers as barber and beauty shops, cleaners, funeral parlors, repair shops, car washes, child care, pet care, etc. I excluded in all years, apartment houses, trailer parks, and professional offices.

41. "Mayor Seeks Resident Investment in Ilion Urban Renewal," OD 8/12/1976, HS.

Chapter 11. Wealth against Commonwealth

1. Each August the Herkimer *Evening Telegram*, the paper of record for the county, runs a legal notice, "Lands in Herkimer County to be Sold for Arrears of Taxes," listing properties on which state, county, local, and/or school taxes have not been fully paid. It is a long list. In 1993 and 1994 county residents could not (or did not) pay all of their tax assessment on nearly 2,000 properties (ET 8/11/93; ET 8/10/94)—in a county with a population of only 65,000.

2. As the U.S. Bureau of the Census explains, the authorities "exist as separate legal entities with substantial administrative and fiscal independence from general purpose governments" (cited in Axelrod 1992:13). The authorities enjoy the powers of government, in that they can issue tax-exempt bonds and exercise eminent domain (i.e., they can take private property for their projects), but they are free of its public accountability.

3. "The American dream" first occurs in print in Adams's book, according to the lexicographers of the *Oxford English Dictionary* (on-line).

4. Neither of these historians speculates on the source of today's Alger myth, but further research would likely turn up a charismatic writer or public speaker who capitalized on Alger's name to make points that had no place in Alger's moral universe.

5. I found little direct evidence of socialist influence in the Valley's historical collections, though there appears to have been indirect influence. The Board of Trade's 1911 rebellion against the trusts coincided with a most interesting development down the Canal, Schenectady's election in 1911 of a Socialist mayor, eight aldermen, and a state assemblyman (Salvatore 1982:241).

Appendix 1. Theoretical and Methodological Orientations

1. These popular sources were the "ten-cent magazines" of the late nineteenth and early twentieth centuries, notably *Cosmopolitan* and *McClures, The Nation, Work of the World, The United Mineworkers Journal*, the fascinating collection of ephemera in the John Mitchell Papers (Tamiment Institute, New York), and numerous newspapers.

2. The professional historians I have most relied on are: Appleby (1984, 1992), Blumin (1989), Cross (1950), Dorfman (1934), Faler (1981), Fink (1983), Foner (1970), Gerstle (1989), Ginger (1949), Goodwyn (1976), Gutman (1963, 1966, 1976), Johnson (1978), Katz, Doucet, and Stern (1982), Lazerow (1995), Licht (1995), Ryan (1981), Trachtenberg (1982), and Wilentz (1984).

3. In the 1970s, spurred by the flurry of history-making that preceded the 1976 U.S. Bicentennial, a group of local people, calling themselves the Friends of the Library put a great deal of effort into organizing the collection ("Volunteers Identify Material at Library" ET 11/12/73:3).

4. In Appendix 2 I list the abbreviations that I use to refer to the materials in the ILHR collection.

5. The collection is ordered by categories; e.g., Ilion Clubs, Ilion Government, Ilion History, Herkimer County, Remington Arms, Remington Typewriter, with parallel categories for photographs. Interestingly, within the categories, all time is compacted into a single "pastness"—dates and periods were not a part of the organizational scheme. I date-ordered much of the material I worked with during my tenure as village historian.

6. It should be noted that Scott explicitly disclaims use of this distinction in contexts of the "impersonal, 'scientific,' disciplinary forms of the modern state" (1990:62). A key text for his formulation, however, explicitly argues the significance of this kind of distinction: There is little evidence, it notes, "for the ideological incorporation of the working class" into "bourgeois ideology" (Abercrombie et al. 1980).

7. For earlier, and related, approaches to regional analysis in anthropology, see Skinner (1964–1965), Smith (1976a,b), Verdery (1976). See Lomnitz-Adler (2001) for a penetrating and sensitive demonstration of this approach.

8. In implicit recognition of these difficulties, for the last couple of decades most ethnographic studies in the United States have been what Louise and George Spindler call "limited context studies"—"microscopic" rather than "holistic" (1983:55–56).

9. This may be less salient for the more recent, more rationalized borders—in the United States this means more westerly borders—that were laid out by urban planners (or their predecessors, the railroad agents). It remains to be investigated, but it is theoretically predictable that at least one edifying Them/Us tale has accreted around any political border. Fargo, North Dakota, for example, is urban to its own hinterlands, but it constructs itself as more "wholesome" and "moral" in contrast to the metropolitan centers east and west of it (Ginsburg 1989).

10. My historical sources for this regionalization are: Katz, Doucet, and Stern (1982), an important social historical study that focuses on Buffalo and Hamilton, Ontario, Canada; Johnson (1978) a groundbreaking social history of morality and commerce in Buffalo; and Zunz (1982), a brilliantly spatialized social history of Detroit. My apologies to other scholars who may have proposed such a regionalization outside the scope of my reading.

11. As Horace Greeley put it (cited in Foner 1970:19).

12. See Livingston 1994:73–74.

13. This formula, C-M-C, refers to the production of a commodity (C), to be sold for money (M), in order to purchase another commodity (C) (Marx 1976 [1866], chap. 4). This is the producers' perspective. The Remington shops, arguably, were not "real" capitalism in Marx's sense. They were what he called a "formal subsumption of labor under capital"; that is, the Remingtons oversaw but did not reorganize the mechanics, who were paid for what they produced, not for their labor per se ("Results of the Immediate Process of Production," appendix to Marx 1976 [1866]:941–1084).

14. This formula, M-C-M', refers to the capitalists' perspective: money (M) is applied to the production of commodities (C) in order to sell them for more money (M'). This formula can be abbreviated, in the capitalists' view, as M-M'—money "works" to make more money; that is, capital is magically productive.

References

Abercrombie, Nicholas, Steven Hill, and Bryan S. Turner. 1980. *The Domi-nant Ideology Thesis.* London: G. Allen & Unwin.

Adams, James Truslow. 1931. *The Epic of America.* New York: Blue Ribbon Press.

Adorno, Teodor (and other authors). 1950. *The Authoritarian Personality.* New York: Harpers.

Appleby, Joyce. 1984. *Capitalism and a New Social Order: The Republican Vision of the 1790s.* New York: New York University Press.

——. 1992. *Liberalism and Republicanism in the Historical Imagination.* Cambridge: Harvard University Press.

Arensberg, Conrad. 1955. "American Communities." *American Anthropolo-gist* 57:1143–1162.

——. 1961. "Community as Object and Sample." *American Anthropologist* 63:240–264.

Axlerod, Donald. 1992. *Shadow Government: The Hidden World of Public Authorities—And How They Control Over $1 Trillion of Your Money.* New York: John Wiley & Sons.

Bailey, Russell D., & Assoc. 1965. *The Master Plan: Village of Ilion, NY.* Utica: Bailey & Assoc.

Baum, Louis. 1991. Memories . . . 45th Annual Homecoming. *Remington Ac-tion* (August) No. 405 (company newsletter; pages not numbered).

Beers, F. W., et al. 1879. *History of Herkimer County, N.Y. with Illustrations . . . , etc.* New York: F. W. Beers and Co.

Beidelman, Thomas O. 1993. *Moral Imagination in Kaguru Modes of Thought.* Washington, D.C.: Smithsonian Institution Press.

Bell, Daniel. 1973. *The Coming of Post-Industrial Society: A Venture in So-cial Forecasting.* New York: Basic.

——, ed. 1971 [1955, 1963]. *The Radical Right: The New American Right, Ex-panded and Updated.* Freeport, N.Y.: Books for Libraries Press.

Benton, Nathaniel S. 1856. *History of Herkimer County, Including the Upper Mohawk Valley, from the Earliest Period to the Present Time.* Albany: J. Munsell.

Blu, Karen I. 1980. *The Lumbee Problem: The Making of an American Indian People.* Cambridge: Cambridge University Press.

Bluestone, Barry. 1984. "Is Deindustrialization a Myth? Capital Mobility ver-sus Absorption Capacity in the U.S. Economy." *Annals of the American Academy of Political and Social Science* 475(September):39–51.

Bluestone, Barry, and Bennet Harrison. 1982. *The De-industrialization of America: Plant Closings, Community Abandonment, and the Dismantling of Basic Industry*. New York: Basic.

Blumin, Stuart M. 1989. *The Emergence of the Middle Class: Social Experience in an American City, 1760–1900*. Cambridge: Cambridge University Press.

Bourdieu, Pierre. 1977. *Outline of a Theory of Practice*. Richard Nice, trans. Cambridge: Cambridge University Press.

———. 1990. *The Logic of Practice*. Richard Nice, trans. Stanford: Stanford University Press.

Bozon, Michel, and Anne-Marie Thiesse. 1986. "The Collapse of Memory: The Case of Farm Workers (French Vexin, pays de France)." In *Between Memory and History*. Marie Noelle Bourguet, Lucette Valensi, and Nathan Wachtel, eds. Pp. 237–260. London: Harwood.

Braverman, Harry. 1974. *Labor and Monopoly Capitalism: The Degradation of Work in the Twentieth Century*. New York: Monthly Review Press.

Brody, David. 1980. *Workers in Industrial America: Essays on the 20th Century Struggle*. Oxford: Oxford University Press.

Bryan, William Jennings. 1913. *The Speeches of William Jennings Bryan*. Vol. 1. New York: Funk & Wagnalls.

Bucki, Cecilia. 1987. "Dilution and Craft Tradition: Munitions Workers in Bridgeport, Connecticut, 1915–1919." In *The New England Working Class and the New Labor History*. Herbert G. Gutman and Donald H. Bell, eds. Pp. 137–156. Urbana: University of Illinois Press.

Buttrick, John. 1952. "The Inside Contract System." *Journal of Economic History* 12:205–221.

Carey, Henry C. 1856. "How to Increase Competition for the Purchase of Labour and . . . Raise the Wages of the Laborer." In *Works of H. C. Carey*. Vol. I. New York: Myron Finch.

———. 1858. *Principles of Social Science*. Vol. 1. Philadelphia: Lippincott.

Carnegie, Andrew. 1889. "Wealth." *North American Review* CCCXCL (391):653–664.

———. 1900a. "The Gospel of Wealth." In *The Gospel of Wealth and Other Timely Essays*. Pp. 1–19. New York: The Century Co.

———. 1900b. "Popular Illusions About the Trusts." In *The Gospel of Wealth and Other Timely Essays*. Pp. 85–103. New York: The Century Co.

———. 1920. *Personal Recollections of Andrew Carnegie*. New York: Fleming H. Revell Co.

Cawelti, John G. 1965. *Apostles of the Self-Made Man*. Chicago: University of Chicago Press.

Chandler, Alfred D., Jr. 1972. "Anthracite Coal and the Beginnings of the Industrial Revolution in the United States." *Business History Review* 46:141–181.

———. 1977. *The Visible Hand: The Managerial Revolution in American Business*. Cambridge: Harvard University Press.

Cohen, Lizabeth. 1990. *Making a New Deal: Industrial Workers in Chicago, 1919–1939*. Cambridge: Cambridge University Press.

Coke, Edward, I. C. 1647. "Against Monopolies, Propounders, and Projectors." In *The Third Part of the Institutes of the Laws of England: Concerning High Treason, and Other Pleas of the Crown, and Criminall Causes*. Pp. 181–185. London: M. Flesher.

Connerton, Paul. 1989. *How Societies Remember*. Cambridge: Cambridge University Press.

Cooper, Patricia A. 1987. *Once a Cigar Maker: Men, Women, and Work Culture in American Cigar Factories, 1900–1919*. Urbana: University of Illinois Press.

Cornell, Robert J. 1957. *The Anthracite Coal Strike of 1902*. Washington, D.C.: The Catholic University of America.

Cross, Whitney R. 1950. *The Burned-over District: The Social and Intellectual History of Enthusiastic Religion in Western New York, 1800–1850*. Ithaca: Cornell University Press.

Dahl, Robert A. 1961. *Who Governs? Democracy and Power in an American City*. New Haven: Yale University Press.

Darwin, Charles. 1859. *On the Origin of Species by Natural Selection: Or the Preservation of Favoured Races in the Struggle for Life*. London: John Murray.

Davies, Edward J. II. 1985. *The Anthracite Aristocracy: Leadership and Social Change in the Hard Coal Regions of Northeastern Pennsylvania, 1800–1930*. DeKalb: Northern Illinois University Press.

Debouzy, Marianne. 1986. "In Search of Working Class Memory: Some Questions and a Tentative Assessment." In *Between Memory and History*. Marie Noelle Bourguet, Lucette Valensi, and Nathan Wachtel, eds. Pp. 261–282. London: Harwood.

Dembowski, Frederick. 1994. "1995–2000: An Enrollment Forecast and Demographic Analysis Study." Report prepared for the Ilion Central School District, December 1994.

De Roover, Raymond. 1951. "Monopoly Theory Prior to Adam Smith: A Revision." *Quarterly Journal of Economics* 65(4):492–524.

Destler, Chester McArthur. 1944. "Wealth against Commonwealth, 1894 and 1944." *American History Review* 50(1):49–72.

Di Leonardo, Micaela. 1984. *The Varieties of the Ethnic Experience: Kinship, Class, and Gender among California Italian-Americans*. Ithaca: Cornell University Press.

——. 1985. "Deindustrialization as a Folk Model." *Urban Anthropology* 14(1–3):237–257.

——. 1987. "The Female World of Cards and Holidays: Women, Families, and the Work of Kinship." *Signs* 12:440–453.

Diss, C. J.. 1935. *Controlled Capitalism: A Cure and Prevention of Depressions*. Ilion, N.Y.: Chas. G. Squire.

Dorfman, Joseph. 1934. *Thorstein Veblen and His America*. New York: Viking.

Doukas, Dimitra. 1997. "Corporate Capitalism on Trial: The Hearings of the Anthracite Coal Strike Commission, 1902–1903. *Identities* 3(3):371–401.

Ehrenreich, Barbara. 1989. *Fear of Falling: The Inner Life of the Middle Class*. New York: HarperCollins.

Fajans, Jane. 1997. *They Make Themselves: Work and Play among the Bain-
ing of Papua New Guinea.* Chicago: University of Chicago Press.

Faler, Paul G. 1981. *Mechanics and Manufacturers in the Early Industrial
Revolution: Lynn Massachusetts 1780–1860.* Albany: SUNY Press.

Fink, Leon. 1983. *Workingmen's Democracy: The Knights of Labor and American Politics.* Urbana: University of Illinois Press.

Fish, Carl Russell. 1929. *The Rise of the Common Man, 1830–1850. Vol. 6 of
A History of American Life.* New York: Macmillan.

Foner, Eric. 1970. *Free Soil, Free Labor, Free Men: The Ideology of the Republican Party before the Civil War.* New York: Oxford University Press.

Foner, Phillip. 1947–1994. *The Politics and Practices of the American Federation of Labor, 1900–1909.* Vol. 3 of *A History of the Labor Movement in
the United States.* 4 vols. New York: International Press.

Fones-Wolf, Elizabeth A. 1994. *Selling Free Enterprise: The Business Assault
on Labor and Liberalism, 1945–1960.* Urbana: University of Illinois Press.

Fox, Richard Wrightman, and T. J. Jackson Lears, eds. 1983. *The Culture of
Consumption: Critical Essays in American History, 1880–1980.* New York:
Pantheon Books.

Frankenberg, Ruth. 1993. *White Women, Race Matters: The Social Construction of Whiteness.* Minneapolis: University of Minnesota Press.

Franz, Eleanor Waterbury. 1987. "Memories of the Revolutionary War: Interviews with the Late Emma Timmerman Recapture the Way of Life of Be-
leagured Palatines." *Legacy* 2(2):3–6.

Galbraith, John Kenneth. 1960. *The Affluent Society.* Cambridge, Mass.: The
Riverside Press.

Gans, Herbert J. 1991. *Middle American Individualism: The Future of Liberal
Democracy.* New York: Oxford University Press.

Geertz, Clifford. 1972. *The Interpretation of Cultures.* New York: Basic Books.

———. 1980. *Negara: The Theater State in Nineteenth-Century Bali.* Princeton:
Princeton University Press.

George, Henry. 1979 [1879]. *Progress and Poverty: An Inquiry into the Cause
of Industrial Depressions and of Increase of Want with Increase of Wealth
. . .* New York: Robert Schalkenbach Foundation.

Gerstle, Gary. 1989. *Working-class Americanism: The Politics of Labor in a
Textile City, 1914–1960.* Cambridge: Cambridge University Press.

Ginger, Ray. 1949. *The Bending Cross: A Biography of Eugene Victor Debs.*
New Brunswick, NJ: Rutgers University Press.

Ginsburg, Faye D. 1989. *Contested Lives: The Abortion Debate in an American Community.* Berkeley: University of California Press.

———. 1993. "The Case of Mistaken Identity: Problems in Representing
Women on the Right." In *When They Read What We Write: The Politics of
Ethnography.* Caroline B. Brettell, ed. Pp. 163–176. Westport, Conn.: Bergin
& Garvey.

Goldschmidt, Walter. 1978. *As You Sow: Three Studies in the Social Consequences of Agribusiness.* Montclair, N.J.: Allanheld, Osmun.

Goodwyn, Lawrence. 1976. *Democratic Promise: The Populist Moment in
America.* New York: Oxford University Press.

Greene, Nelson. 1925. *History of the Mohawk Valley; Gateway to the West, 1614–1925.* 4 vols. Chicago: S.J. Clarke.

Greenhouse, Carol J. 1986. *Praying for Justice: Faith, Order, and Community in an American Town.* Ithaca: Cornell University Press.

Gregory, Steven. 1998. *Black Corona: Race and the Politics of Place in an Urban Community.* Princeton: Princeton University Press.

Grimstead, David. 1971. "Melodrama as Echo of the Historically Voiceless." In *Anonymous Americans: Explorations in Nineteenth-Century Social History.* Tamara K. Hareven, ed. Pp. 80–98. Englewood Cliffs, N.J.: Prentice-Hall.

Gudeman, Stephen. 2001. *The Anthropology of Economy: Community, Market, Culture.* Oxford (UK): Blackwell.

Gutman, Herbert G. 1963. "The Worker's Search for Power: Labor in the Gilded Age." In *The Gilded Age: A Reappraisal.* H. Wayne Morgan, ed. Pp. 38–68. Syracuse: Syracuse University Press.

——. 1966. "Protestantism and the American Labor Movement: The Christian Spirit in the Gilded Age." *American Historical Review* 72:74–101.

——. 1976. *Work, Culture, and Society in Industrializing America.* New York: Alfred A. Knopf.

Hamilton, Richard F. 1996. "The Lower-Middle-Class Thesis." In *The Social Misconstruction of Reality: Validity and Verification in the Scholarly Community.* Pp. 146–170. New Haven: Yale University Press.

Hardin, George A., and Frank H. Willard. 1893. *History of Herkimer County, New York: Illustrated with Portraits of Many of Its Citizens.* Syracuse: D. Mason.

Herkimer County Historical Society (HCHS). 1992. *Herkimer County at 200.* Herkimer, N.Y.: HCHS.

Hatch, Alden. 1956. *Remington Arms in American History.* New York: Rinehart.

Hill, Christopher. 1964. *Puritanism and Revolution: Studies in Interpretation of the English Revolution of the 17th Century.* New York: Schocken Books.

Hofstadter, Richard. 1955a. *The Age of Reform: From Bryan to F.D.R.* New York: Vintage Books.

——. 1955b [1944]. *Social Darwinism in American Thought.* Boston: Beacon Press.

Horowitz, Daniel. 1992. *The Morality of Spending: Attitudes toward the Consumer Society in America, 1875–1940.* Chicago: Ivan R. Dee.

Horwitz, Morton J. 1992. *The Transformation of American Law, 1870–1960: The Crisis of Legal Orthodoxy.* New York: Oxford University Press.

Jackson, Andrew. 1949 [1832]. "Veto Message." In *Jackson versus Biddle: The Struggle for the Second Bank of the United States.* Boston: D.C. Heath.

Jefferson, Thomas. 1944. *The Life and Selected Writings of Thomas Jefferson.* Adrienne Koch and William Peden, eds. New York: Modern Library.

Johnson, Paul E. 1978. *A Shopkeeper's Millennium: Society and Revivals in Rochester, New York, 1815–1837.* New York: Hill and Wang.

Josephson, Matthew. 1934. *The Robber Barons: The Great American Capitalists, 1861–1901.* New York: Harcourt, Brace.

Katz, Michael B., Michael J. Doucet, and Mark J. Stern. 1982. *The Social Organization of Early Industrial Capitalism.* Cambridge: Harvard University Press.

Kazin, Michael. 1995. *The Populist Persuasion: An American History.* New York: Basic Books.

Kimball, Solon. 1955. "Problems of Studying American Culture." *American Anthropologist* 57:1131–1142.

Kolopsky, Marc Steven. 1986. "Remington Rand Workers in the Tonawandas of Western New York, 1927–1956: A History of the Mohawk Valley Formula." Ph.D. diss., University of New York at Buffalo.

Korten, David C. 2001. *When Corporations Rule the World.* Bloomfield, Conn.: Kumarian Press.

Krasniewicz, Louise. 1992. *Nuclear Summer: The Clash of Communities at the Seneca Women's Peace Encampment.* Ithaca: Cornell University Press.

Lamphere, Louise. 1986. "From Working Daughters to Working Mothers: Production and Reproduction in an Industrial Community." *American Ethnologist* 12:118–130.

Lazerow, Jama. 1995. *Religion and the Working Class in Antebellum America.* Washington, D.C.: Smithsonian Institution Press.

Lears, T. J. Jackson. 1994. *No Place of Grace: Antimodernism and the Transformation of American Culture, 1880–1920.* Chicago: University of Chicago Press.

Leggett, William. 1984 [1832]. "The Corporation Question." In *Democratic Editorials: Essays in Jacksonian Political Economy.* Lawrence H. White, ed. Indianapolis: Liberty Press.

Licht, Walter. 1995. *Industrializing America: The Nineteenth Century.* Baltimore: Johns Hopkins University Press.

Lipset, Seymour Martin. 1959. "Democracy and Working-Class Authoritarianism." *American Sociological Review* 24:482–501.

Livingston, James. 1987. "The Social Analysis of Economic History and Theory: Conjectures on Late-Nineteenth-Century American Development." *American Historical Review* 92:69–95.

——. 1994. *Pragmatism and the Political Economy of Cultural Revolution, 1850–1940.* Chapel Hill: University of North Carolina Press.

Lloyd, Henry Demarest. 1894. *Wealth Against Commonwealth.* New York: Harper & Brothers.

Lomnitz-Adler, Claudio. 1992. *Exits from the Labyrinth: Culture and Ideology in Mexican National Space.* Berkeley: University of California Press.

——. 2001. *Deep Mexico, Silent Mexico: Nationalism and the Public Sphere.* Minneapolis: University of Minnesota Press.

Lynd, Robert S., and Helen Merrell Lynd. 1957 [1929]. *Middletown: A Study in Modern American Culture.* New York: Harcourt, Brace, Jovanovich.

——. 1937. *Middletown in Transition: A Study in Cultural Conflicts.* New York: Harcourt, Brace.

Maier, Pauline. 1993. "The Revolutionary Origins of the American Corporation." *William and Mary Quarterly* 50:51–84.

Marcus, George, and Michael M. J. Fisher. 1986. *Anthropology as Cultural*

Critique: An Experimental Moment in the Human Sciences. Chicago: University of Chicago Press.

Marx, Karl. 1971 [1858]. "Critique of Bastiat and Carey." In *Grundrisse*. David McLellan, ed. and trans. Pp. 47–58. New York: Harper and Row.

———. 1976 [1866]. *Capital: A Critique of Political Economy*. Ben Fowkes, trans. New York: Vintage Books.

Mauss, Marcel. 1967 [1925]. *The Gift: Forms and Functions of Exchange in Archaic Societies*. New York: W.W. Norton.

McClure's Magazine Editors. 1902. "Miss Tarbell's History of the Standard Oil Company: Editorial Announcement." *McClure's Magazine* 19(6):588–592.

Moffatt, Michael. 1992. "Ethnographic Writing about American Culture." *Annual Review of Anthropology* 21:205–229.

Moore, Sally Falk. 1987. "Explaining the Present: Theoretical Dilemmas in Processual Ethnography." *American Ethnologist* 14:727–736.

Myers, Fred R. 1988. "Locating Ethnographic Practice: Romance, Reality, and Politics in the Outback." *American Ethnologist* 15:609–624.

Nash, June. 1981. "Ethnographic Aspects of the World Capitalist System." *Annual Review of Anthropology* 10:393–423.

———. 1989. *From Tank Town to High Tech: The Clash of Community and Industrial Cycles*. Albany: SUNY Press.

Nash, June, and M. Patricia Fernandez-Kelly. 1983. *Women, Men, and the International Division of Labor*. Albany: SUNY.

Nelson, Daniel. 1975. *Managers and Workers: Origins of the New Factory System in the United States, 1880–1900*. Madison: University of Wisconsin Press.

———. 1980. *Frederick W. Taylor and the Rise of Scientific Management*. Madison: University of Wisconsin Press.

———, ed. 1992. *A Mental Revolution: Scientific Management since Taylor*. Columbus: Ohio State University Press.

Newman, Katherine. 1985. Turning Your Back on Tradition: Symbolic Analysis and Moral Critique in a Plant Shutdown. *Urban Anthropology* 14(1–3):109–150.

Noyes, Alexander Dana. 1909. *Forty Years of American Finance*. New York: G. P. Putnam's Sons.

Ong, Aihwa. 1991. "The Gender and Labor Politics of Postmodernity." *Annual Review of Anthropology* 20:279–309.

Pappas, Gregory. 1989. *The Magic City: Unemployment in a Working-Class Community*. Ithaca: Cornell University Press.

Parker, Louis C. III. n/d. "Parker Management and Workers, Their Lives and Times at the Gun Works." Manuscript in author's collection.

Peacock, James L., and Ruel W. Tyson Jr. 1989. *Pilgrims of Paradox: Calvinism and Experience among the Primitive Baptists of the Blue Ridge*. Washington, D.C.: Smithsonian Institution Press.

Peterson, Harold L. 1966. *The Remington Historical Treasury of American Guns*. New York: Ridge Press.

Phillips, David Graham. 1964 [1906]. *The Treason of the Senate*. Chicago: Quadrangle Books.

Piven, Frances Fox, and Richard A. Cloward. 1988. *Why Americans Don't Vote.* New York: Pantheon Books.

Plotkin, Sidney. 1990. "Enclave Consciousness and Neighborhood Activism." In *Dilemmas of Activism.* Joseph M. Kling and Prudence S. Posner, eds. Pp. 219–239. Philadelphia: Temple University Press.

Polanyi, Karl. 1944. *The Great Transformation.* New York: Rinehart.

Pound, Arthur, and Richard E. Day. 1930. *Johnson of the Mohawks: A Biography of Sir William Johnson, Irish immigrant, Mohawk War Chief, American Soldier, Empire Builder.* New York: Macmillan.

Rapp, Rayna. 1982. "Family and Class in Contemporary America: Notes Toward an Understanding of Ideology." In *Rethinking the Family: Some Feminist Questions.* Barrie Thorne and Marilyn Yalom, eds. Pp. 168–187. London: Longmans.

Riesman, David, and Nathan Glazer. 1952. *Faces in the Crowd: Individual Studies in Character and Politics.* New Haven: Yale University Press.

Roediger, David. 1991. *The Wages of Whiteness.* London: Verso.

Rogers, Daniel T. 1998. *Atlantic Crossings: Social Politics in a Progressive Age.* Cambridge: Harvard University Press.

Roosevelt, Theodore. 1913. *Theodore Roosevelt: An Autobiography.* New York: Charles Scribner's Sons.

Roseberry, William. 1988. "Political Economy." *Annual Review of Anthropology* 17:161–185.

Roy, William G. 1997. *Socializing Capital: The Rise of the Large Industrial Corporation in America.* Princeton: Princeton University Press.

Russell, Albert N. 1897. "Ilion and the Remingtons: An Address by Albert N. Russell of Ilion." Delivered before the Herkimer County Historical Society, Sept. 14, 1897. Typescript in author's collection.

Ryan, Mary P. 1981. *Cradle of the Middle Class: The Family in Oneida County, New York, 1790–1865.* Cambridge: Cambridge University Press.

Ryerson, Richard Alan. 1976. *"The Revolution is Now Begun": The Radical Committees of Philadelphia, 1765–1776.* Philadelphia: University of Pennsylvania Press.

Salvatore, Nick. 1982. *Eugene V. Debs: Citizen and Socialist.* Urbana: University of Illinois Press.

Sangren, P. Steven. 2000. *Chinese Sociologics: An Anthropological Account of the Role of Alienation in Social Reproduction.* London: Athlone Press.

Scott, James C. 1990. *Domination and the Arts of Resistance: Hidden Transcripts.* New Haven: Yale University Press.

Sellers, Charles G. 1991. *The Market Revolution: Jacksonian America, 1815–1846.* New York: Oxford University Press.

Siskind, Janet. 2002. *Rum and Axes: The Rise of a Connecticut Merchant Family, 1795–1850.* Ithaca: Cornell University Press.

Skinner, G. William. 1964–1965. "Marketing and Social Structure in Rural China." *Journal of Asian Studies* 24:3–43, 195–228.

Smith, Adam. 1982 [1776]. *The Wealth of Nations.* Books I–III. Andrew Skinner, ed. Harmondsworth: Penguin.

Smith, Carol A. 1976a. "Regional Economic Systems: Linking Geographic

Models and Socioeconomic Problems." In *Regional Analysis*. Vol. I. Carol A. Smith, ed. Pp. 1–63. New York: Academic Press.

——. 1976b. "Analyzing Regional Systems." In *Regional Analysis*. Vol. II. Carol A. Smith, ed. Pp. 3–20. New York: Academic Press.

Spindler, George D., and Louise Spindler. 1983. "Anthropologists View American Culture." *Annual Review of Anthropology* 12:49–78.

——. 1990. *The American Cultural Dialogue and Its Transmission*. New York: Falmer Press.

Stack, Carol B. 1974. *All Our Kin: Strategies for Survival in a Black Community*. New York: Harper and Row.

Steward, Julian. 1950. *Area Research: Theory and Practice*. New York: Social Science Research Council, Bulletin no. 63.

Susser, Ida. 1982. *Norman Street: Poverty and Politics in an Urban Neighborhood*. New York: Oxford University Press.

Sutton, William R. 1995. "Tied to the Whipping Post: New Labor History and Evangelical Artisans in the Early Republic." *Labor History* 36:251–281.

Swarthout, Genevieve, and Elwyn Swarthout. 1952. *Highlights of Local History: An Illustrated Dramatic Pageant of the Life and Times of Early Ilion*. Ilion, N.Y.: Ilion Sentinel.

Swinney, H. Jerrold. 1987. "New Notes on Remington's History." *The Gun Report* 32(12):14–24.

——. 1994. "Photographs of the Forge?" Manuscript in author's collection.

Tarbell, Ida. 1966 [1902–1904]. *The History of Standard Oil*. Briefer Version. David Chalmers, ed. New York: Harper and Row.

Thornbecke, Erik, and Chutatong Charumilind. 2002. "Economic Inequality and Its Socio-economic Impact." Paper prepared for the Cornell University Social Science Seminar, 2001–2002, February 2002.

Tonkin, Elizabeth. 1992. *Narrating Our Pasts: The Social Construction of Oral History*. Cambridge: Cambridge University Press.

Trachtenberg, Alan. 1982. *The Incorporation of America: Culture and Society in the Gilded Age*. New York: Hill and Wang.

Trouillot, Michel-Rolph. 1995. *Silencing the Past: Power and the Production of History*. Boston: Beacon Press.

Turner, Terence. 1986. "Production, Exploitation and Social Consciousness in the 'Peripheral Situation.'" *Social Analysis* 19:91–119.

U.S. Bureau of the Census. 1975. *Historical Statistics of the United States, Colonial Times to 1970*. Washington, D.C.: U.S. Government Printing Office.

Veblen, Thorstein. 1979 [1899]. *The Theory of the Leisure Class*. Harmondsworth: Penguin.

Verdery, Katherine. 1976. "Ethnicity and Local Systems: The Religious Organization of Welshness." In *Regional Analysis*. Vol. II. Carol A. Smith, ed. Pp. 191–227. New York: Academic Press.

Wachtel, Nathan. 1986. "Introduction: Memory and History." In *Between Memory and History*. Marie Noelle Bourguet, Lucette Valensi, and Nathan Wachtel, eds. Sharon Romeo, trans. Pp. 207–224. London: Harwood.

Wallace, Anthony F. C. 1978. *Rockdale: An American Village in the Early Industrial Revolution*. New York: Knopf.

194   *References*

——. 1987. *St. Clair: A Nineteenth-Century Coal Town's Experience with a Disaster-Prone Industry.* New York: Knopf.

Wallerstein, Immanuel. 1974. *The Modern World-System I: Capitalist Agriculture and the Origins of the European World-Economy in the Sixteenth Century.* New York: Academic Press.

Warner, William Lloyd, and Paul Lunt. 1941. *The Social Life of a Modern Community.* Yankee City Series, no. 1. New Haven: Yale University Press.

——. 1942. *The Status System of a Modern Community.* Yankee City Series, no. 2. New Haven: Yale University Press.

Warner, William Lloyd, and Leo Srole. 1945. *The Social System of American Ethnic Groups.* Yankee City Series, no. 3. New Haven: Yale University Press.

Warner, William Lloyd, and J. O. Low. 1945. *The Social System of the Modern Factory.* Yankee City Series, no. 4. New Haven: Yale University Press.

Warner, William Lloyd, J. O. Low, P. Lunt, and L. Srole. 1963. *Yankee City.* New Haven: Yale University Press.

Warren, Donald I. 1976. *The Radical Center: Middle Americans and the Politics of Alienation.* Notre Dame: University of Notre Dame Press.

Weber, Max. 1976 [1904]. *The Protestant Ethic and the Spirit of Capitalism.* Talcott Parsons, trans. New York: Charles Scribner's Sons.

Weiner, Annette B. 1992. *Inalienable Possessions: The Paradox of Keeping-While-Giving.* Berkeley: University of California Press.

Wiebe, Robert H. 1967. *The Search for Order: 1877–1920.* New York: Hill and Wang.

Wilentz, Sean. 1984. *Chants Democratic: New York City and the Rise of the American Working Class, 1788–1850.* New York: Oxford University Press.

Williams, Raymond. 1983. *Keywords: A Vocabulary of Culture and Society.* Rev. ed. New York: Oxford University Press.

Willis, Ellen. 1998. "We Need a Radical Left." *The Nation* 266(23):18–21.

Wiltshire, David. 1978. *The Social and Political Thought of Herbert Spencer.* London: Oxford University Press.

Wolf, Eric. 1982. *Europe and the People Without History.* Berkeley: University of California Press.

——. 1988. "Inventing Society." *American Ethnologist* 15:752–761.

Zunz, Olivier. 1982. *The Changing Face of Inequality: Urbanization, Industrial Development, and Immigrants in Detroit, 1880–1920.* Chicago: University of Chicago Press.

Zweig, Michael. 2000. *The Working Class Majority: America's Best Kept Secret.* Ithaca, N.Y.: ILR Press.

Index

Adams, James Truslow, 151–153
Agricultural Works. *See* Remington Agricultural Works
Alger, Horatio, historical misinterpretation of, 152
Aligners' strike (1909), 102–103
All-County Taxpayers Association (ACTA), 29–30
American culture: ideal of classlessness, 17–21; "mainstream," 5, 7, 149, 153, 156; and traditional American values, 6, 7, 14, 60, 72, 90; subordinate, 155; dominant, 159; alleged ahistoricity of, 161. *See also* Old values
American dream, the original, 151–153
American Federation of Labor (AFL), 125, 133
Anti–monopoly politics: English tradition, 68; arguments against corporate privileges, 68–69; exceptions for infrastructure projects, 69; public benefit rule, 69, 176n. 21; anti–trust regulation, 71, 110; national opposition to trusts, 105–106; swells labor union membership, 110; trust prosecutions, 110–111
Anti–trust. *See* Anti–monopoly politics; Trusts
Authorities, the, 146–147, 183n. 2; Industrial Development Authority (IDA), 30; New York Power Authority (NYPA), 146–148

Backyard agriculture, 75–76, 118, 134
Board of Trade. *See* Ilion Board of Trade
Bourdieu, Pierre, 24, 173n. 6

Capital, ideology of, as superior to labor, 100, 115–117, 119, 128, 156
Capitalism, 167–168
Carey, Henry C., 77–79, 176nn. 5, 6;

"harmony of interests," 78–79; opposition to Malthus, 177n. 9
Carnegie, Andrew, 6, 107–109, 179nn. 1, 3, 5
Cavalcade of America, 131
City initiative, 112–113, 118
Civil War (U.S.), 65–66, 82, 116
Columbia, Town of, 46
Combinations. *See* Trusts
Community studies, 25, 163, 172n. 13
Concerned Citizens for Ilion's Environment (CCIE), 27–34, 51–52, 144–145, 148–149, 173nn. 2–3
Consumer society thesis, 164–166
Contractor system. *See under* Remington family enterprises
Cornering. *See* Monopoly
Corporate capitalism, 7; as neo-aristocracy 14; publicly funded benefits, 29–30; as "crony capitalism," 70; and post-World War II prosperity, 131–134; and low-profile PR strategy 132; as threat to American dream, 152–153; proliferation of insecure jobs, 154; export of manufacturing work, 155
Corporate cultural campaign, 5, 13, 14, 116, 149, 153; evolutionary theory, appropriation of, 6–7; social Darwinism of, 14, 96, 107–109; abundance through mass production, ideology of, 109–110; at Remington Centennial (1916), 115–117; at Typewriter Semi-Centennial (1923), 119; post-World War II, 127–128, 131–132; use of Remington story, 131–132. *See also* Capital
Corporate regime, 146
Cross-cultural mistrust, 9
Culture (anthropological perspective), 166
Cunningham, Francis, 122–123, 180n. 15